CONSTRUCTING CHINA'S JERUSALEM

A Series Sponsored by the East-West Center

CONTEMPORARY ISSUES IN ASIA AND THE PACIFIC

John T. Sidel and Geoffrey M. White, Series Co-Editors

A collaborative effort by Stanford University Press and the East-West Center, this series focuses on issues of contemporary significance in the Asia Pacific region, most notably political, social, cultural, and economic change. The series seeks books that focus on topics of regional importance, on problems that cross disciplinary boundaries, and that have the capacity to reach academic and other interested audiences.

The East-West Center promotes better relations and understanding among the people and nations of the United States, Asia, and the Pacific through cooperative study, research, and dialogue. Established by the US Congress in 1960, the Center serves as a resource for information and analysis on critical issues of common concern, bringing people together to exchange views, build expertise, and develop policy options. The Center is an independent, public, nonprofit organization with funding from the US government, and additional support provided by private agencies, individuals, foundations, corporations, and governments in the region.

NANLAI CAO

Constructing China's Jerusalem

*Christians, Power, and Place
in Contemporary Wenzhou*

Stanford University Press · *Stanford, California*

Stanford University Press
Stanford, California

Printed in the United States of America on acid-free, archival-quality paper

Library of Congress Cataloging-in-Publication Data

Cao, Nanlai.
    Constructing China's Jerusalem : Christians, power, and place in contemporary Wenzhou / Nanlai Cao.
        p.   cm. — (East-West Center series on contemporary issues in Asia and the Pacific)
    Includes bibliographical references and index.
    ISBN 978-0-8047-7080-4 (cloth : alk. paper)
    ISBN 978-0-8047-7360-7 (pbk. : alk. paper)
        1. Christianity—Social aspects—China—Wenzhou Shi.   2. Church growth—China—Wenzhou Shi.   3. Christianity and culture—China—Wenzhou Shi.   4. Wenzhou Shi (China)—Church history.   I. Title.
    II. Series: Contemporary issues in Asia and the Pacific.
BR1295.W46C36   2010
275.1'242—dc22

                                                              2010014331

Typeset at Stanford University Press in 9.75/13.5 Janson Text

Contents

Maps, Illustrations, and Tables

Maps

Figures

Table

Acknowledgments

My heartfelt thanks go first to the Wenzhou church brothers and sisters who gave me access to their lives and made this research possible. My dissertation committee—Andrew Kipnis, Philip Taylor, and Nicholas Tapp—provided intellectual guidance and helpful encouragement throughout my years at the Australian National University. I want especially to thank my principle supervisor, Andy, for both mentoring me through the dissertation process and training me as an anthropologist. My thanks also go to Mandy Scott for her editorial help. Chee-Han Lim, my best friend and colleague at ANU, has been a constant source of inspiration and support.

I want to thank my teachers in the United States, especially Mark Warren, Gerald Handel, James Kelly, E. Doyle McCarthy, and Rosemary Cooney. Mark Warren, who was my M.A. thesis advisor at Fordham University, kindled my interest in the study of faith-based community organizations, which subsequently led to my research on Chinese Christianity. Gerald Handel then a professor at the City University of New York, taught me how to study the lives of ordinary people through the production of life history.

Many people helped by reading my draft chapters and papers. I wish to express my gratitude to Helen Siu, Mayfair Yang, Richard Madsen, James Scott, David Buck, David Yamane, Jay Demerath, Ryan Dunch, Peter Ng, Barend ter Haar, Lin Hsiu-hsin, Rodolfo Soriano-Nunez, and Mae Chao. My examiners, Robert Weller and Adam Chau, offered invaluable suggestions for revision.

I am grateful for the funding support of this research from the ANU, the Society for the Scientific Study of Religion, the Religious Research Association, and the Association for the Sociology of Religion. Shi Chenxuan lent helpful research assistance in China and always cheered me up. The Hong

Kong Institute for the Humanities and Social Sciences at the University of Hong Kong furnished vital institutional support during the final stage of writing. I am also grateful to Daniel Bays and an anonymous reviewer for Stanford University Press, as well as the editorial board of the Contemporary Issues in Asia and the Pacific Series at Stanford for their suggestions and criticisms.

I acknowledge two journals for giving me permission to reprint, in revised form, articles that originally appeared in them: *Sociology of Religion: A Quarterly Review* (Cao 2007) and *The China Journal* (Cao 2008). I thank the editors and reviewers of these journals for their helpful comments and suggestions.

My parents have given me enormous support. My father, a historian, has always patiently listened to my endless dissertation ideas; my mother, a Wenzhou native, has been my most reliable source of knowledge on Wenzhou culture and society. My relatives in Wenzhou also helped me in various ways. My maternal grandparents hosted me temporarily during my fieldwork; my maternal grandma always insisted that I go to her place for dinner that she would prepare. Their care made me realize what is truly important in life.

I want to dedicate this work to the memory of my paternal grandmother, Yan Wanyi, who passed away in November 2006, and my maternal grandfather, Wang Xinkui, who passed away in July 2007. In her last months of life, my late grandma was still trying to save every bit of information on Wenzhou for me from the daily newspapers she read. I hope I have not let her down.

Introduction: Putting Christianity and Capitalism in Their Place

On December 22, 2006, the traffic police department of the Public Security Bureau of Wenzhou issued a public notice, "On enforcing traffic control in the downtown area during Christmas."[1] It read, "In order to ensure traffic safety and smoothness in the downtown area during Christmas 2006, a decision has been made to enforce traffic control according to the Law of the People's Republic of China on Road Traffic Safety." The decision was to ban all vehicles except public buses, taxis, and two-wheeled motorcycles in the entire city center from 5:00 p.m. December 24 to 3:00 a.m. December 25. The word "Christmas" (*shengdanjie*) appeared three times in this short magisterial statement. Christmas is not an official holiday in China, but mass participation in the annual Christmas celebration left little room for the local state to maneuver. With memories of hectic traffic jams in previous years, the local police chose to intervene. The naming of this local festival period "Christmas" in the law and the state-controlled media, however, unwittingly granted legitimacy to Christianity. State "recognition" of Christmas is part of the story of the massive resurgence of Christianity in contemporary Wenzhou detailed in this book.

In the last quarter century, the southeast coastal city of Wenzhou has become the largest urban Christian center in China, popularly known as "China's Jerusalem" (*Zhongguo de Yelusaleng*).[2] Wenzhou is home, by some estimates, to as many as one million Christians (Protestant) and more than two thousand churches.[3] However, the state officially designated Wenzhou as an experimental site for an "atheistic zone" (*wu zongjiao qu*) in 1958. During the Cultural Revolution (1966–1976), church buildings were either closed or converted for other uses, and all Christians were driven underground. The great expansion of Christianity in Wenzhou took place over the past two decades. More than five hundred churches were built in the 1980s (*Wenzhou zongjiao* 1994: 27). Although Catholicism, Buddhism, and Chinese folk religion are also on the increase, Christianity's growth has been the most significant in Wenzhou, especially in the urbanized area.[4]

The rise of Wenzhou Christianity is part of a larger revival of popular religious practices during the post-Mao period of political and economic liberalization (Chau 2006; Dean 1998; Jing 1996; Kipnis 2001b; Madsen 1998; Palmer 2007). This book seeks to understand the local significance of Wenzhou's Christian effervescence rather than studying it as an instance of a general religious upsurge. Because of its remoteness from the economic and political center, Wenzhou has been a relatively unique site since ancient times. During the post-Mao era, the development of Wenzhou Christianity has accompanied Wenzhou's evolution from an impoverished rural town to a dynamic regional center of global capitalism, the rapid growth of many small and medium-sized family-owned manufacturing enterprises, the city emerging as a world outsourcing hub, and the rise of an entrepreneurial class in the same region.[5] It is in the context of this changing regional political economy that I interpret Wenzhou Christianity and its relationship to larger discourses of modernity.[6]

Universal Celebration: Christianity as a Popular Participatory Domain

China's Christian population in rural inland areas tends to be homogeneously elderly, female, and illiterate (Li et al. 1999; Leung 1999). In contrast, Wenzhou Christianity constitutes a popular participatory domain in which a great diversity of people articulate subjectivities and interests and interact with one another through belief. This diversity is reflected in the rapid expansion of local religious space and the communal style of Christmas celebrations.

I began my fieldwork in Wenzhou right before Christmas 2004. Although I anticipated something unusual would happen during the celebration, I was still surprised by its grandeur and the combination of various popular cultural elements. Deliberately portrayed as an occasion of universal joy and celebration (*putian tongqing*), Christmas has become a public community event open to all. Local bosses, cadres, migrant workers, students, men and women, young and old, believers and nonbelievers flock to the various church sites as well as hotels and theaters to experience what local preachers proudly claim to be "the [world's] most authentic Christmas." This massive flow of participants in previous years caused the traffic jams that led to the intervention of the local Public Security Bureau in December 2006.

The Wenzhou churches' Christmas celebrations combine grand feasting, performance watching, and evangelical preaching in a festival atmosphere. Most large Wenzhou churches hold Christmas celebrations for several consecutive days, with Christmas Eve being the most elaborate and splendid celebratory gathering. One church in the city center, for example, held an eight-day Christmas banquet and series of performances. People ate while watching a variety of artistic shows on the stage in the main church hall. Each day sixty-five tables of food were served. In all, more than five hundred banquet tables were prepared and five thousand people attended. The church subsidized the 25 yuan admission ticket. At the feasts, hymns were often played as background music. In another large church, a recording of Handel's *Messiah* was played, and hundreds of people gathered while dozens of uniformed female church workers served dishes to each table. At such Christmas banquets, one church member usually pays for an entire table of his or her friends, relatives, or business partners. Wealthy bosses may buy several banquet tables to entertain their extended social networks. Sometimes they also invite their managers and employees as part of a year-end reward for good performance at work. As a vital part of Christmas evangelization, a sermon is usually inserted in the middle of the eating and performances, but it is always kept short. After banqueting one can overhear people enthusiastically commenting on the quality of food and performances and making comparisons with other churches' banquets and the ones they held last year.

This somewhat chaotic Christmas scene has shocked many visitors, including overseas Christians. One cannot help but wonder: How has it been possible for Christianity to achieve such high visibility and popularity among diverse groups of people in one of China's most commercialized regional economies? Who are the key social actors maneuvering behind such high-profile activities? How have they managed to negotiate such a massive space for the local church and refashion a nontraditional religious identity

Figure 1.1 A Christmas banquet held by a local church in a hotel ballroom. Note the robed choir on the stage. (Photo by author.)

in the public arena? This study addresses these questions by presenting an ethnography of the daily practices of local church members. The revival of Christianity among diverse socioeconomic groups points to the multiplicity of attitudes, motivations, and meanings among modern Chinese believers. I detail the diverse subcultures, motivations, and actions of the people involved in Wenzhou's churches. As the church's Christmas celebration suggests, Wenzhou's Christian revival has not taken place in an empty cultural landscape. Instead, it involves a larger cultural system that conditions both local religious forms and state governance and is also transformed by Christianity itself. Although Wenzhou's cadres are officially banned from joining the church, an informal local network of churchgoing relatives and friends can embed them within a shared emotional structure, shaping their values and perceptions of Christianity. A view of Wenzhou Christianity as a popular participatory domain offers a vantage point to critically address the pattern of monolithic depiction of China's Christianity in the literature and ultimately the oppositional binary concept of civil society and the state.

Departure from a Domination-Resistance Model

Popular discourses dominated by journalists often politicize the issue of religious freedom in contemporary China rather than analyze the hybrid local sociocultural environment where the religious revival takes place.[7] China researchers have focused on the post-Mao revival of religion as a politically and ideologically charged process in which the local community resists the totalizing party-state (Anagnost 1994; Feuchtwang 2000; Jing 1996; Mueggler 2001; Yang 2000, 2004). Some studies of Chinese Christianity even embrace a binary construct of state domination and church resistance.

Although Christianity has an established place in modern Chinese history, it has been politically labeled as heterodox for most of the twentieth century. During the Cultural Revolution, Christianity disappeared from public view under the pressure of mass nationalism and militant atheism. Under Mao, Western missionary endeavors were linked to imperialism and colonialism. Today the death of Communism as a faith in China, along with the liberalization of religious policies in the 1980s, has led to a dramatic growth of Christianity. There may be more than sixty million Protestant Christians (twelve million registered) in China today, compared with seven hundred thousand in 1949 (Aikman 2003). The increasing significance of Christianity in local society intensifies church-state interactions.

Despite this "Christian fever," Chinese state restrictions on academic research have made contemporary Chinese Christianity an understudied topic. Political risks discourage scholars from conducting empirical studies of Christianity in China. Ironically, parallel to the party-state's view of Christianity as a "foreign religion," much of the literature has tended to take a more or less politicized, ideological approach to Chinese Christianity. For example, some scholars depict Chinese Christianity as a localized foreign faith, suggesting Christianity and local Chinese culture are two opposing categories (e.g., Gernet 1985; Uhalley and Wu 2001; Whyte 1988). By focusing on the foreign missionary impact, these studies contribute to the understanding of Chinese Christianity as an unfinished Western project. Not unlike early Western missionaries in China, many Western-based journalists and observers today still view Christianity as a transformative social force that has the potential to remodel the life of Chinese society with a single overarching church authority and ideology.[8]

On the basis of their understanding of the history of the harsh political repression of religion during the Cultural Revolution, scholars of Chinese religion have also focused attention on the political context of state-society relationships. Viewed as inherently hegemonic, the state is presumed to have dominated the structure of religious expression and suppressed religious thought and ritual in a mechanical fashion (see MacInnis 1996). Such a politicized approach tends to assume that as the party-state dominates society, the church has two choices: to cooperate or to resist. Therefore, different categories of religious expression can be described mainly as collaboration (usually in the case of the official church), or as resistance (usually in the case of the so-called house church movement), or as a combination of these two. Kindopp (2004: 5), for example, interprets house churches as a form of "the systematic and widespread resistance of the majority of China's Catholics and Protestants." Leung (2007: 283) describes post-Mao church-state relations as an ideological struggle between religious idealism and dialectic materialism. In an essay with the dichotomous phrase "Official vs. Underground Protestant Churches in China" in the title, Wenger (2004) divides Chinese Protestantism into two segments. On this basis, she examines the organizational differences of the two churches and predicts the future difficulty of reconciliation. This stereotypical distinction between the official church and the house church, and the general conception of China's church-state relations as an opposition of resistance and dominance, result from the ideologically specific configuration of China's historical and structural conditions in the high socialist period.

In an analysis of the historical pattern of Chinese state-religion relations, Daniel Bays (2004) has pointed out that the state's registering and monitoring of grassroots religion can be traced back to the Tang dynasty more than a thousand years ago.[9] Therefore, state dominance is not a modern Chinese Communist invention but an ancient requirement of the Chinese political regime. The imperial Chinese state actively shaped and appropriated popular religious cults by imposing its own values and sponsoring the establishment of temples (Duara 1988b; Watson 1985). As popular religion provides an ideological alternative to the Chinese state mode of historization and political rationality (Anagnost 1994; Feuchtwang 2001), the presence of a strong central state power and its unchanging demand for loyalty seems to portend a rather pessimistic future for China's religious freedom, especially regarding Christianity.

However, in contemporary China church-state relations have evolved alongside changing historical and political conditions. First, the state increasingly uses ideological power rather than domination and coercion.[10] A centralized, invasive, disciplinary state is becoming less visible in its exertion of ideological control (Friedman 2004; Yang 2004). This is particularly reflected in the consumer revolution in which a "new mode of governmentality of the Chinese state" has emerged and emphasizes consumption as the drive to modernity and consumerism as the measure of development (Pun 2003: 475). Second, Christianity is no longer a "foreign" religion, because it is mainly local Chinese believers who have revived the faith. In addition, an upwardly mobile stratum is beginning to join the urban churches in China's economically advanced coastal areas (Chen and Huang 2004; Yang 2005). This class generally supports the reformer-era state. Socioreligious dynamics are different in an urban commercialized economy like Wenzhou. Wenzhou Christian entrepreneurs are pioneers in the post-Mao "socialist market economy" and dominant partners of the state development project.

Rather than conduct this research in the conventionally defined political context of state-society relations, I use an ethnographic approach, which enables going beyond an emphasis on the political and symbolic dimensions of religion to examine embodied systems of beliefs and processes of meaning making in daily life.[11] It would be simplistic to take the Three-Self Patriotic Movement (TSPM),[12] the government-sanctioned Protestant organization, as a tool of the Chinese state and treat those who worship or minister "above ground" as state collaborationists.[13] It would be equally unsophisticated to interpret house churches as a form of resistance. The domination-resistance model often reflects the researchers' concern for moral clarity and an old political logic rather than the views of local believers. This model is overpoliticized, not only because things at the local level are much more complex and less directly observable but also because many local Christians defy this hegemonic framework for interpreting their religious experiences as acts of "resistance." Some house churchgoers simply take the label "underground" as an inferior term and claim that they "belong to heaven" (*shutian*). Under this model, scholars tend to ignore the local Chinese Christian experience whenever it cannot be easily categorized as "resistance."

The primacy of the domination-resistance model in Chinese Christian research owes much to Western theories of civil society. Western research has mainly conceptualized civil society in association with voluntary choices of autonomous individuals and in terms of organizational independence from the state. The assumed opposition between state and society has guided much previous research on civil society in China that focused on social resistance to state domination, especially in the wake of the massive public demonstrations of 1989 (e.g., Gold 1990; Strand 1990). However, the concept of civil society is deeply rooted in a Western philosophical tradition that champions Enlightenment notions of individual autonomy (Seligman 1992). It can then be problematic when adopted unreflectively in analysis of non-Western societies. This is particularly true in the context of Chinese East Asia, where "the Confucian traditions of statecraft tended to see family, society, and state as smaller and larger versions of the same kinds of relationships: they related as microcosm and macrocosm, not antagonists" (Weller 2005: 6).[14] As Robert Weller (1999) aptly notes, Chinese social associations that lie between family and state, including business organizations, local popular temples, women's networks, and environmental movements, can all generate forms of civil democracy. Similarly, anthropologists working in other non-Western societies show that communal networks can form a foundation for civic culture and democracy, even though they are not civil society in the classic sense (e.g. Hefner 1998c; White 1996). Therefore, civil society as a liberal Western cultural ideal cannot be taken as given, and China's state-society relationship must be studied on its own terms.

Apart from a much-needed pluralistic understanding of civil association, the notion of the state ought to be thought of in plural terms. The state everywhere is composed of actors with conflicting and contradictory ideas, ideals, and interests. In China there is also a division between the policy-making central state on one side and the local state that implements and often bends the policies on the other (Chau 2006). Moreover, the state has been not only a political apparatus but also a cultural idea in the local community; cultural discourse is thus central to state-society relationships (Siu 1990). A binary construction of resistance and dominance places too little emphasis on the role of local culture, historical context, and the subjectivity of believers. By situating religious expression and representation within the specific context of local history and regional culture, I pursue a meaning-centered and historically grounded analysis of a Christian locality.

From the Anthropology of Christianity to China Studies

Like any other religion, Christianity is not a disembodied faith but embedded in local histories, ethnic memories, social projects, and personal biographies. Nor is it in an empty cultural landscape where Christians interact with one another or with non-Christians. The arrival of Christianity as a transnational religion has been entangled with the life experiences and identities of local Chinese (Constable 1994). Historical studies of local Christianities in the late imperial and Republican periods have shown how local social actors made use of the resources of Western missions to engage in communal politics (Lee 2003) and contribute to the political project of modern nation building (Dunch 2001a). Fully capturing the diversity and complexity of Wenzhou Christianity requires historicizing the phenomenon by viewing it as a cultural process grounded in unequal power relations and differentially related to people in various social positions (Dirks, Eley, and Ortner 1994: 3). By treating Wenzhou Christianity as a cultural fact deeply rooted in local society, I join the efforts of the anthropologists of Christianity to set aside any pre-packed notion of what the Christian experience is (see Cannell 2006; Keane 2007; Robbins 2004).[15] This allows me to explore how macro historical forces of social transformation have been concretized in the everyday practices of Chinese Christians.

Within both the social sciences and public discourse, the relationship of Christianity and China has been generally conceived of as an encounter between two distinct cultural and ideological systems that need to be reconciled. Certain assumptions in Western literature contributed to the boundaries between an anthropology of Christianity and China studies. Making these assumptions explicit enables China anthropologists to integrate the study of Chinese Christianity into the study of Chinese culture and society in general.

Anthropology as primarily a Western mode of producing knowledge about cultures has been deeply influenced by Western cosmology. This can be seen from the production of the modern anthropological category of religion based on the model of Protestant Christianity. Talal Asad (1993) has drawn our attention to the ontological premises on which the notion of religion is founded. He attributes the distinction between "religion" and secular domains such as science, politics, and economy to Christian thinking. For Asad, the modern Western bifurcation of religion and the secular has been taken as given in other parts of the world in the process of state building. By the same token, Marshall Sahlins (1996), through reflecting on the discipline of anthropology as a Western enterprise, aptly points out that Judeo-Christian notions such as human "fallenness" inhabit anthropology and other social sciences, which bedevils Western understandings of other peoples and cultures. Building on Asad and Sahlins, Fenella Cannell (2006) gives an excellent account of the lack of anthropological attention to Christianity as a primary ethnographic object. She attributes this lack to the peculiar relationship between anthropology and Christian theology.[16] Cannell states:

> Anthropology, as part of social science, defined itself in its origins as what theology was not; since the theology it was repudiating was specifically Christian theology, anthropological theory has always carried within it ideas profoundly shaped by that act of rejection, from which there can therefore never be a complete separation. Moreover, because of this uneasy relationship, anthropology has on the whole been less successful at considering Christianity as an ethnographic object than at considering any other religion in this way [Cannell 2006: 45].

Despite the attempt to distinguish itself from theology and understand reality in secular terms, anthropological knowledge carries implicit theological underpinnings. This uneasy relationship of anthropology to theology largely reflects the intertwining of the history of Christianity and that of modernity in the West.

Limited anthropological research on Christianity has tended to focus on its tie to Western modernity in exploring how Western Christianity is adopted, transformed, and localized in a non-Western context. Consequently, there has been a tendency to treat Christianity as a secondary phenomenon of underlying modern political and economic change (Cannell 2006; Robbins 2007). This is particularly familiar to anthropologists who take a historical ethnographic approach to non-Western Christianities (e.g., Comaroff and Comaroff 1991, 1997). These studies tend to place emphasis on colonial agency and modernization, and to show reluctance to view non-Western Christians themselves as producers of cultural knowledge about their everyday realities (cf. Ong 1996).

This reluctance can arguably account for the anthropological neglect of the Chinese Christian experience as a subject in its own right (in contrast to the voluminous anthropological accounts of Chinese popular religion by Western scholars).[17] Instead, a sociological macro structural approach has dominated Chinese Christian studies in the post-Mao era. These studies generally attribute the spectacular growth in church membership during the reform era to contextual factors such as the ideological vacuum left by the collapse of faith in communism, liberalization of state religious policy, and the dismantling of traditional moral systems. In a systematic analysis of Protestantism since 1979, for example, Alan Hunter and Chan Kim-Kwong (1993: 170) emphasize the role of the "spiritual crisis" produced by radical social and political changes. This explanation is confirmed by Bays (2003: 502), who concludes that "different forms of Protestantism can offer for intellectuals or the urban middle class identification with the West and modernization, or an eschatological prospect which may appeal to poor peasants left behind by the economic reforms." In the most recent elaboration of this approach, Fenggang Yang (2005) argues that linking with Western modernity is the main attraction of Christianity to the urban middle class. Such analyses, although valuable for their wide perspectives, cannot explain how local believers participate in the constitution of Chinese Christianity. More important, by focusing on explaining large-scale religious conversion, they tend to deploy prepacked notions of Western Christianity in understanding how (preexisting) Christian rituals, ideologies, and practices are implanted into and reconfigure the local Chinese social order and way of life. To address Christianity's relevance to the negotiation of social power and construction of everyday life in a local world, this study turns the question around by asking how local people produce, consume, and interpret Christian values and symbols that redefine forms of local social organization and local power structures.

In Wenzhou the Christian revival has taken place under the conditions of a modernizing state, lax local governance, an emerging capitalist consumer economy, and greater spatial mobility among individuals. Attention to Wenzhou's religious-economic dynamics recalls Max Weber's classic thesis on the Protestant ethic and the spirit of capitalism (2001). Weber carves out a trajectory of modernization in Protestant Europe, showing a strong organic association between the logic of asceticism in Christianity and secular professional life. However, as Weber also notes, the historical pattern of European modernization characterized by the Protestant-capitalist nexus may not be replicated in other parts of the world. Recent studies show that neither

Christianity nor capitalism forms a unitary power structure that penetrates and dominates local communities (Cannell 2006; Engelke and Tomlinson 2006; Hefner 1998a; Yang 2000). The monolithic notion of a cohesive capitalism and the image of unilateral Christian penetration both should be eschewed for conceptions that emphasize local articulation of capitalist and Christian institutions with power, morality, and subjectivity. In this study, to avoid reproducing either "christianocentric" or "capitalocentric" assumptions, I seek to put Christianity and capitalism in their place (cf. Jacka 2005; Yang 2000) and discuss Wenzhou Christianity in the context of an emerging postsocialist Chinese modernity that is embedded in a state developmentalist project. I show how affluent Christian entrepreneurs negotiate identity while seeking to anchor their feelings and emotions in relation to both a larger meaning system and a state secular order. In particular, I focus on how they interact with the contemporary reformist state that emphasizes individuals' commitment to both the market principle and state ideology. Through depicting a Christian locality that captures the lived Chinese Christian experience in an emerging market economy, this study aims to understand the impact of post-Mao economic restructuring on Chinese Christianity and its relation to the state. By taking Wenzhou Christianity as a historically and spatially contingent process (rather than a pregiven cultural-territorial entity), and Wenzhou Christians as religious individuals with unique cultural histories who confront changes in the macro political economy that encompasses them, I hope to contribute to the understanding of the Chinese Christian experience as a lens for broader processes of sociocultural change in contemporary China.

To take up this challenge, I shift the focus from a narrowly conceived institutional narrative of Christian revival under Chinese state dominance to analysis of the larger cultural processes and social (re)configurations in which Chinese Christians of various backgrounds are situated and differentially related to morality, power, and prestige. Rather than assume monolithic attitudes on the part of any Chinese Christian group, I am interested in how Christians in different social positions, individually and collectively, construct their religious and social identities. This book argues that Wenzhou Christianity is a historically complex regional construct framed by a moral discourse of modernity. This moral discourse tends to justify various social hierarchies and legitimatizes a new socioeconomic order in the making.

To make this point, I show how the vitality and complexity of Wenzhou

Christianity is related to wider transformations that have taken place in the practices of everyday life embedded in the regional capitalist context. I pursue a central question concerning the nature of religious participation in the political economic context of post-Mao reforms—reforms that emphasize a rationalized modernity and in which economic growth dominates all spheres of social life. Following the Weberian turn in anthropology (Keyes 2002), this study delves into the intersection between religion and political economy.

Wenzhou as a Place: The Regional and Historical Context

Understanding the lived history of China's rapid market transition enables fuller understanding of the role of Christianity in Chinese society, particularly in Wenzhou. The city sits on China's southeast coast, two hundred miles south of Shanghai. Geographically, it is enclosed by mountains on three sides and the East China Sea on the fourth. Despite harsh natural conditions, the city has recently enjoyed unprecedented economic development and material prosperity. Wenzhou Christianity received international attention a decade ago for its dramatic growth in a new entrepreneurial world. In a *Wall Street Journal* article, "China's Christians Mix Business and God: Wenzhou Church Thrives on New Capitalists' Wealth," an American journalist described a link between Christianity and capitalism in Wenzhou:

> From a warren of shoe factories and garment shops in this restless city rises a monument to China's ascendant bourgeoisie—a church. . . . Just as they drink Coke and carry Motorola pagers, entrepreneurs show off their cosmopolitan savvy by erecting the finest houses of worship. Taxi drivers sermonize passengers. Factory foremen lure their workers to Sunday services. So the Chinese people are discovering what Max Weber theorized long ago: Capitalism and Christianity can be self-reinforcing.[18]

Political marginality and rapid commercialization have often triggered unusual religious growths in Chinese history (Weller 1995). This seems also to be the case in the reform-era Wenzhou Christian resurgence. Wenzhou was historically not well integrated into the dominant Chinese political economy because of its geographic isolation, linguistic uniqueness, and spatial distance from the state political center. Until a small airport was opened in

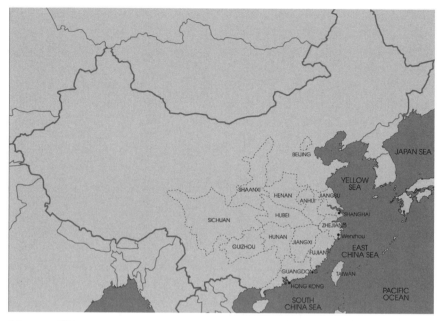

Map 1.1 China

1990, visiting party officials from Beijing had to take a ferry from Shanghai. In 1998 Wenzhou was eventually connected to the rest of the country by rail. The central agricultural state hardly ever had solid control over the region, even during the Cultural Revolution.[19] The "liberation" of Wenzhou in 1949—by local guerrilla forces rather than Mao's Red Army—ensured that native cadres took a leading position in the new local authority (Y. Liu 1992). With strong localist tendencies, Wenzhou's cadres were sympathetic to the regional tradition of capitalism and held strong ambivalence toward Mao's leftist campaigns.

Historically, Wenzhou fit, in Hill Gates' (1996) terms, a weak state tributary mode of production and strong petty capitalist mode of production. According to Gates (1996), because of the difficulty for the state to extract tribute from the coast, a dynamic petty capitalism along with urbanization took shape on the southeast coast of China a millennium ago. This contributed to development of a coastal economy in Wenzhou that has focused on shipbuilding and commercial transportation since the Song Dynasty a thousand years ago, instead of the agriculture-based economy that dominates

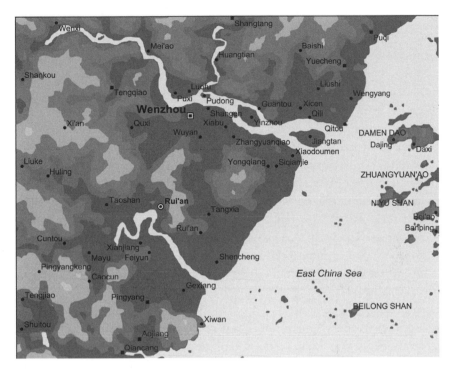

Map 1.2 The mountainous Wenzhou region

most parts of China.[20] The long history of petty capitalist commodity production has contributed to a distinctive regional culture of commercialism in Wenzhou.

The distinctiveness of Wenzhou's regional culture can also be characterized by its dialect. It is a type of ancient *Wu* Chinese influenced by Southern *Min* speakers from nearby Fujian Province. It is unique, and even completely incomprehensible outside the area.[21] This linguistic barrier greatly weakens the central state's ability to serve as an interpretive authority over local culture and society.[22]

As a densely populated coastal port city, Wenzhou became one of the important and vigorous trading centers in southeast China in the seventeenth and eighteenth centuries (Gates 1996: 76). Its trading links with the outside world enabled a long history of cross-cultural religious transmission. Wenzhou Christianity has roots in the early Western mission churches. The Nanking Treaty of 1842 forced imperial China to open up nearby Ningbo

Port to foreign missionaries. George Stott, a Scottish missionary, first started evangelization in this region in 1867 (Soothhill 1907). The original China Inland Mission church he founded still stands in the center of the city today.

Since the late nineteenth century, the local and regional boundaries that hindered centralized political control and communication actually benefited the active presence of Christianity in the Wenzhou region. Such boundaries acted as natural protection for early Western missionary projects and contributed to a local faith tradition. Today Christianity is indigenized because many local believers have inherited faith from their parents or grandparents. In fact, the resurgence of Christianity in post-Mao Wenzhou can be traced to development of the independent sector of Chinese Protestantism in early-twentieth-century China (see Bays 1996). Independent of foreign missions, local Chinese Christian leaders founded three of the six Protestant denominations (or mission groups) existing in pre-1949 Wenzhou.[23]

Wenzhou cultural identity further emphasizes migration and sojourning. Translocal business networks and activities have contributed to Wenzhou's reform-era economic success (see Xiang 2005; Zhang 2001). About two million Wenzhou merchants (30 percent of the current local Wenzhou population) are now doing business in other parts of China, and hundreds of thousands are dealing with other countries, particularly France, Italy, Holland, Spain, and the United States (Shi, Jin, Zhao, and Luo 2002). A recent report in the *Los Angeles Times* portrays Wenzhou people as "China's global go-getters."[24] The mobility and commercialism of the Wenzhou people have given them the name "Jews of China" (Li 1999).[25] Although Wenzhou as a place is on the periphery of the nation-state, it is not marginal to the operation of the global capitalist economy. Nor is Wenzhou a margin in the centralized state discourse of reform.

Wenzhou's privatized economy has experienced rapid growth since 1978. Its GDP increased by seventeen times, with an average annual growth rate of 16 percent, from 1978 to 1997, which is well above that of the nation as a whole (Shi et al. 2002). In 2006, Wenzhou's per-capita income was above $3,000 (*Wenzhou Statistical Yearbook* 2007), about double the nationwide average. Wenzhou's rapid industrialization has attracted two million rural migrant workers from interior provinces such as Jiangxi, Anhui, Hubei, and Sichuan, greatly contributing to the city's GDP accumulation.[26]

Wenzhou's reform-era economic development is mainly characterized by private or family-owned businesses making small merchandise such as shoes, clothes, cigarette lighters, eyeglasses, and household appliances. This economic development has gained gradual recognition from the postsocialist state and has been labeled the "Wenzhou model" of the "socialist market economy" for the rest of the country (Shi et al. 2002).[27] Nowadays the state controls less than 10 percent of Wenzhou's economy.

Many Wenzhou entrepreneurs started small businesses in the early 1980s, well before the rest of the nation. They achieved success under Deng Xiaoping's economic strategy of "letting a few get rich first." The post-Mao state emphasis on getting rich has not only empowered hard-working and risk-taking Wenzhou entrepreneurs but also dramatically reshaped the local Christian landscape. The combination of rapid economic growth and high adherence to Christianity contradicts those who assume Christianity to be a savior only of the poor. Many Christian entrepreneurs give their wealth to the church and spread faith as they travel across China. Hundreds of sumptuous "unofficial" house churches, decorated with conspicuous red crosses, operate openly in suburban Wenzhou. They are the visual representations of sacred power, showing the salience and importance of religious identity in local society. In their analysis of the Christian communities in the greater Wenzhou area, Chen and Huang (2004) indicate that a new type of Christian, known as "boss Christians" (*laoban jidutu*), has emerged since the end of the 1980s. In contrast to the uneducated farmers and elderly city dwellers who have traditionally made up the majority of the Chinese Christian population, these boss Christians are private business owners or white-collar workers with wealth.[28] The forms and meanings of Christian practices in the Wenzhou area relate to the rise of this new entrepreneurial class and the emerging regional modernity they have constructed.

Doing Fieldwork in Wenzhou

This research is based on a total of nineteen months of ethnographic study in the church community of Wenzhou city between 2004 and 2006. There are thousands of churches and gathering points in the Wenzhou area that offer various services and activities daily. Given the size and diversity of the local church community, I decided against focusing on one church. As a sole researcher, I often rushed from one church site to another by taxi and visited three or four sites within a day. Therefore, I did not take the traditional approach of congregational studies. Instead, my research largely depends on collection of individual Christians' life histories and life course study.

I combined participant observation at various churches with life-history interviews to understand the meaning of everyday life among Wenzhou Christians and to examine the symbolic presence of state power and state relations in the local church community. I did life-history interviews, both semistructured and informal, with about seventy church members (I repeatedly interviewed many of them). I designed major interview questions to reveal the relationship between religious participation and daily practices influenced by class, gender, age, place, and popular culture. In presenting my data, I employ a narrative approach to religious experience (Harding 1987; Keane 1997; Yamane 2000) and explore languages of faith and state ideology among Wenzhou Christians.[29] As Robert Wuthnow argues, meaning is "a product of the regularities present in speech and actions themselves" (1991: 2). The respondents come from a variety of backgrounds, with entrepreneurs, migrant workers, state-ordained pastors, local party cadres, house church leaders, and ordinary church members. The interviews were conducted in Mandarin Chinese, and all quotations are my translations from Chinese. To protect the respondents' identities, all names were changed and occupations altered to similar ones.

Having studied at a Catholic university in the United States and done extensive research on the immigrant Chinese church in New York City (see Cao 2005), I identified myself as a "cultural Christian" (*wenhua jidutu*), a term well understood by local evangelical Christians to mean someone who appreciates the doctrine and the faith but has no personal commitment to the church. I attended various church services just like an ordinary church member, listening to sermons, singing hymns, studying the scripture, and saying prayers. But I never participated in Holy Communion, a service for baptized church members only. From time to time I encountered individuals who asked me to be baptized in their church. Whenever this happened, I made it clear to them that I was in the Wenzhou church to conduct my doctoral research, which requires a certain degree of objectivity, and that I would leave baptism as a possibility for the future. On a number of occasions, my respondents told me that they would not have shared their personal views on certain church leaders and the internal politics of the Wenzhou church were I an insider to the local church community.

I was fortunate to be able to gain the trust of a group of entrepreneurial church leaders who granted me much freedom to take photos, tape-record interviews, and even videotape their activities. They are open-minded, powerful, and eager to build prestige and further expand their influence and networks in the religious and business domains. They welcomed me to work with them in order to promote the *culture* of Christianity and kindly offered a platform for my research.

I was also aware that my fieldwork took place at the historical juncture when local church development was starting to emphasize worldly engagement. The younger generation of Christian businessmen sought to reach out to renowned Christian scholars outside of Wenzhou, to (in one businessman's words) "reformulate the basic attitude towards economic wealth through using authoritative scholars' study and interpretation of the relationship between faith and economics."

During my fieldwork, I acted as a reporter by writing for the newsletter of a fellowship of businesspeople and the newspaper of a Christian-led factory. Occasionally, I was also asked to write banquet speeches and furnish English translations of local Christian slogans. These activities facilitated data collection and allowed me to understand and assess the *quality* of their cultural resources and moral commitments (see Madsen 1993). In particular, I benefited greatly by sitting through the fellowship's numerous planning meetings, listening to their concerns and observing closely their private interactions and discussions. Furthermore, I accompanied an energetic young Christian businessman who drove around the city to talk to major Christian bosses in order to spread the vision of combining business with Christian faith.

Gradually I became part of the process I went to study and found myself being able to identify with my Christian respondents in some of their pursuits and interests, particularly in their efforts at self-refashioning. In this sense, I was both an outsider and an insider to the local Christian community. The inner circle of the local church leadership not only accepted but also encouraged my researcher identity. It was also through this entrepreneurial church leaders' network that I gained much greater access to other groups of church members, including many migrant worker Christians in their factories. The present work is the result of my prolonged ethnographic engagement with Wenzhou Christians and an effort to retell their stories to a wider audience.

A Note on Romanization and Units of Measurement

In this book, I use the *pinyin* system of romanization of Mandarin Chinese. In many cases, I have given both pinyin and original Chinese characters to avoid confusion. In several places, Wenzhou dialect expressions are romanized in their Mandarin equivalents.

The official exchange rate between Chinese yuan (¥) and U.S. dollars was about 7 yuan to a U.S. dollar in the early 2000s. One Chinese *mu* equals one-sixth acre.

Definitions and Book Outline

When I use the term *Wenzhou*, it refers to the prefecture-level city of Wenzhou, which currently contains three city districts (Lucheng, Ouhai, and Longwan), two county-level cities (Rui'an and Yueqing), and six counties (Yongjia, Pingyang, Cangnan, Dongtou, Wencheng, and Taishun). The city of Wenzhou, as an administrative region, covers both urban and rural areas. It is noteworthy that as Wenzhou's pace of rural industrialization and urbanization continues to accelerate, it is increasingly difficult to draw a clear line between the urban and the rural in the region.

Throughout this study, the term *Christianity* refers to Protestantism. In reference to the entire Wenzhou Christian community, the phrase "the Wenzhou church" or "the local church" is used. Although the local church usually measures its membership in terms of the number of baptized participants, it does consider all who "confess with their mouth and believe in their heart" (*xinli xiangxin kouli chengren*) to be Christians who have attained salvation.[30] This is in accordance with their evangelical emphasis on the doctrine of "justification by faith" (*yinxin chengyi*), which means salvation is a gift from God, and the only criterion is "belief" (*xin*). By emphasizing the notion of belief, the Wenzhou church takes a rigid stance on who has salvation and who does not. Here it should be made clear that most Wenzhou Christians, like conservative evangelical Protestants elsewhere, are religiously intolerant and critical of those who do not share their faith.[31] Many Wenzhou Christians hold the view that even Catholics cannot be saved, owing to the Catholic emphasis on good deeds as one's ticket to heaven. Wenzhou Christians strive to practice the faith in what they believe to be the most exclusive and orthodox manner.

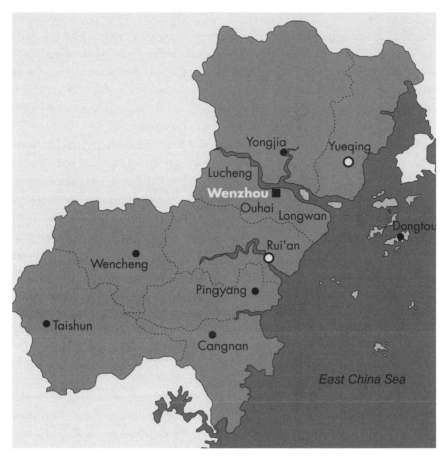

Map 1.3 The administrative region of Wenzhou

They consciously avoid visiting Buddhist, Daoist, or popular religious sites or engaging in any religious activities they consider un-Christian, especially ancestor worship.[32] This sets them apart from many rural Christians, whose practices bear strong popular religious flavor (Bays 2003; Hunter and Chan 1993; Leung 1999). The fact that there is little room for hyphenated religious practices in Wenzhou Christianity has become a source of great pride for many local churchgoers as testimony to the authenticity of their belief. However, Wenzhou Christians' anxiety about boundary making and maintenance places their religion in fierce competition with non-Protestant religions.

Given the common assumption that defines Christianity as a matter of inner spirituality, it is necessary in the beginning to supply a working definition of the term *Christian*.[33] In viewing Christian identity and practice as an ethnographic object, I have relied on local people's self-description. I did not attempt to distinguish between devout believers and others. When I use adjectives involving a sense of judgment, such as "devout," "pious," and "committed," I refer to how my respondents described themselves or others.

Wenzhou Christians unanimously address male believers as brothers (*dixiong*) and female believers as sisters (*zimei*), regardless of their age. These terms are used to distinguish Christians from non-Christians in daily practice. I have adopted these titles in referring to Wenzhou Christians.

The Wenzhou church claims to believe in the doctrine of biblical inerrancy and engages a literal reading of the Bible. However, local church members have pursued this fundamentalist orientation in diverse, mutually contradictory ways. There have been severe conflicts regarding interpretation of particular biblical verses, in part due to the use of different Chinese versions of the Bible.[34] The Chinese Union Version of the Holy Bible (*hehe ben*), first published in 1919, is the predominant Chinese language translation of the Bible used in the Wenzhou church. However, the New Chinese Version (*xinyi ben*) of the Holy Bible, completed in 1992 by the Worldwide Bible Society, has gained great popularity among the younger generation of Wenzhou Christians today, partly for its accommodation to modern Chinese. Many local church members anticipate that the New Chinese Version will replace the older Chinese Union Version in the future. The Bible verses in this book all come from the Holy Bible New International Version. Citations made by my respondents are followed with the pinyin and Chinese characters of the original verses from the New Chinese Version.

In addition to this Introduction, the book has six chapters. Chapter Two introduces the entrepreneurial class of Christians in reform-era Wenzhou by using personal biographies that illustrate journeys of upward mobility, paths of identity formation, network building, and engagements with state power. Chapter Three explores the close interrelationship among power, prestige, and Christianity in contemporary Wenzhou. Chapter Four explores the intimate cultural linkage between the entrepreneurial outlook of the boss Christians and processes of local church development. Chapters Five and Six show how Wenzhou Christianity not only encapsulates the aspirations of China's new rich class but also symbolically dominates the underprivileged, particularly non-elite local women and migrant workers. Chapter Five seeks to understand how religious identification and commitment emerges and is experienced differently among non-elite women and elite male bosses. It also explores the role the regional political economy plays in shaping gendered identities within Christianity. Chapter Six portrays how, on the one hand, rural migrant workers remake and contest boundaries of urban belonging through participating in Wenzhou Christianity. On the other hand, it examines how the boss Christians' practices mark their socially advantaged and morally superior status in relation to unconverted or newly converted migrant workers. Finally, in the concluding chapter, on the basis of Wenzhou people's heterogeneous and mutually contested practices of Christianity, I highlight a moral discourse of modernity in which emerging socioeconomic groups struggle to negotiate their social status and refashion and legitimate their identity in this period of radical transition. In particular, I show how the beliefs and practices of the boss Christians illuminate larger processes of postreform social reconfiguration.

Chapter 2

The Rise of "Boss Christians" and Their Engagement with State Power

Let a few people get rich first.

— DENG XIAOPING

Doing business is serving God.

— A WENZHOU CHRISTIAN BUSINESSMAN

The reality of the Wenzhou church is distinctively different from that of the rural Chinese church that has largely shaped the Chinese Christian landscape. For many rural believers, Christian identity tends to draw a sharp distinction between the worldly and the spiritual (Leung 1999). Being a Christian requires taking a spiritual approach to all worldly issues. Such a conservative faith creates tension with the profane business practice of urban-oriented Christian entrepreneurs and with their public identity in the emerging market economy. The role of the growing capitalist consumer economy has not been explored in previous ethnographies of Chinese Christianity because of their focus on village-centered Christianity in rural China (Constable 1994; Diamond 1996; Kipnis 2002). Unlike marginalized rural churchgoers who favor the conservative idea of withdrawing from the world, Wenzhou Christian entrepreneurs publicly acknowledge having been blessed by both God and the state in their business success.

Private Entrepreneurs Blessed by God and the State

The Christian revival has been intertwined with regional development for the past two decades in Wenzhou. As the Wenzhou model of economic development became an emblem of the post-Mao reform in the state-controlled media in the late 1980s, for the first time in history Wenzhou emerged as a center on the political map of China. There is also a "Wenzhou model" in the post-Mao Christian revival, which can be characterized by Christian entrepreneurs playing a leadership role in the local church community. Although showing a certain degree of caution, today's Wenzhou Christian entrepreneurs have little fear of revealing their religious identity in the public arena. Many have named their enterprises after individuals and places in the Christian Bible, such as the Jianan (Canaan) shoe factory, the Boteli (Bethel) button factory, the Yisila (Ezra) bookstore, and the Mijia (Micah) valve factory. They have earned much recognition and respect for their rising economic power, from the reformist state and the local populace. This contributes to their growing confidence and assertiveness in dealing with local government authorities on religious issues.

Brother Liu, in his forties, owns one of the largest furniture factories in Wenzhou and leads a local church at the same time. He started his own enterprise in the mid-1990s. Before that, he was an ordinary worker in the state sector. Liu describes his success story of expanding the factory, from a family workshop in a rented apartment to the current one with its several modern production lines and seven hundred employees, as "God's special care." As he puts it:

> We seized a good opportunity to run this factory at the time when this industry just started and there was much space for development. We saw the prospect of the market so we made it. If we did it today it may have difficulty. Each year we have a new wish and we have always been able to fulfill it. Our development is quite smooth. First of all, this is due to God's blessings. Second, it has to do with the efforts of our shareholders and workers. Today we enjoy a good reputation both in Wenzhou and in the same industry. This is not due to my personal efforts, but completely to God's special care.

Liu became a Christian as a teenager under the influence of family. Although he attributes his dramatic accumulation of wealth primarily to God's work, he is aware that when the state started to bless the private economy early in the reform era, he was able to seize an unprecedented opportunity for business development. As a main beneficiary of the post-Mao economic reform, Liu holds a positive attitude toward the reform-era state and toward being integrated into the current socioeconomic mainstream.

As one of the founders of a local church, Liu has sought legal and public status for his church. He elaborates:

> Currently our church takes a different view [of the government] compared with other house churches. I believe we are also a house church, but we need to face the government with courage. I found that some churches are afraid of the government. Their attitude is that when the government puts some pressure they just escape and disappear. Some churches are like that. They are afraid of having a dialogue with the government. They go underground if the government represses them. But I think we should be able to use the rights the state gives us, the freedom to believe. Also we know that we are not an evil cult, and we should be legitimate. So relatively speaking we can face the government with ease. In recent years, the government also tends to recognize us because we are all taxpayers and have made, more or less, some contribution to society. Furthermore, they know our ways of doing things and our background. They must believe that we won't do things like an evil cult or become anti-government. We follow all official rules, pay taxes, and obey political orders. In addition, we are serving society. Now there are social problems. The government is trying to build a harmonious society. In a harmonious society the religious force cannot be neglected. Due to this, the government fairly recognizes us. Thus, our church has such a large space. Seriously speaking, our church is not officially approved or registered. But as a house church we have certain connections with government.

Liu seems to be talking about his church, but his entrepreneur identity is even more salient in his language, as if he were commenting on the role of his enterprise and his rights as a state-sanctioned private entrepreneur. This is particularly so when it comes to his "contributions to the society," "paying taxes," and "connections with the government." He is well aware that the state's recognition of his church is based on his success as a boss or, in his words, a "taxpayer."

Three years ago, Liu and several other contributors purchased the current 1,500 square meter church space in an office building for ¥8 million. The Wenzhou municipal building is just a few blocks away. Liu originally wanted to register his church with the local Religious Affairs Bureau (RAB), a state apparatus for religious governance, but the RAB officials declined his request, reluctant to grant his church legal status. This new type of urban church is in between the officially registered church and the traditional "un-authorized" house church. It constitutes a third way, as a state-recognized but unregistered "house church." Though the church failed to receive a "re-ligious venue certificate," an embodiment of state regulation of religion, Liu used the smooth relationship he has developed with the local government through business to obtain informal recognition from the authorities con-cerned. "Those cadres like to maintain good *guanxi* [good relationships] with the bosses," he said with confidence. In fact, it happens that the head of the local RAB has a relative who has been a business partner with Liu's factory. It is often the case across China that local party cadres are envious of the eco-nomic power of the new rich and seek to ally with them for personal material benefit (see Wank 1995). Liu is satisfied with the current status of his church, since it already has the state's recognition to conduct services openly. More-over, its unregistered status has pleased many elderly churchgoers who still have the traumatic memory of state persecution under Mao and thus strongly reject any form of state involvement in church affairs.

As both a successful businessman and influential church leader, Brother Liu fits the Wenzhou model of the boss Christian. Although few Wenzhou boss Christians can balance their roles in the business world and in the church community as well as Liu does, they are important actors in Wenzhou's post-Mao Christian revival. As an older local church leader reluctantly remarked, "During the Cultural Revolution the workers and farmers played a leadership role in the church, while today it is bosses who are playing that role." He at-tributed this change to God, saying "the context of God's work changes" and "bosses have the special vision from God" (*yixiang*). The so-called changing context of God's work mirrors the ideological change from the Maoist lead-ership of the worker-peasant to the current leadership of entrepreneurs and scientists. In such a rapid transition period, Christian entrepreneurs have surpassed the older church members in authority and leadership. This can be clearly seen from those Christian entrepreneurs who hold a certain political influence in local society.

Brother Chen, in his early fifties, owns the largest Wenzhou Christian en-terprise, Shenli (literally, "God's power") Group Ltd. Founded in 1984, Shenli currently consists of more than twenty manufacturing companies, with total assets of more than ¥1 billion. Chen is a model private entrepreneur whom the reformist state eagerly seeks to incorporate. As such, he has played several politically significant roles in the state bureaucratic system and received the title of "national outstanding private entrepreneur," an award the post-Mao state uses to encourage the private economy. Earlier, his economic ambitions were severely punished under the Maoist state, which prohibited private business activities; he was jailed for "economic crime" for sixty-nine days. Today he recounts his experience of God in the jail as a miracle and his quick release as a result of his continuous prayer. However, his personal transformation from a poor three-wheeler driver to one of the wealthiest entrepreneurs in China appears to be a more miraculous story. In testimony he gave in a fellowship meeting mainly for entrepreneurs, he recalled his previous hardships and offered a supernatural explanation for his current success:

> I used to be out of work, but now I am the president of the Shenli Group. Of course, God must have used me to do his work. I didn't have any social status as a three-wheeler driver, but now God has given me the positions of the president of the Wenzhou Chamber of Commerce, the vice president of the Wenzhou committee of the People's Political Consultative Conference, a commissioner of the National People's Political Consultative Conference, and a council member of the Zhejiang Provincial People's Political Consultative Conference. These are all things that an ordinary person cannot imagine. In the past, I also could not think about it. But they all have happened. I think God must have his arrangement, and he let me do what he wanted to do. . . . So I believe God has loved me throughout the years and as a shepherd he won't let any single sheep get lost.

As seen in the way he named his enterprise, Chen believes God's power enables him to get ahead in the emerging market economy. Chen has publicized his Christian identity on local TV and in the newspaper, and I have heard his personal testimonies retold by a number of Wenzhou Christians who take him as a public symbol of high official tolerance of Christianity in Wenzhou. He has emphasized the harmonious coexistence of faith and the state on various occasions. He even once said, "The stability of the state is the foundation of our faith." His recent experience of accompanying President Hu Jintao on a visit to North America as part of a private entrepreneur delegation made him an even more highly respected figure in the local Christian community. Although as a busy entrepreneur he is not actively involved in daily church affairs, his presence in the local church often leads to enhanced confidence among local believers and signals that they are practicing a socially and politically approved faith.

In contrast to the symbolic political influence of Chen, Brother Gao has served as an actual partner of the state in governing the local community. In his forties, Gao has run a garment factory for more than a decade. A year ago the party superior selected him as the party secretary of his district to govern its three thousand residents. At the time, he was taking a six-month theological training course in a local church with a plan to be fully committed to serving the church one day. He has established his reputation as a local business leader with the capacity to help the local populace get rich. Although the Chinese Communist Party officially bans religious faith among its members, local government leaders often see the conflict between the party and religion in a less ideological, more pragmatic light. For Gao, service to the party and local government is also a chance to serve God, even if it costs him financially as a businessman. As he said:

> If the populace agrees and God supports, I will do my best based on justice and love. I may lose millions of yuan during the three-year term but if I can promote the development of the district, the honor is far beyond the loss. I know that the development opportunity comes. . . . If I were not a Christian, why should I work so hard [as the party secretary]? Everything we do is for the glory of God and the love of Christ . . . to use this position to show the light of Christ and to let people see that we are Christian so we have power and determination to do it. We won't feel tired but will pursue it with happiness.

Gao's Christian faith energizes him to take care of the community and act for justice. By "following God's standards," Gao has successfully dealt with local gangs in a road construction project and refused various types of bribes. When one of his political opponents challenged him by reporting his Christian faith to his party superior and accusing him of believing in superstition, Gao made no compromise. He even took the opportunity to attack the internal conflicts and problems within the local government and stress that a Christian-dominated government would be much more efficient, since Christians treat each other as brothers and sisters and value truth.

Gao's attack on the local government is an example of Christian entrepreneurs' increased assertiveness, which is prompted by their rising economic power. In fact, his Christian identity is more salient and helpful than his party secretary identity in dealing with various local issues. The local people generally view the party cadres as corrupt and self-interested, and the position of the party secretary as highly profitable. Indeed, his rival for the same office attempted to get the position through bribery. Although it is still too early to say whether the state and the church have co-opted one another in their common pursuit of social stability and economic development, Christianity certainly has gained recognition from the state as a useful social force in local governance. In this case, the local government preferred a cadre who follow the Christian ethic and seek to promote local development rather than a greedy, rent-seeking, but ideologically trustworthy atheist official.

These are portraits of several Christian entrepreneurs whose experience of rapid upward mobility is not uncommon in reform-era Wenzhou. The dramatic personal transformation from deprived state worker to wealthy private entrepreneur, and even state partner, corresponds to Wenzhou's development from an impoverished town to a dynamic regional center of global capitalism in the post-Mao market transition. Having been empowered by state policy change, Wenzhou Christian entrepreneurs began to interact more vigorously with the state and take a pragmatic approach to religious governance by the state. Moreover, their modern capitalist cultural logic has greatly facilitated the production and management of various church-related activities, of which evangelization constitutes the core.

Evangelization in the Context of Development

Preachers have the noblest status in front of God as God's servants; entrepreneurs are the most glorious in the field of business. It would be much better if we can combine the two parties.

— A YOUNG WENZHOU BOSS AND CHURCH PREACHER

In response to "God's calling," many Wenzhou Christian entrepreneurs have pursued evangelization in and outside Wenzhou with the same fervor with which they have pursued their economic ambitions. Some have even quit business to be fully engaged in spreading Christianity across China. More have found a way to promote evangelization as an integral part of their economic development plans. In practice, the Christian entrepreneurs apply their strategic vision and managerial experience in organizing evangelization work. For example, they take advantage of the existing Wenzhou business network in the target region to learn more about the political economic conditions of the community before going there, which parallels a regular market survey. As a matter of course they would make careful arrangements to avoid police harassment in the local community and seek permission from the local government.

An interchurch evangelization group was established in Wenzhou in 1989 to coordinate efforts and resources. Well-funded by local entrepreneurs, it has three main goals: to spread the Good News, to develop local evangelization initiatives, and to build Wenzhou businesspeople's evangelization network across the country. They have successfully evangelized in many poor inland provinces, where their economic power plays a central role in gaining entry from local cadres and state agencies and in attracting local people to conversion.

During one sermon Brother Dai, a middle-aged preacher and former businessman who had just returned from an evangelization trip, shared his experience in the impoverished regions of southwest China. Surprisingly, the southwest township government, local RAB, and police department all supported his high-profile evangelization in a stadium and even encouraged him and his fellow Christians to return in the future. Behind the local state support and encouragement were the investment and material benefits Wenzhou Christians brought with them. This closely parallels trading behavior in the market economy. In fact, Brother Dai's evangelization was conducted in the context of "Western Development and Poverty Reduction," a central state-promoted regional development program. For the same reason, individual Wenzhou Christian businesspeople have seldom encountered official obstacles in establishing house church gathering points while they do business across China. On the basis of their economic advantage and their knowledge of the actual workings of state bureaucracy, Christian entrepreneurs have developed a distinct strategy of facilitating evangelization by responding to the local government's call to "attract investment and enterprises" (*zhaoshang yinzi*) and approaching high-ranking local officials as their top priority.

With eleven years of evangelization experience, Sister Chang summarized her strategy as a "top-down" approach characterized by building *guanxi* with local party officials from the highest level to the lowest before evangelizing the local populace. According to Chang, this helps circumvent the local police, RAB, and other potential barriers to evangelization at the community level. Chang used to run a shirt factory but later transferred the business to her relatives to "work for God" on a full-time basis. On behalf of a private Wenzhou enterprise, she persuaded the mayor of a poor inland city to establish an orphanage-based evangelization center there.

Unlike the older generation of believers, who tend to view the local state as a major enemy of their faith and prefer to conduct evangelization clandestinely, Christian entrepreneurs in Wenzhou sometimes take the local state as a potential partner that can greatly facilitate their work in spreading the faith. This parallels development of their positive working relationship with the state in the "socialist market economy." Brother Luo once shared an episode in his negotiations with a local government in central China:

> They invited our Wenzhou entrepreneurs to invest in a local high school based on 500 mu of land. As a Christian, I requested they provide an investment environment that included three sacred things. First, I asked for a sacred school there, a Christian-culture-based school like Harvard and Cambridge, and they agreed. Second, I asked for a sacred hall, a church for gatherings, and they also agreed. Third, I asked for a sacred mountain like the Prayer Mountain in Korea. Korea's rapid development has resulted from their prayers. The local government promised me 5,000 mu of mountain land.

Luo is an ambitious, middle-aged businessman who owns an investment company headquartered in Shanghai. He also acts as the head of a district-level Christian council, a government-sanctioned Protestant organization under the RAB's direct supervision. The local government has recognized him for his donations to various relief and public development projects. In line with his conspicuous businessman's style, Luo has his luxury council office on the top floor of a high-rise commercial building furnished by a Christian entrepreneur friend. As both a devout, long-time Christian and a current local state-authorized church leader, he serves the church by acting as a bridge between believers and the state.

For Christian entrepreneurs, the experience of successfully combining evangelization with economic development is something they like to brag about. Indeed, they feel so empowered that some even imagine conducting evangelization in the Great Hall of the People in Beijing. Their assertiveness and boldness in dealing with the local state is a result in part of their well-internalized notion of economic development as the fundamental principle in society under the contemporary reformist state. Since the mid-1980s, local party and government leaders have been under great pressure to promote economic development in order to politically legitimate themselves in the eyes of both the populace and their party-state superiors. In this context, some local and regional governments encourage faith-based charities to meet the huge need for social services caused by the collapse of the education and health care systems in poor rural areas and the bankruptcy of state-owned enterprises in the city.

Another way of combining evangelization with business development among Wenzhou Christian entrepreneurs is the creation of a Christianity-based enterprise culture that they perceive as modern, progressive, and productive. Translated Western books dealing with employer-employee relations from the perspective of the Bible (e.g., *Management by Proverbs*, by Michael Zigarelli) are popular among Wenzhou Christian entrepreneurs and have even become required reading for managers in several Wenzhou enterprises. Some Christian-headed Wenzhou factories periodically invite small evangelization groups from the local church to proselytize among their employees, most of whom are migrant workers from poor inland provinces. During a sermon in front of a group of uniformed workers who had just finished that day's assignments in a factory making glasses, a young boss preacher stated:

> There are many bosses in Wenzhou. This is God's special blessing to them. Coming from other provinces, you may also have the urge to become a boss here in the future. . . . It is not for your boss that you work hard. Instead, you should be grateful to your boss who has provided such a good work environment. The value of a person is to be someone who is being needed. Our jobs are arranged by God. Everything we now are doing should be God's special calling.

This type of Christian teaching proves both an effective way of evangelization and a new method of discipline and factory governance. The notions of hard work as God's calling and high economic status as God's blessing serve as a motivation for ambitious poor workers (cf. Weber 2001). For practical reasons, the workers often feel a strong urge to follow their Wenzhou employers' faith. Some even convert to Christianity in a rather short period after entering Christian-led Wenzhou factories.

As a forward-looking businessman, Brother Liu tries to apply his Christian faith in the operation of his furniture factory and promotes Christianity as the enterprise culture among his seven hundred employees. The aim, in his words, is to "raise the quality [*suzhi*] of the uneducated migrant workers and purify their minds" and to "let God's words govern the factory." He believes that this will help lower the cost of daily management by cultivating a strong sense of self-motivated work ethic among the workers and eventually enhance productivity. He maintains a chapel inside the factory that holds services every morning and can accommodate more than a hundred people. He preaches there once a month, and as the head of the firm his presence unsurprisingly attracts strong attendance among the workers. To further implement the idea of a Christian enterprise, Liu requires all his managers and directors to attend a small weekly Bible study group to learn the *culture* of Christianity. The class is designed to enlarge their managerial know-how; accordingly, he makes it clear that he does not care whether they really believe.

The practice of combining secular enterprise management with faith ideally not only serves the economic ends but also fulfills the evangelistic goal. As Liu once stated, "I sincerely hope that all workers not only pursue material improvement but also think carefully about the value of their life. Through listening to the Good News they can accept Christian faith, change their life, and truly become a person filled with God's blessings." More than one hundred workers have been baptized under Liu's consistent influence. It is noteworthy that evangelization under the guise of modern enterprise culture and factory governance is apparently detached from the politicized context of state religious governance. It has particular legitimacy in the post-Mao state space in which economic development constitutes the party's central task but traditional moral teachings and political education have lost their effectiveness in disciplining and motivating the workforce.

Engaging the State and Reforming Church Culture

Although the state politically appropriates and promotes the Wenzhou model as an integral part of its developmental project (Shi et al. 2002), regional development contributes to depoliticizing the local religious context and reshaping church-state relations. Individual believers today can legitimate their faith identity through engaging in capitalist commercialism. As one boss Christian said, "Doing business is not equal to serving God, but doing business is just serving God for those who have real Christian faith." When asked to comment on the relationship between economic development and Christian faith in Wenzhou, the boss Christians frequently refer to the correlation between the number of churches and economic advancement in Europe and the United States as an obvious answer. Several have even cited Max Weber's *The Protestant Ethic and the Spirit of Capitalism* (2001) in their preaching to highlight the connection. Yet they turn Weber's classic thesis on religion and capitalism upside down to legitimatize their Christian faith and their entrepreneurial identity simultaneously in the post-Mao market transition. Here the Protestant ethic appears to be a cultural "tool kit" (Swidler 1986) for Wenzhou bosses to bring transcendent meaning to a rationalized market economy. In this sense, unlike Chinese Christianity in rural areas, Wenzhou Christianity serves more as a symbol of Western modernity than as a symbol of salvation or a medium of resistance (Constable 1994; Diamond 1996; Kipnis 2002).

Wenzhou Christian entrepreneurs seek to reposition themselves through faith in the changing political economic context. As people who were among the first to get rich under the reforms, they have found a supernatural justification for their newfound wealth. They attribute their own economic success and Wenzhou's rapid development in the reform era to "the work of the Holy Spirit," "God's guidance," "God's mercy," and "God's blessing for Wenzhou's long Christian tradition and large Christian population." The hard-working and risk-taking spirit of the Wenzhou model is rarely mentioned. This supernatural attribution also corresponds to their enthusiasm about evangelization. Many truly hold a deep belief that God will bless their enterprises if they support evangelization work, and that the more they give, the more God will give back. The Wenzhou Christian notion that "doing business is serving God" mirrors the reformist state language of "letting a few people get rich first" and "getting rich is glorious." Their success in the entrepreneurial world not only fulfills a Protestant's duty to work hard for the glory of God but also meets the secular demands of the reformist state, which emphasizes economic development. Therefore, they find their economic status glorified in the Christian and state discourses alike. From their strong sense of agency, developed in daily business practices, Wenzhou Christian entrepreneurs collectively renegotiate the boundaries of religion and politics through blending personal faith with economic development.

Affluent urban-oriented Christian entrepreneurs seek to play a much greater role in the church and also to greatly expand the influence of faith beyond the physical boundaries of the church. To achieve these ends, they must cope with a conservative faith tradition in rural areas that discourages socioeconomic involvement. While some individuals who face the conflict between entrepreneurial and religious identities resolve it by abandoning one or the other, many are trying to find a way to combine them. As an advantaged urban-oriented Christian group, they can afford to construct a dual identity by reshaping the church culture and distancing themselves from traditional rural Christianity.

A newly established monthly meeting of entrepreneurs, called "the professionals' fellowship" (*shiyeren tuanqi*), best shows such initiative. According to one of the Christian entrepreneur organizers, the goal of the fellowship is to "serve as a platform for professionals to socialize with one another and to integrate and share resources for the sake of Christ." By their definition, the professionals refer to the "high-end" (*gaoduan*) people in the church, among them entrepreneurs, teachers, lawyers, doctors, government officials, and pastors.[1] But they explicitly give priority to big entrepreneurs. A social gathering for local Christian elites, the fellowship is an invitation-only event. The organizer invites people by phone or sends a formal invitation a week before the scheduled meeting. All participants are expected to sign in, leaving their title and contact information. The fellowship meeting lasts for four hours. A speaker invited from outside gives a lecture, which is always followed by a lively, interactive discussion session. The invited speakers are all Christians and have expertise in the relationship between faith and economics, particularly in promoting business management on the basis of biblical principles. Recent speakers have included a professor who lectured on the importance of Christian faith in developing a healthy market economy and a writer who talked about the proper view of Christians toward wealth. The highlight of the fellowship was the day when the former president of Motorola China, a well-known Chinese-American Christian, came to speak on the opportunities and responsibilities of Christian entrepreneurs.

The monthly professionals' fellowship usually attracts hundreds of participants from different parts of the city. It helps them feel involved and engaged in church affairs. Many say the invited experts help them clarify questions about their faith in the context of a market economy and correct their attitude toward the relationship between faith and business. After attending a fellowship meeting, a young businessman commented, "We used to think that only preaching and evangelization are serving God. In fact, developing personal business is also a way of serving God and exhibiting the love of Christ." A middle-aged boss echoed, "If I could have heard this lecture ten years ago I would have developed a much larger enterprise and have made much more money by now." Previously, he was blamed by older churchgoers for "worshiping Mammon" and "loving the world" when his enterprise was doing well financially.

This conservative tradition has had less influence on the younger generation of churchgoers, those who grew up in the post-Mao era and thus have little historical baggage. Brother Tian, in his late twenties, represents the younger generation of boss Christians who are dissatisfied with the socially isolated condition of the church. He severely attacked the older conservative church members for their "old-fashionedness" and strong antistate emotions. He stressed use of the current context of development to promote the influence of Christianity in society. As a main planner of the fellowship, he raised a number of challenges for today's Christian professionals:

> As the Bible says, I am sending you out like sheep among wolves. Therefore, be as shrewd as snakes and as innocent as doves. Tracing the historical development of the church, we could not find any period of time when shrewdness and innocence were well integrated. Is Jesus' demand too high, or do we need to reflect on ourselves deeply? How can a church without a good sense of management and strategic vision be shrewd and resourceful? How can a church without concern about society and responsibility testify innocence and love? The whole society is now supportive of "building a harmonious society" [jianshe hexieshehui] and the enterprises are focused on making plans to fit their brands to the current context. What can Christian professionals do for the church and society? What will the Beijing Olympics and Shanghai World Expo bring for China? How should we expect and pray for it?

By talking about "building a harmonious society" and mentioning Beijing Olympics and Shanghai World Expo, Tian shows his great familiarity with the state's vocabulary and puts God's decrees in the context of China's development. He has a positive attitude toward the future role of the church in contributing to China's social development. This contrasts sharply with many elder church members, who maintain the victim mentality developed under Mao and are passive about social participation.

As entrepreneurs, the organizers of the professionals' fellowship are shrewd in positioning the group. Although it is held usually in a local church, the fellowship has its own organizational structure, independent of any church. In Chinese, a fellowship is called *tuanqi*, a term that carries the meaning of a social gathering or organization. The fellowship therefore violates current state law, which restricts religious organizations or gatherings beyond officially registered churches. The fellowship organizers were aware of this potential legal problem. Brother Tian explained to me that this was why they decided to replace "fellowship" with "lecture series" (*jiangtan*) in their forthcoming newsletter. In fact, the organizers have used "professionals' fellowship" constantly in conversation but "profession and faith lecture series" in all written communication, even on the background curtain, the hymn paper, the fellowship logo, and participant badges.

Although many Wenzhou Christians are still struggling in the spiritual-secular binary, the fellowship participants are developing a dual identity and a new shared vision of faith and business activities. Unlike other social clubs or gatherings for entrepreneurs, the professionals' fellowship is conducted strictly in a spiritualized framework, with the ultimate goal of "bringing people to God." It always starts with a half-hour of hymn singing and then simultaneous individual prayers, which is no different from regular church sessions in Wenzhou in terms of the ritual form. A slight contrast is that, in the fellowship, a Wenzhou Christian entrepreneur usually leads a prayer to thank God for guiding the guest speaker to Wenzhou and let God empower the guest speaker to say the truth. Then the guest speaker offers another prayer as a prelude to the lecture. The hymns they select for the meeting are much more socially significant than those sung in a typical Wenzhou church session; for instance, they have repeatedly sung "China's Morning" and "A Heart for China." Both convey a Christian's faithful prayer and blessing for a peaceful China. Brother Tian briefly commented on the selection of these patriotic hymns: "We want to show concern about the fate of the nation from a Christian's stance." The final discussion session often produces divergent and even conflicting views, but all disagreements are formally reconciled and (ideally) unity is achieved in the simultaneous prayers and singing of hymns that conclude the meeting.

This regular gathering constitutes a cultural ritual of identity reconstruction for the Christian entrepreneurs, and it offers a local context in which they can transcend moral and spiritual restrictions on secular business dealings. The wealthiest Christian entrepreneurs are among those receiving the most attention at the meeting. They are recognized not for service to the church but mainly for combining personal faith and business achievements. As the biggest Christian entrepreneur in Wenzhou, Brother Chen was always asked to sit in the first row in front of the speaker and sometimes to sit on the stage to engage in a dialogue with the guest speaker in front of the audience. The fellowship is an emotionally supportive community that reconciles religious and professional identities. By singing hymns, offering prayers, listening to a lecture, and engaging in a postlecture discussion together with fellow Christian professionals, individual Christian entrepreneurs experience a range of rituals that are significant for maintaining their reconciled identities. Here they find cultural resources and mutual recognition unavailable in the traditional church setting and collectively engage in creating a new church culture.

This new church culture is consistent with a modern entrepreneurial logic. Several Wenzhou Christian entrepreneurs have privately talked about using the professionals' fellowship as an opportunity to "build attractive faith products," "provide high-quality, professional faith service," and "make Christianity a Wenzhou brand." In practice, the professionals' fellowship is an important opportunity to exhibit Christian faith in a highly sophisticated atmosphere and enhance the cultural capital of the entrepreneurs. As mentioned earlier, the guest speakers are all well-known, accomplished professionals. Accordingly, the monthly meeting takes the form of a professional business conference. This is particularly reflected in the well-sequenced ritual program of registration, speaker's introduction, tea break, group discussion, and concluding remarks.

A planning and managing committee (*cehua zhixing zu*) comprising several Christian entrepreneurs supervises all meeting-related issues and operations, from the speaker's invitation and reception, coordination, technical support, and finance to selection, design, and decoration of the meeting place. Throughout the process of producing and managing a fellowship meeting, these Christian entrepreneurs highly value specialist skills and knowledge and rely on the modern specialized division of labor that is also the basis of their private enterprises. The imported stereo system, the overhead projectors, the stylish exhibition boards displaying the speaker's biography, and the specially designed fellowship logo and participant badges further contribute to the modern, professional look of the meeting. There are also young girls carrying Christian ribbons greeting people at the entrance. Moreover, to further its influence, the meeting produces and circulates a newsletter afterward, with large color photos and short essays portraying the event. The fellowship's modern style embodies Wenzhou Christian entrepreneurs' self-image as leading members of society and encodes components of their understanding of the economic modernization in which they play a major part.

Although there is no room for religion in the official state discourse of modernity, the Wenzhou professionals' fellowship demonstrates that Christianity, as a so-called great religious tradition, represents high culture and constitutes an ethical basis for everyday life—in contrast to "feudal superstition," the officially constructed category of excluded ritual practices (Anagnost 1994). Christian entrepreneurs are using their socioeconomic advantage and market-based discursive power to attract potential converts and influence the state and society by presenting living examples of high-quality believers. As Brother Liu commented, "We want people to rethink the view of Christianity as a faith for the ignorant and those who have nothing else to do, so they can reposition Christianity."

An essential character of the postsocialist mode of governance is its stress on individuals' commitment to both the market principle and the state ideology, a commitment encoded in the official rhetoric of spiritual civilization (*jingshen wenming*). However, the ambiguity and pragmatic use of such language often encourages new state interventions in local society, especially as "the cultivation of civilized, high quality citizens" comes to be seen as the key to China's modernization (Friedman 2004). Through the success of the Wenzhou model of economic development, these entrepreneurs demonstrate nationwide their abilities in modern capitalist production. Through the organization and management of the high-profile professionals' fellowship, Wenzhou Christian entrepreneurs display both religious piety and an entrepreneurial spirit. In positioning themselves as committed simultaneously to religious faith and rationalized modernity, they defy the dichotomous categories of the modern, "civilized," and secular versus the poor, "superstitious," and religious.

Conclusion

Adding to the post-Weberian literature on religion and capitalism, I argue that regional capitalist development enabled by post-Mao reforms has both depoliticized and promoted local practices of faith. The emerging market economy plays a mediating role in church-state interaction by molding the postsocialist popular consciousness in which both the state and church are embedded. Because of its remote geographic location and private sphere-centered economy, Wenzhou traditionally occupied a marginal place on the political map of the state-controlled socialist economy. As a successful model of market economy championed publicly by the postsocialist developmental state, Wenzhou is undergoing a recentering process in which its people are gaining the confidence to assert and display their local cultural tradition and religious identity. Rapid regional development is neutralizing the sociopolitical context in which local religious individuals had to confront state power, and it has greatly empowered local Christianity through the role of many urban entrepreneur believers.

By focusing on the entrepreneurial class of Christians in post-Mao Wenzhou, this study presents an example of religious innovation and growth in modernity. The current Christian entrepreneurs are mostly middle-aged men who were teenagers during the Cultural Revolution. They were too young to have memories of the brutal elimination of religion by the Maoist state. As the beneficiaries of post-Mao reforms, they have internalized the postsocialist mode of governance and adopted a strategic approach to engaging with state religious governance. Some highly ambitious individuals have taken advantage of the existing political and economic system to disseminate faith; in so doing they engage in remaking church-state relations. Many have acted as local church leaders and preachers, translating the economic capital, social knowledge, and civic skills they acquired in the modern marketplace to their capacity in church management. They can be compared to the older generation of churchgoers, many of whom have internalized a culture and embraced an identity of martyrdom that is based on their endurance and sufferings during the Cultural Revolution. Unlike marginalized rural believers, the entrepreneurs seek to be integrated into the current socioeconomic mainstream and play a greater role in the public arena. Rather than conform to institutionalized religious authority, they shape church culture to suit their emotional and identity needs. They actively and creatively seek to integrate their religious and entrepreneur identities, thereby depoliticizing Christianity in the state-authorized context of business development.

Chapter 3

Of Manners, Morals, and Modernity: Cosmopolitan Desires and the Remaking of Christian Identity

The rise of the entrepreneurial Christians in the late '80s and early '90s was influenced by the work of the Holy Spirit in the '70s. After they got rich and obtained social status, they realized it was God's blessing and got to know Christianity better. They want to redeem [huikui] the blessing. Many had already experienced and been involved in the Christian revival in the '70s when they were still young. But later they left the church and started businesses. After years of efforts in the [business] world, when both their status and Christianity's status was enhanced, they then returned to the church.

— A MIDDLE-AGED FORMER FACTORY BOSS AND CHURCH ELDER.

Just as this boss Christian suggests, private entrepreneurs and Christianity gained prestige and prominence almost simultaneously in Wenzhou. As the notion of "redeeming the blessing" implies, the rise of powerful boss Christians contributes to the social prestige associated with Christian identity. This chapter explores the interrelationships of social power, prestige, and Christianity in contemporary Wenzhou.

Although it was once denigrated by Maoist anti-imperialism campaigns, today Christian identity implies both a superior spirituality and social prestige, at least among Christians. This process of identity remaking was enabled by the post-Mao reforms and China's vigorous integration to a global economy. It expresses the unfulfilled cosmopolitan desires of the newly ascendant capitalists of rural origin. Christianity is a prestigious cosmopolitan faith that embraces both global capitalism and an idealized notion of Western civilization and modernity. These stem in part from Christianity's historical roots in early Western missionary projects that emphasized civilizing the minds of the locals. Today Wenzhou Christianity has become a precious cultural and moral resource for the upwardly mobile bosses to reposition and distinguish themselves in the process of catching up with the capitalist West and shedding uncouthness. It is also an integral part of Wenzhou's urbanization, industrialization, and modernization processes. Wenzhou's capitalist development and rising Christianity have dismantled traditional social hierarchy and led to new forms of differentiation in local society.

Rural Origin, Cosmopolitan Desires

In the context of post-Mao market liberalization, Wenzhou has become the country's biggest manufacturing center of low-end products such as shoes, clothes, lighters, and spectacles. These items are then exported around the world. The mobility of Wenzhou merchants played a central role in fueling Wenzhou's reform-era economic miracle. Although Wenzhou's urbanization and industrialization began just three decades ago, it has been a transnational society actively engaged in trade and commerce for many centuries. Some half a million people of Wenzhou origin currently reside in more than one hundred countries, mainly in Europe and the United States.[1] There are streets named Wenzhou in Paris, Rome, New York City, Vienna, Madrid, Sao Paulo, Dubai, and Budapest. The large expatriate community of Wenzhou people around the world maintains close social, economic, and cultural ties with their hometown; consequently, Wenzhou people often take Western cities (rather than the Chinese metropolises of Beijing and Shanghai) as a reference point for the latest fashion trends and new business concepts. These transnational networks enable Wenzhou to look outward and stay at the forefront of China's capitalist development.

After years of struggling for survival and success overseas, many Wenzhou emigrants have made it and now can afford to bring the symbols of Western modernity back to their hometown like a gift. Upscale local residential communities in Wenzhou bear such names as Paris Mansion, Athens Garden, Prince Garden, and Earl Hill estate. Newly built shopping centers are called the World Trade Center, Union Square, and Times Square. Europe Town, a mixed commercial and residential building complex covering 144 mu, is still under construction in the city center, with an already erected copy of Michelangelo's statue of David, a miniature Arc de Triomphe, and dozens of gigantic, ornate roman columns.

Nearby, the supposedly fanciest local villa project, "Manhattan," is about to begin construction on the land of an old state-owned shipyard that a syndicate of local businessmen bought for ¥1.5 billion. It will become the site of ultra-luxurious villas designed for rich entrepreneur customers. One of the project developers, a member of the local syndicate, proudly said to a newspaper, "America has Manhattan, Shanghai has Oriental Manhattan, and Wenzhou also needs a Manhattan."[2]

New social classes are forming in this intensely urbanizing society. Wenzhou is also an openly competitive society in which a person of rural origin has a chance of upward mobility and can make a claim to cosmopolitan modernity. In fact, the overwhelming majority of current Wenzhou entrepreneurs are of rural origin and started their businesses from scratch in the beginning of the reform era.[3] Nowadays Wenzhou's new rich are well known for their conspicuous and symbolic consumption of Western brand-name products. According to statistics supplied by the Wenzhou municipal department of motor vehicles in July 2006, Wenzhou residents currently own more than thirty-six hundred BMWs, two thousand Mercedes, and six thousand Audis.[4] These figures do not even include those Wenzhou people who have registered their cars outside of Wenzhou. Besides owning luxury cars, Wenzhou bosses are enthusiastic about buying prime real estate in Shanghai, Hangzhou, and Beijing, taking foreign vacations, and sending their children to study abroad, particularly in the United Kingdom and Australia.

Although Wenzhou seems to be ahead of the rest of China in the process of catching up with Western-style capitalist consumption, it retains small-town character. Administratively, it was recently elevated to a national-level city from a prefecture-level city. But local people have maintained a strong sense of communal solidarity based on the unique cultural and linguistic traits that distinguish Wenzhou from the surrounding areas. This communal solidarity has become an important source of social capital among Wenzhou businesspeople worldwide.

Wenzhou has also become a hub of informal lending in China. Outside the official banking system, money flows among relatives and neighbors in

Figure 3.1 Europe Town in Wenzhou. Note the Roman columns lavishly used to decorate not only upscale local residential and commercial buildings but also local church buildings. (Photo by author.)

the form of informal loans to finance the starting of small local enterprises.[5] Family-owned enterprises dominate the Wenzhou model of economic development. Wherever they travel and sojourn, people of Wenzhou origin build their ethnic enclave in the form of Wenzhou markets, streets, and towns. Family and neighborhood connections are essential to the social organization of the daily economic life in Wenzhounese societies. Wenzhou currently has ¥300 billion in private capital, of which nearly two-thirds is floating capital that constantly moves across regional and national borders for speculation in real estate, coal mines, the cotton industry, petroleum wells, power stations, and even taxi licenses (Hu 2004). Other Chinese have accused groups of Wenzhou speculators of inflating housing prices across the country. Wenzhou business and financial practices are founded on a notion of community that is described by Tonnies (1974) as *Gemeinschaft*. Wenzhou's networked capitalism operates on a transnational scale, with globally distributed social networks facilitating the global circulation of Wenzhou capital, commodities, and people. The business ties and networks across national boundaries enable Wenzhou people to celebrate their long-standing spirit of self-reliance and autonomy from the state—and sometimes to circumvent restrictions imposed by the state. The Mao-era decision not to base large state enterprises in this area left a vacuum for these risk-taking merchants to get a head start in the fledging market of the post-Mao era.

Although the local people enjoy increasing affluence, Wenzhou resembles a rural town, owing to its poor infrastructure and dilapidated public spaces. Wenzhou's small-town character is further reflected in the daily life of the local inhabitants. It is a common scene in winter to see people of different ages and sexes driving cars, riding motorcycles or buses, or wandering around outside in their pajamas. When it is hot, some men go half-naked and just wear underwear outside. Such scenes have become a subject of derision for outside visitors. Furthermore, petty squabbles and rivalries pervade everyday life in Wenzhou, where shrewdness is a much-celebrated personal virtue. In the neighborhoods adjacent to the central commercial district, where many boutique shops sell luxury Western branded goods such as Rolex, Gucci, Lacoste, Montagut, and Boss, families set their dinner and mahjong tables by the street, people bargain with the peddlers, neighbors sit outside gossiping, and they even hold funeral rituals there. Wenzhou combines rural tastes and sensibilities, commercial wealth, cosmopolitan desires, and bourgeois pursuits. Such contradictions are partly a consequence of the rapid urbanization of the countryside.[6]

Wenzhou's intense commercialism and utilitarian culture along with its poor educational facilities and infrastructure are responsible for a reputation of being a "cultural desert." As part of the local state civilizing project, the municipal government has envisioned developing a "cultural Wenzhou" (*wenhua Wenzhou*). Anxiety about uncouthness (*tu*) is intense among people of rural origin across China. This desire leads to commoditization of Chinese social life, consumerism, hedonism, and social inequality as well as pursuit of Western fashions, particularly among those who are wealthy and powerful enough. In Wenzhou, the local state and the upwardly mobile classes share these desires. The party chief of Longgang township in Wenzhou once commented on "the key to the success of complete urbanization" in a *People's Daily* news report titled "civilizing Longgang" (*wenming Longgang*). As the head of "the first peasant city" in China, he states:

The previous success of Longgang depended on the building of the city. Now it is time to enhance social and comprehensive quality [shehui zonghe suzhi], the key to which is to build people [zaoren]. By enhancing people's quality, the "peasant city" will eventually shed its uncouthness [doudiao yishen tuqi].[7]

The report concludes by championing the fact that the township, with a population of 150,000, owns twelve hundred pianos, indicating that "Longgang people are increasingly acquiring more Western style" (*yangqi*). What the major state newspaper fails to mention is that this "piano fever" has been felt most deeply in the Christian community.[8] A piano is always used to accompany hymn singing, an indispensable part of church services in Wenzhou. According to local Christians, almost all well-to-do Wenzhou Christian families own a piano and take it as a must-have item in the household. Sometimes a piano even appears as part of a dowry. Christians are the main patrons of local piano stores. During my fieldwork, I found that many boss Christians had a piano in their living room, a display of their high-class Western taste. Here the piano is not simply a Western musical instrument; it serves as a Western cultural symbol.

Not surprisingly, local Christians also participate in this process of symbolic consumption. Indeed, Wenzhou Christians often represent themselves, particularly to nonbelievers, as having the most authentic reason to embrace the West. Their unfulfilled cosmopolitan desires make Christianity an ideal symbolic product. Many entrepreneurs I encountered in the field were not new converts but were born to the faith. They seem to have just gotten serious about their faith recently, perhaps due to the perceived association between Christian universalistic values and cosmopolitan modernity. The notion of the West has played a profound role in shaping local Christian discourse and identity, and the landscape.

Maoist Past and Missionary Hauntings

Under the impact of Mao's anti-imperialism campaign, the notion of Christianity as a tool of imperialism imposed a profound stigma on many local believers. However, it also reinforced the connection between Christianity and the West.

In June 1951, on the eve of a campaign to systematically eliminate religion,

Figure 3.2 A piano in the living room of a boss Christian's house for home decoration purposes. Note the framed Bible verses written in Chinese calligraphy on the wall. (Photo by author.)

the Wenzhou municipal police department issued a top-secret document regarding Wenzhou Christianity. After a review of the backgrounds of some Wenzhou Christian denominations and the socioeconomic composition of local Christians, it concluded:

> The Wenzhou church was without exception controlled by the imperialist forces of England and the U.S. in terms of its organization, institution, economy, ideology, and operation. Given the anti-revolutionary view of this so-called apolitical, non-international church and their various criminal activities under the legal guise of evangelization that has undermined the people's interests since the liberation of the mainland, the church should be an important target of our anti-American imperialism campaign.[9]

Whether inadvertently or not, local believers swallowed the state's denigration of Wenzhou Christianity. Soon some were using an even more radical tone to denounce their religion.

In the early 1960s, some religious groups were forced to attend a series of political study meetings. At a local government meeting to "strike those who conduct anti-revolutionary sabotage activities under religious clothes," Xie Shengtao, who was then head of the Wenzhou TSPM, confessed:

> We cannot deny that imperialism has taken advantage of religion. In the past the clergy have listened to decrees on everything and taken imperialism as God. Now the poisonous elements of imperialist thoughts still persist. So we need to completely eliminate them. Without engaging anti-imperialism, speaking of patriotism is false.[10]

Hu Guiye, the vice head of the Wenzhou TSPM at the time, echoed this view:

> This meeting has taught me a lesson. I have been deeply affected by the poison of imperialism, only knowing the Kingdom of Heaven and the United States. Regarding the class struggle within religion, I have been unclear and have had ambiguous stances. Without the Party's education, I would be very dangerous.[11]

Maoist discourse on class struggle and anti-imperialism pervaded public opinions on Christianity. Although the colonial face of Wenzhou Christianity changed during the post-Mao era, local Christians continue to be haunted by a derogatory model of the West. Today, many Wenzhou Christians will not even admit that Christianity is a Western religion (*yangjiao*), even though the image of Jesus in Wenzhou is always a white man with blond hair and blue eyes. They learned in school that Christianity was the running dog (*zougou*) of imperialism. A young preacher's memory of such stigma is still fresh; he told me this story in a self-derisive tone. Born into a preacher's family, he used to hate preachers because this calling made their family poor. He felt ashamed in school during the 1980s when the textbook said that Christianity was an imperialist running dog the West had brought into China during the Opium Wars, and that Western religion equates to "flood and feral animals" (*hongshui mengshou*).[12] In public he was afraid of revealing his Christian identity; before meals he would either drop his chopsticks intentionally or pretend to feel tired so that he could close his eyes to pray in silence without others noticing.

State pressure not only imposed a stigma on the local Christian community but also deeply divided it. Given the history and memory of the TSPM's submission to and cooperation with the party in the Maoist era, nearly half a century later many elderly churchgoers still see TSPM as a tool of the state and a betrayer of faith. This blame and distrust was also passed on to the younger generation. Some young believers today hold the view that those who go to the TSPM church will not be saved because they place the CCP at a higher status than God and preach Marxism more than the Bible, even though they have never been to a TSPM church.

Because of such prejudice, members of the so-called official church always endure more pressure to defend their faith than members of house churches do. Consequently, the official church in Wenzhou tends to downplay its ties with the government by emphasizing ties with "authentic" Western Christianity and membership in the international religious community. As the chair of the Wenzhou Christian Council states:

> Actually the so-called orthodox churches overseas have connections with the
> two committees [lianghui][13] because the China Christian Council is a member
> of the World Council of Churches. The so-called house church is not a member
> of the World Council. Actually overseas orthodox churches like the Anglicans
> and Presbyterians have no connection with the house church. Put plainly,
> the authentic white church doesn't have connections with them. Only these
> unorthodox [busan busi de] overseas Chinese, particularly those originally from
> Wenzhou, have connections [with the house church here]. For example, the
> People's Republic of China is a member of the United Nations. The so-called
> Republic of China has no seat there. Similarly, China's two committees are part
> of the World Christian Council. They, the house church, are not. We all take
> part in the commemoration of World Prayer Day. The house church doesn't.
> Christians, Catholics and the Orthodox from all over the world all attend this
> annual event on the first Friday of March. We all attend, but they don't.

The "we" and "they" clearly characterize the differentiation between the so-called official and unofficial churches in Wenzhou. Nevertheless, it also shows the importance of the West in legitimizing Christian identity. There is further an assumption that authenticity is linked with the notion of Western whiteness, while those hailing from Wenzhou may be viewed as unorthodox because of their lack of foreignness. This statement comes not from a minor leader of an unorthodox church but from the head of the state-sanctioned Protestant organization. Wenzhou Christian communities, regardless of their divergent attitudes toward state religious governance, all resort to the West for legitimacy.

The perceived links between Western Christianity and cosmopolitan modernity reinforce this search for legitimacy. With a passionate and somewhat unquestionable tone, a young preacher in his thirties elaborated a Christian theory of cosmopolitan modernity under the title "the origin of faith." Wearing pressed black jeans and the English word "cowboy" conspicuous on the back of his red T-shirt, he preached:

> Many people believed in Jesus after they went to study abroad. Why? There are many people without knowledge and culture in China, but those who go to study in the West mostly have knowledge and culture. Some Wenzhou people don't want to accept the Gospel no matter how hard we have tried, but when they migrate to Italy they soon believe in Jesus. One said, "Ah, I believe in Jesus now." I asked him what had happened since he did not believe at home. He answered, "You have no choice [buneng buxin] in Italy, bosses and people who have knowledge here all believe in Jesus." Similarly, there are many migrant workers in Wenzhou whom we call the new Wenzhounese [xin wenzhouren]. They didn't believe in God in their hometown but all convert after they came to Wenzhou. They say that the bosses here all believe in Jesus and the people who have knowledge and culture all believe in Jesus. So in a civilized nation, Jesus is the source of wisdom. Civilized nations take Christianity as their state religion; many developed countries believe in Jesus. England has had Christianity as the state religion since the Roman Empire. Now the United States has the highest percentage of Christians among its population in the world. You have to admit that the Americans are the smartest people. For example, two out of three world-class scientists are Jews.[14] Why do people with wisdom and culture also believe in Jesus? The U.S. is a superpower. Look at how it was founded by the Puritans. England wanted to kill Jews and Christians. So the Puritans fled to the place now called the U.S. In just two hundred years, it became a superpower in the world. So when a newly elected U.S. president is sworn in, he will put one hand on the Bible and swear to use biblical principles to govern the nation. So a nation, a civilized nation, a civilized people all believe in Jesus. . . . Christian-

ity can also help develop civilization. A backward nation can be changed by faith. If you know a little bit about Chinese history, you will have to admit that schools, hospitals and orphanages, rest homes and other charitable organizations were established by Christians. When the Gospel reached China, schools were established. Why do we have pinyin that can facilitate our study of Chinese? I tell you this was not invented by the Chinese but by the missionaries who found Chinese so hard to learn and created pinyin based on their alphabet to help spread their faith. In fact these are all foreign inventions. Our hospitals were all established by foreigners, and China didn't have hospitals before. China didn't have schools before.

The preacher presents his argument as resting on evidence that is both self-evident and obvious. In Wenzhou, modern schools and hospitals were indeed introduced by Western missionaries. Two of the three major Wenzhou hospitals were operated in the first half of the twentieth century by Western missionaries, and a high school established in 1903 by the United Methodist Free Church accommodated three hundred local students at its peak, making it one of the largest schools in Zhejiang Province at that time (Soothill 1907).

In Wenzhou, school education used to be part of the privileged experience associated with Western missions. Today, in Wenzhou dialect Christianity is called "reason" (*daoli*); Christian faith is called "belief in reason" (*xin daoli*), and going to church is called "listening to reason" (*ting daoli*). This notion of reason involves a dual process of knowledge production and consumption in which the West acts as the center. Such Western (or Western-related) names as Isaac Newton, Albert Einstein, Thomas Edison, George W. Bush, Bill Gates, John Rockefeller, and Sun Yat-sen frequently appear in local preachers' sermons and send powerful messages to the audience. By connecting Christianity with the West, Wenzhou Christians are regaining their lost prestige in the post-Mao era.

The local church's embrace of biblical fundamentalism cannot be viewed as just an integral part of its evangelical orientation but must be considered in association with the fact that the great majority of Wenzhou Christians hail from rural villages and had little schooling. The Bible serves as the ultimate source of all knowledge for them. A middle-aged former boss preached on the authority of the Bible in a factory evangelization meeting in front of hundreds of workers:

> The Bible is the best seller in the world. The Bible is very important. The Bible is required reading at universities today. Such foreign countries as America and

Figure 3.3 A local Christian bookstore promoting the book *The Faith of George W. Bush*. (Photo by author.)

England, those developed countries all use the essence of the Bible to influence their culture. Their culture has the Bible as the background. So we see that the Bible is God's words telling you where you are from and where you are going. What have you come to do in this world? You can find out all the answers about your life in the Bible. The Bible is the Lord's words. The Bible tells us that you cannot change even one dot or stroke in it. We see there are so many books in China. They were popular before. Everyone had them. But a hundred years later they were found in the trash bin. No one would read them. Many books such as novels and students' textbooks always change, but the Bible won't change a single word. The Bible tells us that it is a time of change and Jesus will come to this world.

Usually, the TSPM church preachers appear to be more reserved when commenting on Christianity's Western connections.[15] In one of the two Wenzhou churches directly managed by TSPM, a female preacher who graduated from a state-approved seminary stated that "the West learns from God, so we should learn from God directly rather than learn from the West. Those who plan to go to graduate schools won't choose India, a Buddhist country, but the West. This is because countries that have Christianity have knowledge and are advanced." Similarly, a boss Christian said, "Westerners all use the Bible in management. Let's look at Israel. They have a population of twenty million but have the most Nobel Prize winners. However, China has 1.3 billion people, but not a single Nobel Prize winner. This is because Israelis use the Bible. The most influential person in the entire world is Jesus. The Bible is a gold mine that you need to dig." It seems there is a template that most local preachers depend on, since I have heard many similar sermons in various local church meetings.

The training of the younger generation of preachers is a primary concern of the Wenzhou church community. Brother Huan is viewed as one of the most promising future preachers in the Wenzhou church. As a young boss, at the age of twenty-eight, he currently runs an international trading company; his sister in Italy is helping him. Before that, he joined his father in running an auto parts shop. Every Monday night, carrying his laptop and overhead projector, Huan drives his Audi from work to an eyeglass factory forty minutes away. There he holds a Bible study class for a group of workers, taking this opportunity to sharpen his preaching skills. On one night, using his IBM laptop, he projected these Bible verses on the wall:

PROVERBS 8 ON WISDOM'S CALL
14 Counsel and sound judgment are mine; I have understanding and power.
15 By me kings reign and rulers make laws that are just;
16 by me princes govern, and all nobles who rule on earth.
17 I love those who love me, and those who seek me find me.
18 With me are riches and honor, enduring wealth and prosperity.
19 My fruit is better than fine gold; what I yield surpasses choice silver.

His topic was "belief in Jesus gives you status and wealth." Huan first started by presenting the idea, wrongly perceived, that "only those who have illness and no money go to church to sing songs." Using the Bible verses projected on the wall, he raised the examples of President George W. Bush and Donald Tsang, the chief executive of Hong Kong SAR, both of whom are "faithful Christians and take prayer as the most important thing." He added:

The richest people are all Christians or Catholics. This is because they know the purpose of making money. Those who have made big money did it for God, for the nation and for society. Those who make money for their own private interests are short-sighted people and cannot make big money. The Jews have used God's words to educate their younger generations. This is why they can perpetuate their wealth in later generations. But in China, rich people usually cannot pass their riches beyond the third generation [fu buguo sandai]. Thus we need to pray to make money for God and work hard to live a positive life.

In the sermon, he showed many photos of Christian celebrities that he had found through search engines. But he does not limit himself to associating wealth and faith:

I think our generation of Christian entrepreneurs has a big responsibility. We should not only use our success to demonstrate our faith but more importantly use our morals to convince people. Many people believe if you really do things based on biblical principles you will fail. But if we succeed while behaving morally, this would be a good testimony, a wonder. We always like to use the examples of successful entrepreneurs, but seldom investigate if the person indeed has followed Bible principles in doing business. To be direct, I very much dislike Christians who depend on the testimony of the president of Shenli Corporation. The logic is quite simple, he is a Christian, and he is also very successful. He may be the biggest [local Christian entrepreneur]. Rather persuasive. This is pragmatism. In the past there was another person, whose name is Su, but he is now in prison. What a big irony. He was the first person to run a credit cooperative in Wenzhou and was one of the richest persons at that time. He is also a Christian. But he was jailed for business crime. Now people don't mention him anymore. This is called fragmented life [zhiliposui de shenghuo]. One is very warmhearted in church but does not distinguish himself from non-Christians at work. This is a rather big problem our church is currently facing.

However, Huan does not question the link between wealth and faith. Rather, he affirms the assumption that good faith and high socioeconomic status should go together, further adding that morals should be integrated as part of the Christian whole since it would be a "fragmented life" otherwise.

Making a Claim to Cosmopolitan Modernity

In the context of globalization, foreigners (in particular Westerners) serve as useful and catchy shop signs for local churches wishing to attract potential converts who seek to learn Western culture and English. For many local churchgoers, good preachers are necessarily Western preachers. This is reminiscent of a popular Chinese saying that "monks from foreign countries are good at reciting scriptures" (*waiguo de heshang hui nianjing*). Although overseas Christians represent the highest form of modernity, morality, and civility, the upwardly mobile class of Wenzhou believers makes a claim to that status through their transnational connections and cosmopolitanism.

Despite state opposition, the Wenzhou church has developed a Sunday school system for children and youths from preschool age to college. The most complete Sunday school system in the nation, it was entirely copied from overseas. Many Wenzhou Sunday school teachers were trained by their experienced overseas counterparts through short courses. According to local church leaders, Wenzhou's Sunday schools began in the 1980s but did not become formalized and standardized until 1990, when a local boss preacher obtained a series of Sunday school textbooks from Hong Kong. Nowadays all Sunday school textbooks in Wenzhou are imported from Hong Kong, Taiwan, and Singapore. A Sunday school usually divides children and youths into classes in which they not only learn Bible knowledge but also receive artistic education such as singing, dancing, performing, and playing (mostly Western) musical instruments.

Seeking to follow the style of worship found in overseas churches, many local churches have organized their own youth choirs and introduced youth electronic bands to perform and accompany the hymn singing at the beginning of service. A Christmas stage performance has become a major occasion for such performers to display what they have learned for a large audience. Because of minimal state support of educational infrastructure for decades in Wenzhou, today many local churches have better musical equipment than local public schools do. Violin teams and horn choirs are popular among the church community. Local Christians strongly advocate the notion of Christianity as a religion of music. In a report published in *Tianfeng* (Heavenly Wind), the official TSPM magazine, a local Wenzhou preacher observed that the majority of Wenzhou churches could perform choruses in four-part harmony (see Ouyang 1996). In early 2006, two local church choirs were allowed

Figure 3.4 A church choir performing at the 2006 Wenzhou Lunar New Year Ensemble Concert. (Photo by author.)

(after strict professional screening) to perform classic Western hymns at the Wenzhou Lunar New Year Ensemble Concert in a main local theater, an event organized by the propaganda department of the municipal party committee for the purpose of "using music to build a harmonious Wenzhou."

The privileged experience of church education can be confirmed by the account of a local Christian woman, Sister Miao. In her early thirties, she recalled how her church education gave her much privilege over her secular peers at school.[16] Miao could already play piano, read music staves, and sing songs at the age of ten. When she was fourteen, most of her junior high classmates did not know how to read musical notes, and one of her teachers even turned to her for help. She also played a leadership role in her class by introducing many activities she learned in the church, and she felt quite welcomed by her classmates. According to Miao, church education is far more advanced than school education in Wenzhou in cultivating artistic and dramatic skills.

"The average level of [education of] church youth is much higher than those non-churched in society and there is at least a five- or six-year gap," she said. Advanced church education contributes to the making of desired cosmopolitan subjects.

Like the Christian faith, both believers and nonbelievers in local society view English as an essential part of cosmopolitan modernity. This is particularly true for Christian parents. Many let their children attend summer camps in Wenzhou led by foreign teachers who are native English speakers. One church in the city center even set up a long-distance online class for church youth to learn oral English and biblical hermeneutics from a Chinese American preacher based in southern California. People paid ¥300 for the service. Bible English classes are popular among the younger generation, though many young church members also want to learn English for international trade and business. A boss Christian preacher recently sent his teenage daughter to attend a high school in Australia by herself. He told me that the girl's grandmother could not understand for a long time that this was for the good of the child, who might not be able to test into a good university in China but could at least master English after studying abroad. The child's grandmother blamed this "cruel decision" on his frequent communication with foreign pastors.

A common belief in the church community is that one cannot be a qualified church worker in the twenty-first century without learning English and computer skills. There are even ambitious and fanatic college youths who choose to major in English in order to be prepared to evangelize in foreign countries. The popular use of English writing in decorating churches and naming Christian fellowships is also a public display of the prestigious Western connection of the faith. I have been to a Wenzhou outer suburban church that has the gilded English verse "return to Jehovah to be holy" on the façade and English "up" and "down" signs in the stairs, even though most church members are illiterate elderly who cannot speak Mandarin, let alone English.

For Wenzhou Christians, rather than being imperialistic Christianity, as part of globalization, can be a patriotic force to build a modern, strong China.[17] Overseas Chinese Christians play a key role in mediating transmission of Western modernity in the current context. With their Chinese ethnic and cultural background, fluency in Chinese, and knowledge of contemporary China, they sometimes act as a filter for Western Christian values by means of selective presentations, making them more palatable to local believers.[18] Messages from Chinese American Christian entrepreneurs appear most acceptable to Wenzhou believers.[19] Here are testimonies from two Chinese American Christian entrepreneurs, as retold by a local boss preacher at an evangelization meeting titled "meeting in the Lord" at a local church. In front of an audience of hundreds, he started by deploring the popular perception of Christianity as a low-class rural pastime for elderly women:

Today we may have many new believers. In fact a lot of people around here have not believed because there used to be such a view that those who believe in Jesus must be illiterate, or have some misfortunes such as illness or poverty. In sum, one must be in a desperate condition before choosing to believe in Jesus. In Wenzhou dialect, those who believe in Jesus are of no culture and no knowledge and are elderly women, who are such a disadvantaged group. But this is wrong. Let me introduce two figures to you. The first is Zhang Rujing; you can see his photo on the screen. He is the president of China Chips International. He is originally from the U.S. In 2001, he brought about one thousand returnees to Shanghai's Pudong and started to manufacture semiconductor chips. Our cell phones [he points to his] and computers all have imported chips. Our cell phones basically have no China-made chips. So his brand is called "China Chips." This is a remarkable enterprise, because it fills a blank area in the Chinese market and gains honor for the Chinese people. He is a Taiwanese who loves China. He was born in Nanjing. That is why his name has a "Jing." When he first invested in Shanghai, he brought 1.4 billion US dollars. This is a very huge amount. It equals more than 10 billion renminbi. It was such a big investment. Although he has such huge capital, he is a very down-to-earth, pious Christian who even lives a puritan life. He once said that "we never do anything that will not please God and we believe that God must bless us." His company has never done anything that violates laws or faith. Once there was a big client who was in the process of negotiating a big contract with them. But the client made a request for a sexual service. But the manager said their company would never allow this to happen. He was willing to risk losing such a great order and reached a firm decision to decline the request because they didn't want to do anything that will not please God. Later it turned out that they not only won the order but gained more respect from the client. Maybe today is your first time coming to church. Don't think that believing in Jesus is a very simple thing for those with too much time on their hands. Zhang Rujing could not be busier every day [rili wanji, a laudatory term usually reserved for high-ranking party leaders]. His company has branches in Shanghai, Beijing, Tianjin, and Shenzhen. In Shanghai, there are more than seven thousand employees. He is really a big boss. But he is very pious and prays for everything. He once said that "I have experienced countless difficulties and many times I pray to God to help me. Then there are miracles for which I thank God."

The second figure is Shi Dakun. He is the vice president of Motorola and the president of Motorola Asia. From 2004 to 2005 he helped Motorola achieve a 60 percent growth rate. This was the highest production value among all the foreign enterprises in China. . . . As a very pious Christian, he is very good at praying and shedding tears. Once, in front of thirteen thousand employees, he shed tears when making a speech and saying a prayer. He has been to our church. That day his sermon greatly moved us. Because he really takes faith as his top priority. Due to his good relationship with God, he has a very good family and very successful career. He also maintains good relationships with central government officials such as Vice Premier Wu Yi and even Premier Wen Jiabao, as well as Beijing's mayor and Party chief.

These two Chinese American Christian entrepreneurs visited the Wenzhou church to give talks. The boss preacher noted that "they are both first-rate speakers who would otherwise charge 2,500 US dollars a day if they were not invited in the name of our church." Indeed, they might not have come to Wenzhou at all if Christian faith were not the key "status bridging social capital" here (Wuthnow 2002). Not surprisingly, those who are able to connect to, invite, and host overseas Christian elites can greatly enhance their own authority and status in the local church community.

Not only the overseas Chinese Christians' high morals but also their politeness and humble manners deeply impressed local believers. When the boss Christian drove his white BMW to pick up Zhang Rujing at 8:00 a.m. at the local airport, he was surprised by Zhang's low-key style. "It was like he came from Anhui [an inland province that the majority of rural migrant workers in Wenzhou hail from] rather than the U.S.," recalled the Wenzhou boss Christian with a big grin. "He wore an old shirt under his suit, and his shoes were even less shiny than mine." He was also amazed by the fact that such a billionaire really enjoyed fish ball noodle soup (*yuwan mian*), a cheap Wenzhou local dish.

The two Chinese American brothers represent the ideal image of Christians in the post-Mao context and in an age of global capitalism. Local Christians' respect for these overseas Christian entrepreneurs comes from deep in their hearts; they fulfill the locals' desire for modernity, morals, and manners. Compared with the many high-end overseas Christian enterprises specializing in information technology, almost all Wenzhou enterprises are low-end labor-intensive ones facing fierce local competition and increased tariffs from Europe (the major destination for Wenzhou-made products). The pervasiveness of rent seeking and bribery is a central part of the Wenzhou model of development. Without such illegal practices, or what Wenzhou scholars term the "original sins" of Wenzhou capital (Zhou and Dong 2003), most Wenzhou entrepreneurs would not be able to enjoy today's material prosperity and economic growth. Many local Christian entrepreneurs are reluctant to comment on how they negotiated with local state agents in seeking enterprise development. Instead, they often use "God's good will" to romanticize their accumulation of capital. Many are suspected of buying prostitutes to treat officials and business partners in response to their requests.

The perfect testimonies from overseas Christian entrepreneurs help construct a dichotomy between the category of the "Christian-modern-elite masculine" and the "superstitious-backward-rural feminine." Such a narrative reconstruction of Chinese Christian identity gives local Christian businessmen much legitimacy to pursue connectedness with privileged overseas Christian elites and an "entrepreneurially comfortable" lifestyle. It enables them to further distinguish themselves from the rural class of believers and place the entrepreneurial class of Christians at the center of socioeconomic change as they strive to promote the influence of Christianity in local society.

Building Prestige and Distinction in a Postsocialist Modernity

In the early 1990s, the party-state issued several policy statements that started using the term *mutual adaptation* to describe the desired relationship between religion and socialism.[20] Such documents, along with the public speeches of several top CCP officials, stressed guiding religion to better serve the current phrase of socialist development. In a meeting with leaders of national religious organizations on the eve of the Chinese New Year of 1997, Li Ruihuan, then chairman of the National People's Congress, stated that "all religions advocate ethics and morality and contain elements of renouncing evil and embracing the virtuous" (*qi'e yangshan*) and "religious groups can make a proper contribution to building a socialist spiritual civilization by using the positive elements of their doctrines" (quoted in Li et al. 1999: 219). In his speech to nationwide RAB directors in February 1998, then-Premier Li Peng said, "We welcome and would like to absorb all the fine cultures in the world. Superstition and religion cannot be confused with each other. Many religious doctrines represent philosophical thoughts, a type of ideal, social ethics and morality, which can be transformed into positive elements" (ibid: 218). Such top CCP officials' statements reflect the principle in the party-state's current religious work of promoting mutual adaptation between socialism and religion, albeit always with an emphasis on how the latter should adapt to the former. The state has singled out the moral and ethical aspect of religion as a positive factor in facilitating social stability and economic development; it is even trying to incorporate religion in its discourse on spiritual civilization. Wenzhou Christians also appreciate the need of Christianity to guide morality.

Taking advantage of the political weakness on the periphery of the state, Wenzhou's highly privatized economy took off in the early 1980s, along with a booming sex industry and various illegal business activities such as smuggling, bribing, tax cheating, and making counterfeit products. Wenzhou is famous nationwide for its "hair salons that do not do hair" (*bu lifa de falang*), which have inspired sex workers in other parts of the country. Such hair salons, along with massage parlors, night-clubs, and Karaoke bars, dominate the surroundings of the local churches. This is perhaps not a coincidence. Both the local sex industry and church development greatly benefit from lax local governance, though not without cost.

Local state agents derive financial benefit from these technically illegal institutions. The sex industry, backed by local authorities, facilitates Wenzhou's embrace of capitalism. It is no exaggeration to say that Wenzhou is now in an age of mass consumption of commercial sex. Karaoke hostesses and massage parlor girls play an indispensable part in negotiating business contracts in today's capitalist Wenzhou. Gambling and drug use are also prevalent social problems, as reflected in public posters all over the place prohibiting such illicit activities.

Perceptions of the "original sins" of Wenzhou capital accumulation and the moral fading of the larger society are intense among the local church community. Not surprisingly, evangelical Christians believe their faith to be the only alternative, and they preach an overarching Christian morality. As Brother Liu stated in a sermon titled "We Are Destined to Serve Jehovah," "real spiritual civilization and utopia must be found in Christ, and then our original sins can be forgiven."

Wenzhou Christians generally believe that they now live in a world of decadence, darkness, and sin, which is a sign of the second coming of Jesus Christ. But belief, more than moral action, is the key to salvation. Therefore, as several Wenzhou preachers mentioned in their sermons, such national moral models as Lei Feng and Wang Jie cannot be saved. They are convinced that "those who do not believe will go to hell and those who do will go to heaven." There is a notion of inevitability in their belief, and their submission to the inevitable affords them maximum certainty and privilege over those who fail to anticipate the ultimate trend. By taking belief as the only means to attain eternal salvation, Wenzhou Christians adopt a meaning frame that allows them to interpretatively understand their immediate circumstances and the institutional condition in which they are embedded. "Authentic" belief involves adoption of canonical language in explaining one's immediate situation. By stressing the ultimate authority of the Bible, they engage in such interpretive practices with constant reference to notions and verses from the sacred text, even in daily gossip with fellow Christians.

The overwhelming emphasis on divine agency and the doctrine of "justification by faith" naturalizes the moral hegemony of Wenzhou Christianity and contributes to constructing a prestigious religious identity. Anything that comes from human flesh and spirit (*xueqi*) rather than from God is deemed inappropriate and not authentically Christian. Christians should "follow Jesus's style" (*yesu de yangshi*) and bear the "morality of Heaven" (*shutian de pinge*). Moral behavior is not enough for salvation, but it is taken as a sign of faith. Those who are known to have serious moral problems in the church community are viewed as fake Christians who still do not know enough about faith.

BUSINESS AND SOCIAL MORALS

Wenzhou Christian businessmen often flexibly position themselves along a continuum between religious and secular, depending on specific purposes and tasks in daily life. Brother Cheng, a young boss Christian, said his wife should be happy with a Christian husband in a society where "debauchery [*fangdang*] has become a normalized way of life." His way of engaging in social and business activities and dealing with worldly seductions is to disclose his Christian identity. Sipping a cup of iced cappuccino in a local café called La Defence, Cheng said:

> Many people in Wenzhou know what Christians are supposed to do. Once you make it clear . . . For example, right after a banquet, many businessmen would prefer to go to sing Karaoke or for a sauna. But if they know you are Christian they say, "He believes in Christianity, don't ask him to go, he is no fun." If you go, some ask for hostesses [xiaojie] there, but they would say directly "Don't ask him, he doesn't want one." I try as early as possible to let my business associates know I believe in Christianity. Then they will not bother me about things like drinking, particularly if they are really interested in doing business with you.

However, sometimes Cheng has to confront business partners who are less sympathetic about his faith. He described one such moment: "They always bring hostesses or girlfriends to banquets. They wonder why I come alone and show no interest in talking about this. One made fun of me, saying, 'Either you go to have fun by yourself without our knowledge or you are not a real man.'" Cheng responded by saying, "I also like to watch beautiful girls on the street, but I have a different lifestyle. Maybe you enjoy your current life, a life of debauchery. But how will you face your family and wife when you return home? If you are too happy now, you may end up with a sad story [*leji shengbei*]. You won't be able to enjoy family life. The difference is that I am a Christian."

According to Cheng, leading a life of debauchery was purely for fun in the past, but today it has become a necessary part of business dealing:

> When you want to treat a cadre or an important client to a banquet, you feel it necessary to get several hostesses as company to drink and eat together. It has become a necessary thing. It is so natural that you can just tell your wife. One even said to his wife confidently that he went to a Karaoke bar and asked for three hostesses. He thinks that this is his work and what a man should be like. Three hostesses are OK as long as you don't get a second wife [ernai]. This is the larger social environment.

Like other evangelicals, Cheng attributes his moral standard to his personal relationship with God. It is "God's love" that makes him "feel afraid of doing such things." It is no wonder that local Christian women all try hard to convert their nonbelieving boss husbands.

In another case, the moral superiority of Christian faith was reflected in resistance against illicit business dealing. Brother Guo, a middle-aged part-time preacher, once shared a story of his moral struggle on a business trip to Xinjiang, in northeast China, and how he resolved it through faithful prayer. He had received what he called "gray income" (*huise shouru*) for the trip before leaving Wenzhou, but he was unsure if he should have accepted it. Once he arrived at a hotel in Xinjiang, he received a phone call from home saying that his daughter had a high fever caused by faucitis (inflammation of the fauces). He immediately linked this to his business misdeed. He then prayed to God, "If it is due to taking gray income, I will return the money right after I get back." According to him, as a result of this prayer his daughter completely recovered that evening. He interpreted this as "God's protection of me from making more serious mistakes."

Wenzhou boss Christians such as Brother Cheng and Brother Guo link the fundamental morals of life with their submission to God. Many church-goers hold the view that there are bad people in the church, but those who don't believe are even worse. In Christian Wenzhou, being Christian means being good, and one can be good only by believing in the Christian god. From the local Christian point of view, although other religions, particularly Buddhism, also teach people to be morally good, Buddhists do not realize and admit they are sinners, and the fundamental difference is that they do not know the only true god and worship idols. Local Christians believe that only they can truly sacrifice for the public good because they do it for God, not for people. Consequently, even though local Buddhist groups conduct many charitable activities and emphasize doing good deeds, Christians view their motives as suspicious and worldly. Christians do good deeds only because "they are moved by God." Accordingly, any personal achievement or contribution to society and others is ultimately the work of the Holy Spirit. Christians' good deeds always add to the glory of God and not to themselves. One preacher put this moral superiority of Christianity in the context of a comparison of China and the West: "Why are there differences between us and the West? This is due to the fact that we don't have Christ's teaching and discipline. The West has the Christian spirit and there is Jesus in their culture and thoughts. So they can give up their own interests for the sake of others."

Having a conservative evangelical faith, the Wenzhou church stresses belief as the sole criterion to attain salvation. Given their belief in the certainty of salvation, good morality and manners are viewed only as evidence of one's true Christian faith and have nothing to do with one's status as the elect. Therefore, many local believers see current social problems and the moral crisis as a consequence of bad human-God relations; they think that only continuous prayers to God can resolve Satan's attack. "In the 1970s and 1980s, people were holy and pure" (*shengjie*), said Sister Miao, a thoughtful believer, "and thus there were many good testimonies and wonders, due to their intimate relationship with God. Today people are after their own interests and less pure, and their hearts are far away from God."

Local Christians also display and apply their superior Christian moral vocabulary in the process of capitalist production and enterprise management. Many Christian entrepreneurs are enthusiastic about "applying Bible principles to enterprise management" and "transforming faith to productivity." Brother Liu is one. He designed the Chinese aphorism *yidao zhichang*—literally, using the Word to govern the factory. Four huge Chinese characters were put on a wall in his spacious factory conference room, which is also used to hold various church services. In the monthly factory newspaper, Liu explained:

> To use the Word [dao] to govern the factory is more fundamental and thorough than the use of laws or people. Currently our government advocates using morality to govern the country and build a harmonious society. The school advocates moral and quality education. General Secretary Hu Jintao has brought up the notion of "Eight Honors and Disgraces." These all reflect and confirm the value of morality. However, the foundation of morality is the Word. The Word anticipates morality, The Word anticipates reasoning. The Word anticipates the way. So we need to return to the true Word, to be united with the Word and to submit to the heavenly Word, which should be the only goal of our society, our country and even all humankind. . . . Particularly as a labor-intensive enterprise, our employees' quality determines the quality of the products. Using the Word to govern the factory cannot only enhance the overall quality of the people but more importantly change lives and renew minds, so that people can live a more meaningful life and find out what their personal values are.

Liu's factory has about seven hundred employees, one fourth of whom are Christian. Most of them converted after entering the factory. The factory is also eager to recruit workers who are already Christian. Almost all labor-

Figure 3.5 A Sunday morning service in Brother Liu's factory church. Note the aphorism in the background: "Using the Word to govern the factory." (Photo by author.)

intensive factories in Wenzhou prefer young laborers and set an age limit (usually thirty) when recruiting new workers, and Liu's factory is no exception. Liu added a question on religious faith in the job interview, however, and preference is given to those who have Christian faith. In some cases, applicants who far exceed the age limit entered the factory thanks to their Christian background. In fact, many church brothers and sisters have secured jobs in the factory through local and translocal Wenzhou church networks. There is also an explicit rule stipulating that Christian workers have priority over nonbelievers for promotion to higher positions and for receiving further technical training. Some Christian workers I talked to interpret the notion of "using the Word to govern the factory" as "using Christians to govern the factory" and take Christian identity as a privilege. In my conversations with such workers, they frequently switched between the title of "brother" (*dixiong*) and "president" (*dongshizhang*) in referring to Liu. The fact that some workers have converted for practical benefits associated with this privileged religious identity does not bother or discourage Brother Liu. Like many other local Christian leaders, he believes that "God uses many different methods to bring people to Him."

When the socialist morality campaign known as the Eight Honors and Disgraces (*barong baru*)[21] was launched and propagated through continuous state media coverage in March 2006, it almost immediately became an idiom in the circle of Wenzhou boss Christians, as reflected in Brother Liu's speech. They use this official phrase to celebrate their superior Christian morality and identity. For them, Christian morality has a much higher standard than the recent concept of socialist honor. Socialist morality can therefore be perfectly subsumed into Christian morality. As a big boss Christian proudly said in a church meeting, "The Eight Honors and Disgraces are just what the Bible taught long ago." Another young businessman echoed, "The Eight Honors and Disgraces just show the progressiveness [*xianjinxing*] of Christianity, since Christians have already achieved them." He even suggested that the church use the slogan as a backdrop to talk about the greatness of the Bible. There are also forward-thinking local believers who respond to each new socialist morality campaign as an opportunity for the church to conduct social outreach and promote its social power. Wenzhou boss Christians not only readily reproduce dominant state discourses but also actively seek to refashion Chinese national modernity in religious and moral terms.

SEXUAL MORALS AND WEDDING MANNERS

Sexual conservatism remains a central part of Wenzhou Christian identity. Local church services segregate gender in seating arrangements (men always on the right, seemingly a challenge to the standard Confucian order that places men on the left). Even wives and their husbands must be seated separately. The church has also established a rule regarding church wedding rituals. It says that only couples who are virgins and are baptized believers can be allowed to have a wedding ceremony in a church and receive prayers and blessings from the pastor and fellow churchgoers. This rule is often bent in reality. For example, a preacher's son, even if not a churchgoing person, may be allowed to have a church wedding because of his father's connection to the church.[22] Many, though, take the rule seriously. A Christian woman said proudly, "People currently in their thirties like me were all virgins when they married. Today one-night stands are popular and girls only get married after they are tired of that." To my surprise, she did not have a church wedding herself because she was married to a non-Christian, although she was an active member of a church evangelization group before her marriage. Many church youths do not publicize their love affairs until they are ready to get married. Others are urged by their church and Christian parents to get married early on so that the possibility of engaging in premarital sex can be minimized and they can lead a holy and pure life. Concern about the integrity of morality and Christian identity sometimes even outweighs the importance of evangelical faith per se. In one case, a twenty-four-year-old girl said that her preacher father did not allow her to get baptized because she was sexually active.

It is a local Wenzhou tradition that one needs to hold an engagement ceremony some time before the wedding ceremony. However, many churches hold a church wedding ritual for newly engaged youths as if they are already married. One local Christian respondent spelled out this seemingly contradictory arrangement: "The church often offers marriage prayers for those who are just getting engaged, in fear of the possibility of cohabitation before marriage. This is certainly an ethical expedient" (*quanyi zhiji*).

Christian youths' moral purity is rewarded with a holy and romantic wedding ritual characterized by Western elements and forms such as a choir, a pastor, Mendelssohn's "Wedding March," a flower arch, and a bride in a long frilly white dress and a veil walking down the red carpeted aisle on her father's arm to meet her groom in a Western suit. White signifies death in traditional Chinese culture and used to be avoided at weddings. The adoption of white bridal dress and veil is an imitation of Western Christian weddings in which the color symbolizes holiness and purity rather than misfortune. Such an "authentic" Western wedding enhances one's status and prestige in the church community. The ritual of a church wedding itself is so important and memorable that many church youths said they would feel it a disgrace if they were denied the ritual on the grounds of lacking sexual purity. Besides the church ritual, a "morally pure" Wenzhou Christian wedding also includes a hotel banquet that resembles what secular newlyweds enjoy, particularly in its seeking of extravagance and a heated social atmosphere.

Weddings in Wenzhou are generally a display of class signs and symbols and a means of prestige building.[23] "The richer one is, the more the dowry one gives," said one man; "some give a million yuan as dowry." An elaborate church ritual testifies to one's moral privilege, modern tastes, and social

Figure 3.6 A church wedding in Wenzhou. (Photo by author.)

status. It also reinforces the connection between one's Christian identity and Western tradition.

The standard procedure of a local Christian wedding is that the groom first picks up the bride and her relatives and friends in her home with a fancy motorcade and then they all go to visit the newlyweds' apartment together. After saying prayers in the new apartment with both families, they leave for the church ceremony and afterward go directly from the church to a hotel for the dinner banquet. All the parts of the wedding must be conducted properly, both in a Christian style and in a socially acceptable way.

The degree of ritual extravagance depends on one's level of wealth. There is also competition in marriage transfer, which churchgoers seem to take for granted.[24] Some spend tens of thousands of yuan decorating the church hall with flowers, ribbons, balloons, and candles. The desire for an elaborate wedding is particularly strong among Wenzhou church sisters. A newlywed Christian girl once told me enviously that another church sister had recently had an engagement banquet of thirty-five tables and a wedding banquet of fifty tables, both at the Overseas Chinese Hotel, the only five-star hotel in Wenzhou. According to her, the lucky girl was married to a preacher's son who "runs a clothing business" and "drives a Mercedes." Girls who marry up to a rich boss are often the envy of fellow church sisters. The difference between a Christian marriage and a non-Christian marriage is the extra standard about faith, with everything else the same. Those who have good faith tend to marry a church brother, but the economic condition of the young man's family is still a paramount concern for Christian girls.

Elaborate weddings constitute a central piece of urban middle-class identity (cf. Kendall 1996). In such weddings, the number of banquet tables in the hotel usually ranges from twenty to thirty. Each banquet table costs around ¥4,000 and usually has lobster, crab, shrimp, deep sea fish, expensive Chinese liquors, red wines, and Chunghwa cigarettes.[25] Through articulation of modernity and morality, the two-step Wenzhou Christian wedding symbolizes a turning point in one's life course, displays economic and social might, and implies Christian moral identity.

EVERYDAY RHETORICAL STRATEGIES AND SYMBOLIC DISTINCTION

In daily life, Wenzhou Christians take great pains to distinguish themselves from non-Christians. Given the dislocation between Protestantism and traditional Chinese secular culture as well as the church's heavily evangelical orientation, Wenzhou Christians consciously avoid infusing Chinese cultural components into Christian rituals. In some sense, the church community has embraced white American evangelical subculture.

For example, Wenzhou Christians try hard to avoid using anything that bears the patterns of the dragon and phoenix, the combination of which symbolizes auspiciousness in traditional Chinese culture. (Sometimes the dragon and phoenix are viewed as not only un-Christian but also earthy and backward.) The dragon is seen as evil in the Christian Bible. Some new converts have even changed their names because the word for dragon (*long*) is a popular male Chinese name. They further avoid questions about the Chinese zodiac. If asked which sign they belong to, they reply, "I belong to God" (*wo shu shangdi*) or "I belong to Heaven" (*wo shutian*). An answer of any one of the animal signs of the Chinese zodiac would sound un-Christian and superstitious. Some even use such questions to judge one as being more or less authentically Christian. In this case, Chinese traditional cultural identity along with traditional moral order seems to fade out in favor of conspicuous display of Christian piety. As one preacher proudly put it during a Sunday service, "People say that Christians have a high spirit. That is true. Our status is way high up in the sky. We should take Jesus Christ not as shame but as the highest honor, happiness, and glory."

Sometimes, Wenzhou Christians' high moral stance becomes a double-edged sword. A non-Christian girl from a Buddhist background said to me that she has good Christian friends and she prefers Christianity to Buddhism because "Buddhists are too secular while Christians have a higher standard." Such a positive perception of Christian piety and morality is not uncommon among local non-Christians. Some are reluctant to accept the faith themselves but encourage their friends and relatives to attend church and convert. This claim of moral superiority becomes a burden when nonbelievers ridicule and nitpick about daily behavior. A middle-aged male Buddhist and party member who acted as my housing agent in Wenzhou complained at length about his elder sister, a Christian who lacks common decency. She has been unjust on family economic matters and once threw away his incense burner at their mother's funeral. "The good thing about Christians," he says, "is that they go to visit and pray for strangers who are ill, while the bad thing is that a daughter and her mother who attend church together would call each other 'sister.'"

Conclusion

Christianity is an integral part of Wenzhou's regional culture. The unique regional capitalist development has produced not only an upwardly mobile class with cosmopolitan experiences, practices, and visions but also a growth in Christianity that stresses and celebrates Wenzhou's ties with Western Christianity.

This integration into the global capitalist economy and increased general affluence in the reform era have driven many local entrepreneurs to go beyond conspicuous consumption of material products to redefine personal identity and privilege. In such a highly stratified and intensely commodified society, Christian faith produces symbolic distinctions and enables upwardly mobile people to achieve status enhancement and privilege building in the context of a globalizing modernity. For many, good manners and morals are derived from an authentic Christian faith that forms the basis of Western modernity, and Christian faith with its Western connections naturally constitutes a way to display privilege and produce distinction in a region where transnationalism has been under way since ancient times.

Wenzhou boss Christians have come to terms with modernity and civility through their faith. Few of them have completed high school. They tend to take the Bible as the most authoritative source of knowledge; some try to reposition themselves as a type of "scholar merchant" (*rushang*), as a distinction from non-Christian Wenzhou bosses, particularly as Wenzhou bosses have a bad reputation nationwide for their poor manners and lack of civility.

The resurgence of Christianity among the entrepreneurial class of the Wenzhou people is part of a process of celebrating their distinctive and once marginalized place identity. As Wenzhou bosses try to make sense of and legitimate their capitalist and cosmopolitan distinctiveness in Christian terms, Wenzhou becomes a wealthy, religious, "cosmopolitan periphery" (Taylor 2007a). This is not the first time in Chinese history that a local community envisioned a linkage of Christianity to Western modernity. In late imperial and Republican periods, Fuzhou Protestants in southeast China actively participated in building a new China following the model of the West (Dunch 2001a). The Christian faith was tolerated and increasingly accepted among the progressive elite circle, primarily for its association with modernity in the form of Western-style schools and hospitals. What is new here is that the upwardly mobile class of Wenzhou Christians not only views Christianity as a symbol of Western modernity but has reflexively exercised their agency to transform the faith from a social stigma to a holistic superiority in local Chinese society.

Chapter 4

The Business of Religion in the "Wenzhou Model" of Christian Revival

Faith without works is dead.

—JAMES 2:20

Those who are busy outside are all capable entrepreneurs, so they are also busy in the church.

—A TWENTY-FOUR-YEAR-OLD WENZHOU CHRISTIAN MAN

Since the 1990s, Wenzhou boss Christians have emerged and spearheaded local church development. They were among the first to get rich under the reformist state. Like non-Christian Wenzhou bosses, they started their businesses from scratch in the beginning of the reform era as village en-trepreneurs.[1] Though Wenzhou's economic success has received nationwide acclaim, Wenzhou sometimes gives the impression of "a society obsessed with making money at the expense of all else" (Forster 1990b: 62). Wenzhou bosses are frequently stereotyped as uncouth, uneducated new rich (*baofa hu*), sarcastically characterized by the saying "they are so poor that they only have money left" (Shi et al. 2002: 373). In part, the spirituality of the boss Christians is an attempt to prove this stereotype wrong; in this sense it reflects a desire common to many new rich across China.

The rise of Wenzhou boss Christians remade Christian identity and trans-formed the local Christian landscape. Many boss Christians are success-ful private entrepreneurs and influential Christian leaders. They explicitly promote production and management of church development in consumer-ist and entrepreneurial terms. During my fieldwork in Wenzhou, some boss

Christians proudly talked about "the Wenzhou model of church" (*Wenzhou moshi de jiaohui*) as a parallel to the renowned Wenzhou model of economic development. In this chapter I take "the Wenzhou model of church" as a central metaphor for examining the cultural linkage between the entrepreneurial outlook of the boss Christians and local church development.

By examining the linkages between economic and religious practices, I might remind the reader of Weber's famous argument in *The Protestant Ethic and the Spirit of Capitalism* (2001). Ironically, the Chinese translation of this work is sold in Wenzhou's Christian bookstores and has been widely read by Wenzhou's boss Christians. As mentioned in Chapter Two, they see it as a how-to manual that lends moral support to their dual identity as entrepreneurs and Christians rather than as a critical commentary on capitalism. My view of the relationship between economic and Christian practice differs from those of both Weber and the boss Christians. On the one hand, unlike Weber I do not posit a causal relationship between religious ethics and capitalist practice, in either direction. I merely explore the overlaps and congruencies. On the other hand, unlike the boss Christians I do not accept that the Wenzhou model of the church proves the uniqueness and superiority of Wenzhou Christianity; rather I see this concept as a metaphor through which boss Christians express their conflicting identities as entrepreneurs, Christians, Wenzhou citizens, and new rich.

Rather than focusing on what Christians believe and why they do so, this chapter examines what boss Christians do when practicing religion and how these religious practices relate to local business practices. I build on Adam Chau's study (2006) of a popular religion in rural Shaanbei, in north-central China. Chau notes the importance of understanding diverse actors' desires and actions in the process of collectively "doing" religion. This approach is especially appropriate for Wenzhou, where local people are proud of their pragmatism, a way of life that emphasizes practical action (locally called "doing rather than thinking").[2]

The analysis shows how newly rich entrepreneurs supply the vital financial capital for church-building projects, evangelical organizations, and church initiatives.[3] These boss Christians, rather than the preachers or pastors, actually lead the governing committees of Wenzhou Christian organizations. The advantaged believers often promote the city's fame as "China's Jerusalem" and use the notion of "constructing China's Jerusalem" (*jianshe Zhongguo de Yelusaleng*) to unite the local church communities. I further discuss how boss Christians use locally developed entrepreneurial logic in investing in infrastructure, establishing investor control over churches, managing church brands, networking, and outsourcing production of church activity. Local church development has benefited directly from the practical logic of boss Christians.

Investment in Space and Centralized Control

In the last quarter century, the Wenzhou church has focused on building its institutional structure and establishing and expanding religious space. According to a local preacher, after churches were allowed to reopen in 1979 there was an initial wave of church building to meet the needs of local church gatherings. However, since 1990 competition has developed among local Christian communities to "build the most costly church, the most beautiful church, and even the tallest cross." In Yueqing County, Wenzhou's most industrialized and prosperous area, most unregistered house churches have erected church buildings. The house churches in the center of the city have all purchased real estate; some have spent ¥5–6 million, and some more than ¥10 million, to purchase their gathering sites, in defiance of central state regulation of religious venues.

This "fever for church building" (*jiantangre*) highlights the dynamic process of Wenzhou Christian development in which regional political economy, local cultural tradition, and religious meaning closely intertwine.[4] It also reflects the specific way in which local believers simultaneously negotiate secular social identity and divine power.[5] Individual church members see acquisition of new church property as an expression of faith, a main indicator of Christian revival, and a reflection of the church leader's personal capacity. Consequently, Wenzhou church leaders brag about the high cost of their church buildings and furnishings. When church leaders report their evangelical work at church meetings, acquisition or construction of new church sites is frequently mentioned as both a main strategy and the most tangible outcome of their evangelization.

For Wenzhou Christians, the notion of the Wenzhou church extends beyond Christian sites in Wenzhou to other parts of China, and even other countries. A prideful local Christian saying explains: "Where there are Wenzhou businesspeople, there are Wenzhou Christians, and where there are Wenzhou Christians, there are Wenzhou churches." Wenzhou Christians doing business in other places are eager to establish their own churches and are reluctant to cooperate with local Christians in their church-building projects. A Christian businessman who does business in a North China city said: "I advocate that we Wenzhou people build our own Wenzhou church in other places [*waidi*] to establish a brand. Through this brand, others will say the Wenzhou people are powerful [*lihai*]; they can build such a luxurious church elsewhere to let others attend. This is very good testimony." This Christian boss, the vice-head of the Wenzhou chamber of commerce in that northern city, told me how he used the chamber's network to spread the Gospel in the city in order to "let the city be blessed by Wenzhou people." He firmly rejected the request from the city's two committees, the government-sanctioned Protestant organization, to erect a church building together with a local church. By building an independent church, he hoped to hang out the "Wenzhou church" sign. According to this Christian boss, "Building churches is more influential than evangelization" and "using the name of the Wenzhou people and of the Wenzhou church to cultivate a positive image is more meaningful." In the end, the two committees approved purchase of land for the new Wenzhou church project in this North China city.

In line with this cultural logic, there are also large Wenzhou churches in Europe, particularly in Italy, Spain, and France, the three main destinations for Wenzhou migrants.[6] These costly immigrant churches are a source of great pride for local Christians in Wenzhou. Instead of being integrated into Western (or even other overseas Chinese) Christian communities, the "Wenzhou model" of church in Europe operates on the basis of autonomy and maintains close transnational ties to the church communities back in Wenzhou, resembling the business dealings of Wenzhou immigrant enclaves in Europe (Wang and Béja 1999).These immigrant Wenzhou churches regularly invite Wenzhou preachers to preach in Europe in Wenzhou dialect, and pay their travel expenses.[7] Expansion of translocal Wenzhou church space accrues enormous moral prestige to Wenzhou Christians (cf. Fisher 2008).

THE BIG CHURCH DREAM AND ITS FULFILLMENT

Many Christian leaders are also real estate bosses, who are commonly known in the church community as having "the gift of buying church buildings" (*maitang de enci*). They profit from dealing in real estate in Wenzhou and across China.

Simply sharing and promoting an imposing church-building plan can be thrilling for those real estate bosses who like to dream big. Brother Luo is a Christian boss who has an investment company in Shanghai and made a fortune through investing in real estate. Luo always carries a portfolio in his leather business case that contains a project description titled "Proposal for Constructing a Ten-Thousand-Person Church in Shanghai," and he is always ready to share this big plan with great zeal in meetings and encounters, formal or informal. Thinking about this great vision makes him too excited to sleep at night. On a number of occasions, he has also shared a dream of building a church in central China so large that it could make the *Guinness Book of Records*. The big-church dream reflects the popular ideology of petty entrepreneurialism and consumerism in Wenzhou society that emphasizes extravagant new spending on housing and other conspicuous consumer goods (Parris 1993).[8] The big-church dream reflects as well the Wenzhou desire to worship in large group settings for a fervent spiritual atmosphere (locally called *huore*).[9]

Boss Christians finance and promote big-church dreams. They often promise a great amount of money well before the idea of a building plan is finalized. One big garment factory boss (who also has real estate in several parts of the country) announced in a church meeting that if his church decided to purchase a local badminton stadium as a new church site (which would cost about ¥7 million), he would contribute ¥1.5 million immediately. Local believers earnestly view such a public display of piety and wealth as a reflection of both "God's grace" and one's "great confidence in God's plan."

Raising funds for church building also parallels local practices for raising capital for family business. Wenzhou church projects usually combine donations and informal lending.[10] Informal lending enables a great number of local Christians who lack immediate financial capital or ministry and pastoral resources to set up their own church. The practice greatly shortens the period between planning for a new church and completing church construction or a church-space purchase.

Quite often, acquisition of new church property rests on the decision of a few entrepreneurs, or even just one. Brother Liu recalled the process of buying a 1,500 square meter church space in an office building, and how ardent church members urged him to make the largest contribution:

> Initially I was unsure but I was moved by their great confidence and zeal. They said if I decided not to buy, they would find it very difficult [to buy the site].

They said, "You are not only one of the church leaders but more importantly you are the main source of finance." In the end, my contribution to the church accounted for more than one-third of the total funding needed.

Like many other local churches, Liu's church followed standard business procedures in financing church acquisitions. Table 1 is the annual account summary information sheet posted in Liu's church, displayed as a PowerPoint presentation at the church's annual believers' general meeting (*xintu dahui*).[11] Its format resembles an enterprise's year-end fiscal report. The church took out loans from several sources, including banks, other local churches, individual believers, and a private enterprise, and rented out more than half of its purchased space (800 square meters) to a well-known garment company.[12] In 2005 the church collected ¥249,000 in rent to help pay for its loans. The rent was to go up to around ¥300,000 in 2006. Liu plans to reclaim the space from the company in three years.

Though such religious space is not for productive use, the congregation often views it as a collective commercial asset that will appreciate in China's booming real estate market.[13] The economic logic of such fixed-asset investments has contributed to the dramatic revival of Christian sites in Wenzhou.

Liu's congregation used to be a youth fellowship affiliated with a major local church. Before moving into the new office building in early 2004, they met in a rented peasant house that was later torn down during an urban renewal campaign. By acquiring the large church space, the new church gradually gained legitimacy among local church communities and established its own independent institutional structure. As a result, church membership rose from several dozen to a few hundred in a short period. One of the church's immediate goals is to achieve a thousand registered members. This is an example of how acquisition of church worship space greatly facilitates formation and development of Christian subjects (see Lefebvre 1991). A middle-aged pastor explained the connection between expansion of church space and the growth of church membership: "In Wenzhou, if you build a new church, it immediately fills up. You build another church, and it fills up too. That's the way it is here."[14] Indeed, Wenzhou Christianity expresses its intense religious energy and expands its influence through massive reappropriation of sacred space (Yang 2004).

TABLE 4.1
Annual Account Summary Information Sheet (2005) (in Yuan)

Previous debts (by the end of December 2004)	3,620,000
Balance	9,444.9
Revenue	1,211,344.7
Contributions	745,634.7
Rent	249,000
Personal mortgage	124,000
Other revenue (hymn book sales and waste recycling)	2,710
Interest-free loan	90,000
Expenditure	1,118,494.6
Church affairs	179,914.1
Reimbursement*	830,000
Interest paid	108,580.5
Balance	98,850.5
Total debts	2,880,000
Hu's company	1,000,000
The Jianan meeting point	100,000
The Nancheng church	200,000
The Beicheng church	200,000
Brother Yu	40,000
Interest-free loan	40,000
Bank loan**	1,300,000

*Reimbursement (Sister Liu 20,000; Brother Chen 400,000; Sister Lin 20,000; Brother Hu 40,000; Sister Zhu 50,000).

**Bank loan (300,000 without interest, 1,000,000 with interest).

SOURCE: Data from a Wenzhou church.

OWNERSHIP, CONTROL, AND THE "CHURCH MANAGEMENT RESPONSIBILITY SYSTEM"

Fast expansion of church property has fostered new power relations within the church community. The multiplicity of investment sources inevitably leads to ambiguous church ownership. In fact, conflicts over control of the church are commonplace in the reform era. Unlike corporate organizations, churches often lack the legal status to purchase real estate and have great difficulty in obtaining ownership, unless they are registered with the state.[15] To get around this requirement, ideally the church selects the most trustworthy individual to assume the role of the "legal" person who signs the contract on behalf of the church. The common practice is that person signs two contracts: a formal one to obtain the property, and an informal one for the church to claim its ultimate ownership. This arrangement helps the church circumvent state restrictions on church property acquisition. However, such ambiguous ownership often results in conflict within the church. It is not uncommon for churchgoers to buy an apartment for a church gathering but later to be reluctant to transfer ownership to the church. In some cases, multiple ownership is introduced, which causes more conflict among the various churches involved in financing the property acquisition. For example, when one church recently relocated because of urban redevelopment, a Christian boss contributed ¥500,000 to buy a new apartment for their fellowship meetings near the city center, but still more funding was needed from others. At this juncture, a sister from another church contributed ¥60,000 (¥50,000 from herself and ¥10,000 from her church group) in the name of her own church. The first donor, however, later returned the latter's money for fear that she would attempt to use the apartment for her own church services at some point in the future; the shared underlying logic is that the person who purchases the property has the say in the church. Certainly it is not easy to reject a donor's request to use church property, but it is even harder to refuse the offer of such donors and founders to assume a leadership role in the church. Patterns of investment greatly shape the church's ownership and control.

Brother Liu offered this account of his church's small council meeting (*xiao yihui*):

> If we decide to do something and it costs less than ¥2,000, there is no need to pass it to the small council for approval. It is enough for me to sign. If spending ¥20,000, I need the small council to approve it by raising their hands. In such cases I spread the vision to them and tell them why we should do it. This year we planned to invest ¥200,000 in Fuquan [Guizhou Province] to do charitable work and open up a new field for evangelization. Most of our small council members said it was not necessary, that we still owed money, and asked why we should be so kind. But I know that without standardization [guifan hua],[16] we cannot do things successfully. This problem exists in many churches today.

You see, we have bought such a large church space, the current value of which cannot be compared with what we owe. The church is worth more than ¥10 million, but we only owe ¥2 million or so. This level of debt is very normal. It should not even be considered as debt at all. I think we, just like an enterprise, should operate on borrowings [fuzhai jingying]; it is not a problem. If you pay off all the money, you will feel you have nothing to worry about and won't be motivated to work hard. Since we owe debts, we should work hard to motivate more people to make contributions. However, the debts should not restrict the development of other church work. If you pay off all the debts, then your enterprise—oh, not enterprise; your church development—will be restrained. When I made this clear, basically all of them agreed. This is a procedure we must observe. That is, to approve by voting.

Though a seemingly democratic process, it is hard to ignore the fact that Liu, as the biggest donor to the church, enjoys the power to persuade those who may not agree with the logic of "operating on borrowings." According to him, the current market value of the church space is almost twice the cost of when they bought it three years ago, an achievement Liu likes to talk about. The appreciation of the church property gives the Christian bosses particular leverage among the congregation. Liu speaks just like a chairman of a board of directors.

As his narrative shows, Liu sometimes confuses enterprise with church. This is not surprising, given that Liu is also the chair (*dongshizhang*) of his family-owned enterprise. In addition, three members of the church's small council have opened a shoe factory together under Liu's direct financial support and guidance, and the church members collectively hold two hundred shares in the factory at ¥10,000 per share. The boundaries of the entrepreneurial and Christian worlds are quite blurred in the operations of the Wenzhou model of church development. However, symbolically these boundaries remain in the consciousness of most local Christians. They reflect a fundamentalist belief in the sacred-secular binary. One preacher said, "We don't talk about the issue of preacher remuneration in the church, only the divine work [*shenggong*], though remuneration is the basis of divine work." Nevertheless, personal economic relations shape the politics behind the church scene. Liu's mention of the democratic voting procedure has little to do with his notion of "standardization."[17] Standardization is what Liu personally perceives as the right direction in developing the church, rather than his reference to a democratic church structure. In fact, the members of his church's small council are not elected. In this way, Liu's church resembles most Wenzhou churches today.

The committee of church affairs (*tangwu weiyuanhui*) is the highest authority in the power structure of most large Wenzhou churches. Many local believers explicitly call this committee system a "system of patriarchy" (*jia-zhang zhi*), since the chair of the committee (*tangwu zhuren*) is the "general responsible person" (*zong fuzeren*), in charge of the church's central affairs such as the development plan, budget making, church spending, coworker employment and compensation, and preacher invitation. According to some critics within the church, such leaders often use church resources to build personal connections. Though Brother Liu enjoys preaching regularly, his formal title in the church is "general responsible person," a term that resonates with the "enterprise contract management responsibility system" (*qiye chengbao zeren zhi*) introduced in the early years of economic reform. As the main donor and founder of the church, the general responsible person is often viewed as having full control over the congregation.

Similarly, when I asked one local church sister why her church does not elect its leader, she replied without any hesitation that the responsible person (a middle-aged male former boss) is not subject to election because he was the founder of this church after separating from his previous church. "He runs the church like his factory, and he has sovereignty" (*zhuquan*), she said somewhat helplessly. "Our church won't have much further development, but it won't be very bad either, because he has good *guanxi* with several other churches." According to her, the church does have elections for church committee members below the level of the responsible person. However, such elections can also involve a lot of *guanxi* building (cf. Kipnis 1997). As she recalled, the responsible person's wife was elected as the deacon after privately giving gifts such as fine peanut oil and expensive traditional Chinese tonics to many church members. As perhaps one of the few who rejected the gifts, she commented derisively on the direct link between the wife's gift-giving acts and her victory in the church election: "Those who lack knowledge think she has a very good, loving heart."

These examples illustrate how the operation of many Wenzhou churches mirrors not only a private enterprise but also a family-owned enterprise. Leaders tend to view their churches as their own children and cannot restrain their intense desire for control. Consequently, the patriarchal culture of Wenzhou family-owned enterprises has successfully permeated the religious boundaries of the church.

By pointing out the close connections between donor/founder status and a leadership role in the church, I do not intend to deny instances of rich bosses giving unconditional help to fellow church members or contributing to church development. In fact, I have heard from several sources the story of a Wenzhou Christian boss in Italy who continually sponsors thirty-five full-time preachers in a local Wenzhou parish and who "is not even interested in gaining control over them and seizing power." Local believers praise him for his refusal to exercise entrepreneurial control; some commented that "he is not even superrich" and "works hard for his money there," which apparently gives his financial contribution greater spiritual and moral weight. These believers, however, framed the entire story as an exception rather than a common practice. As this tale also reveals, it is usual practice for businesspeople to give money privately and directly to full-time preachers to support their livelihood, an informal arrangement that influences lay-clergy relations in a way that neither party wishes to discuss.

CHURCH SPLITTING, FAILURE, AND MULTIPLICATION

As some churches grow large, they divide into smaller groups and fellowships based on age groups or residential communities and neighborhoods. These new church groups may grow rapidly under the leadership of a few ambitious and resourceful believers and eventually claim independence from the home church. Severe conflicts over such fission and independence are common. According to local church leaders, one of the main reasons is financial management. The numerous fellowships and gathering points are supposed to turn in their financial contributions to the mother church. However, churchgoers are often not clear about, or are dissatisfied with, how the money is spent by the central church leaders. Some church members ridicule the leaders as "religious hegemonists" (*jiaoba*) and the church structure as "religious autocracy" (*jiaohui zhuanzhi zhuyi*). Gradually discontent mounts, often culminating in creation of new churches facilitated by aggressive practices of property acquisition. Great pressure and antagonism from the former church authorities results in the new independent churches tending to place strong emphasis on cultivating horizontal networks with other new churches and avoiding the vertical organizational structure of the traditional church.

In some churches, especially house churches, division is exacerbated by church leaders' kinship ties and personal tactics. For example, a middle-aged local house church leader described how certain house church leaders act like "commanders-in-chief " (*siling*) who are in charge of huge wealth and human resources and who demand absolute obedience from members. He sharply criticized one of them for his corruption and despotism, taking his wrongdoings as a sign of his lack of fear of God. Comparing some audacious and arrogant house church leaders with the stigmatized (by house church members) official TSPM church, this leader said with obvious sarcasm that "the TSPM church may not fear God, but at least they have to report to the government."

There are certain implicit rules governing the dynamics of interchurch relations. The fundamental ones can be summarized as reciprocity and mutual respect. Whoever disregards or transgresses such rules has to pay a price. A young local church leader used to be one of the most popular preachers in the Wenzhou church community but then gained a bad reputation for "stealing sheep" (*qiangyang*) from other churches in trying to establish his own independent church with some limited foreign funds. At that time he was an invited guest preacher for another church's youth fellowship on Fridays, but he took the opportunity to persuade the young people to visit his own church in an office building. After negative news about the young preacher spread, church leaders no longer welcomed him. As a full-time preacher leading a small church whose congregation mostly came from outside Wenzhou and whose members were not as rich as the locals, he found his financial situation worsening. He was said to have unabashedly attempted to borrow money from a local Christian entrepreneur and leader who had previously invited him.

Recounting the story of this young preacher, some local Christians took it as a negative lesson on how important it is to maintain smooth *guanxi* in the Wenzhou church. They attributed his failure to gain more new members to his isolation, his lack of good *guanxi* with local entrepreneurs, and his church's small size and lack of "momentum" (*shengshi*). Though several others praised the courage he demonstrated in breaking away from traditional church forces, it is clear that he damaged his support networks. Without ties to enterprises, entrepreneurs, or other church organizations, either domestic or overseas, it is difficult to survive as a newly independent church. As one Christian businessman and church leader said, "The bosses are the driving force behind [*houfang*] church work, while full-time preachers are at the forefront [*qianfang*] of evangelization."

Ironically, independent churches sometimes unite with one another to counter the pressure of the "hegemonic" traditional church structure. As they grow bigger, however, they sometimes reproduce the centralized vertical organizational structure of the traditional church. The breakup of a large church into separate ones not only energizes local Christian development but also resembles the complex interrelationship among Wenzhou's family-owned enterprises.

Outsourcing Church Work

As the case of the disappointed young preacher discussed in the previous section illustrates, a church without good relationships with other churches and parachurch organizations falls behind in the competitive faith market, in part because it cannot (to use a local Christian boss's favorite term) "optimize resource integration" (*ziyuan youhua zuhe*). Some boss Christian leaders have been explicit about the process of "outsourcing" (*waibao*) church work through networks when striving to "integrate resources for the sake of Christ" (*wei jidu zhenghe ziyuan*).[18] In fact, almost all Wenzhou churches, whether house churches or the TSPM churches, small or large, are embedded in networks. Their pastoral services and evangelization work are mostly "outsourced" to established local Christian networks that link preachers, entrepreneurs, churches, and enterprises. This is particularly reflected in the arrangements for sermons and production of various large-scale evangelical activities. This "specialized division" (*zhuanye hua fengong*) of church work has contributed to increasingly professionalized church services in the reform era. For example, preachers regularly rotate among churches, reducing the need for each preacher to come up with a new sermon every Sunday. Similarly, one would never see an evangelization meeting organized by a single Wenzhou church. The underlying organizing principle is "coordinated service" (*peida shifeng*) based on specialized division of labor.

Since the withdrawal of the Western missionaries, an administrative division in parishes (*muqu*) has replaced the Wenzhou church's denominational structure. Each parish is responsible for dispatching preachers to different churches and gathering points to conduct services.[19] The preacher-dispatch system is called *paigong* or *paidan* and is actually a system of outsourcing pastoral services because churches do not necessarily need their own preacher.

Each church has a timetable (*dan*) that records the names of the preachers and times of their preaching over half a year or an entire year. Almost all the preachers under this system work on a volunteer basis and have daytime jobs. According to a Wenzhou preacher's report published in 1997 in *Tianfeng*, the official Chinese Protestant magazine, there were only about a hundred full-time pastoral workers and thirty-four ordained pastors in Wenzhou, and the ratio of these pastors to believers was 1:20,000. As a result, daily pastoral work heavily depended on a large group of volunteer (*yigong*) preachers, whose number was around thirty-five hundred (Shi 1997).[20]

The volunteer preachers can rely on only limited lecture notes for their sermons, since none of them will be dispatched to a particular church more than twice a year. Many of them therefore recycle their sermons in front of different church audiences. This enables busy entrepreneurs and those with little education, religious or otherwise, to contribute to pastoral work.[21] Over the past decade, many Christian businessmen have attended various short-term training courses to sharpen their preaching skills.[22] For boss Christians, preaching is often a way of conspicuously displaying their spiritual (which is to say, cultural) capital.

Outsourcing of Sunday sermons and other services to volunteer preachers from other churches resolves the biggest problem inherent in fast church growth: the lack of professional pastoral care (*muyang*) for individual believers. It is impossible to know who first designed the preacher-dispatch system or contributed to the idea, but according to local churchgoers this is a unique Wenzhou Christian invention under God's special tutelage. As one preacher said:

> God has let these volunteers rise in the 1980s when there was an explosion of believers and churches . . . if there were no such volunteer coworkers to help with the church's Sunday pulpits, the situation of the church today would be unimaginable. This unprecedented phenomenon is the miraculous work of God Himself.

Nevertheless, the underlying logic is arguably entrepreneurial rather than religious, given the city's international fame as a base for outsourcing production, a local entrepreneurial reality in which tens of thousands of family-controlled firms engage in flexible, fast, and competitive production of small merchandise.[23] These small firms rely heavily on a massive number of Wenzhounese itinerant traders who organize production through subcontracting (Y. Liu 1992; A. Liu 1992).[24]

Just as in business enterprises, outsourcing decisions are usually based on a mixture of factors: the location of the planned activity or ministry, church leaders' personal connections, past experiences of cooperation, and the "comparative advantage" of conducting various church services. For instance, to enhance members' commitment, one local church leader proclaims in a church council meeting that his church will seek to "provide the best pastoral services" and "build a brand church" (*dazao pinpai jiaohui*). To achieve this end, his main strategy is to invite the best preachers he can find from other places to engage collectively in the church's pastoral work on a weekly basis, rather than train someone from his own church.

In addition to daily pastoral work, large-scale evangelization events in Wenzhou are also heavily outsourced. Annual Christmas Eve events are a good example. On Christmas Eve 2006, an evangelization meeting held in a local theater drew more than a thousand participants from around the city, a grand scene not uncommon in the Wenzhou church's celebration of Christmas in recent years. A group of local Christian entrepreneurs from several churches funded and organized the event. To ensure that the local authorities did not interfere, at the beginning of the event the head of the district-level two committees donated ¥20,000 to the district-level charity federation on behalf of these Christian entrepreneurs. As planned, this worked as a cover to label the evangelical meeting a "charity show." The event took the popular form of a variety show, in this order: first "ballet dancing on a person's head" (*dingshang balei*, a form of acrobatics), followed by a house church choir performing three hymns, and then a one-hour modern dance drama titled "The Star of Bethlehem" and performed by a professional troupe invited from Nanjing. An itinerant preacher acted as the host of the show, and a Singaporean piano teacher and seminary graduate served as an invited advisor supervising the entire program. Dozens of youths from a local church's youth fellowship acted as ushers.

Many parties all with their own agendas and interests are involved in producing such large evangelization meetings. The main organizers need to decide which choir, troupe, preacher, or foreign teacher they should invite, and when. They coordinate these efforts in a series of planning and preparation meetings to ensure a well-sequenced program. They also furnish trained church workers to maintain order at the meeting site. Last but not least, the main organizer needs to be ready to negotiate with local state agencies in the event of unwelcome state intervention.

Although heavily dependent on outsourcing networks, Wenzhou Christian entrepreneurs act innovatively in manufacturing various evangelical activities that appeal to the Christian consumer self. They seek to exert greater control over the overall design of the evangelical program by designating specific speech topics for the invited guests and particular themes for the invited performances. For example, when they invited a Chinese American Christian and the head of a high-tech joint venture as a guest speaker for an evangelical banquet targeting local entrepreneurs, they asked him to talk about his enterprise development, since "this is his specialty," and "our local Wenzhou preachers can lecture better than he does on the cultivation of spirituality" (*lingming de zaipei*).

As the case of Christmas Eve evangelization reveals, Wenzhou Christian entrepreneurs and local churches often collaboratively sponsor a range of evangelical activities and initiatives.[25] In this context, shop fronts, office spaces, factory workshops, and chambers of commerce can all become important spiritual resources (*shuling ziyuan*). Moreover, the mix of hosts, partners, sponsors, preachers, and performers in these various activities and events can vary, giving the Wenzhou Christian organization great flexibility. Religious production in Christian Wenzhou can therefore react quickly to consumption-driven chains of changing religious desires. Flexible production of pastoral work and evangelization contributes to the Wenzhou church's sophisticated adaptability to local situations, and it represents an innovative structure resembling that of the Wenzhou model of enterprises with their global-distribution-driven commodity chains.[26]

Learning and Copying from Overseas Christian Models

Wenzhou people's transnational networks not only enable Wenzhou's reform-era economic takeoff but also foster the resurgence of Wenzhou Christianity. Wenzhou Christians have imported Bibles and other Christian materials from overseas when such things were still hard to find within China. Over the last few decades, Wenzhou churches have received advice or guidance from a great number of overseas Christians.

Today there are overseas Christians who come to preach and teach in the local church almost every week. During my time in Wenzhou, foreign Christian bands and musicians also performed regularly, producing a "Christian fever" among local youth. The Wenzhou church invited some of these performers, while it was Wenzhou's international fame of being "China's Jerusalem" that attracted others. These overseas Christians came from Hong Kong, Taiwan, Korea, Singapore, the United States, Canada, Australia, and Holland. Their presence in the local church always drew large crowds, and they often received applause and flowers when they ended their speech or performance. Some enthusiastic young believers took photos of them or with them and asked for autographs, treating them like pop stars.

Over the past half-century, since the withdrawal of Western missionaries and the founding of the TSPM in an attempt to fend off foreign funds and influence, the role of (mostly clandestine) foreign evangelists in Wenzhou has been transformed by both the restrictive state religious policy and the consumerist local reality. The local Christian community today treats foreign visitors as exotic speakers, lecturers, experts, celebrities, and performers rather than as missionaries in the traditional sense of such activity. By representing the highest form of Christian modernity, these overseas Christians have become a significant and constant source of inspiration and legitimacy for the local Christian community. Wenzhou Christian entrepreneurs often talk of the need for the Wenzhou church to introduce more overseas Christians to Wenzhou and encourage more local Christians to go abroad (*yin jinlai, zou chuqu*). In fact, they have made a claim to the high status of overseas Christians through mass "copying" (*mofang*), "learning" (*xuexi*), and "introduction" (*yinjin*) of Western or Western-derived cultural and religious forms in local church development.

Desired Western styles are most tellingly reflected in local Christian architecture. Wenzhou church architecture, with its clearly Western design, always impresses overseas Christians visiting for the first time. "These are often gigantic, ornate structures evocative of large European or North American churches, topped by huge red crosses that are landmarks as you make your way out of the center of town," commented a Christian journalist from the United States (Aikman 2003: 187). One preacher from southern California expressed similar amazement that Wenzhou church buildings reminded him of the orthodox churches of the eighteenth and nineteenth centuries. He said that in the West today church buildings are not like that any more.[27] The profound economic and technological advancements in the reform era also contribute to rapid development of many modern auditorium-style churches in Wenzhou. Many local churches feature prominent theatrical elements such as proscenium arches, stage curtains, marquee lighting, imported stereo systems, and sound-mixing rooms, mirroring the nineteenth-century middle-class theater-style church in the United States (Kilde 2002). The beauty of the site draws potential converts to the local church in numbers. This architectural style is partly due to Wenzhou's extensive historical exposure to Western (missionary) influences. More important, however, images of Western Christian architecture brought back by Wenzhou Christians doing business overseas strongly inspire local church designs. Take the case of a newly built local church. The founder (a middle-aged entrepreneur) said that the design of the church was based on many church photos he took while traveling in Europe, and that a local design company helped realize the plan by following his "direction of thought" (*silu*).

Another prominent example of the influence of Western Christianity is the founding in early 2006 of a ministry center in a local parish. The founder, a former factory boss, borrowed the idea of a ministry center from the Hong Kong church in order to promote professionalized, centrally managed pastoral services in Wenzhou. Since its establishment, this ministry center has received numerous visitors and guests, both domestic and from overseas, and has served as a showcase for the open and modern image of Wenzhou Christianity. When a middle-aged Christian boss, known for his big dreams, shared his plan to set up an elderly activity center in Wenzhou, I heard a middle-aged preacher who was friendly with him make fun of him by saying that he could make his plans "simply by visiting Hong Kong and returning to hold a preparatory meeting in Wenzhou." Albeit a bit of exaggeration, this comment vividly characterizes a Wenzhou model of both business and Christian infrastructure building that often relies on copying ideas and concepts from overseas.

Ambitious Wenzhou Christian leaders view learning and copying from overseas Christians not as their ultimate goal but as an essential means for elevating the status of the Wenzhou church in global Christian development. In fact, many anticipate the rise of a Wenzhou church model comparable to the status of the Wenzhou economic model, which would also be widely studied and copied by others. The elite circle of entrepreneurial leaders is most enthusiastic about overseas Christian models in the local church, given their extensive cosmopolitan experiences. Foreign names, places, examples, and

Figure 4.1 A landmark church under construction in the heart of Wenzhou's City District. The building and furnishing project will cost about ¥15 million. (photo by author)

references keep cropping up in their conversation. The recently established Wenzhou Christian entrepreneurs' fellowship was modeled on the U.S.-based Full Gospel Businessmen's Fellowship. There the organizers share bold vision in fellowship meetings, including founding a Christian culture school as important as Harvard or Cambridge, acquiring a sacred mountain similar to the Prayer Mountain in Korea, building a big landmark church like Korea's Yoido Full Gospel Church (known as the biggest church in Asia), and establishing a Christian foundation as successful as the Amity Foundation.

The desire to copy overseas models of Christian development does not imply lack of desire to export their own models. Boss Christians envision an entrepreneur-led Wenzhou model of evangelization in the global Christian mission of what they call "bringing the Gospel back to Jerusalem." They are convinced that Wenzhou's status as "China's Jerusalem" and the existence of a global business network will lead Wenzhou people to "take over

Figure 4.2 A newly built church in suburban Wenzhou. It cost about ¥12 million. Surrounded by rice paddies and family-owned factories, this is a district from which many big Wenzhou entrepreneurs hail and from which a great portion of the local population have emigrated overseas. On the façade of the church building, there are two English words: "Evangel Hall." (Photo by author.)

the last relay baton" in the great mission of global evangelism, a mission that was started by the Christian West but never completed.[28] One Christian boss commented, "The world looks at China, China looks at Wenzhou, and Wenzhou looks at our Christian entrepreneurs."

This strategy of imitation in local church development, however, is not a Christian invention; nor is it a new invention in the reform era. Wenzhou bosses themselves view the ability to imitate (*shanyu mofang*) as a defining feature of the "Wenzhou ethos" (*wenzhouren jingshen*). It is also championed publicly in the nationwide fever for "Wenzhou study" (Cai 1999). This characteristic of Wenzhou culture has been shaped by the historical practices of household handicraft industry and trade, by which Wenzhou emerged as a main regional center during the Song Dynasty (960–1276; Cai 1999). The historical continuation of this entrepreneurial culture appears to be closely associated with Wenzhou's geographic isolation and linguistic uniqueness.[29]

Figure 4.3 An interior view of the auditorium-style church. It features rows of fancy oak pews, granite walls, central air conditioning, an electronically controlled vertically moveable stage (for choir performances), and modern theater lighting and audiovisual equipment. (Photo by author.)

In the early years of post-Mao reform, imitation was the starting point for many Wenzhou village entrepreneurs in low-end family-owned manufacturing enterprises.[30] Feeling especially blessed, boss Christians speak positively of imitative efforts in both church development and business development. Some view it as evidence of the powerful entrepreneurial capacity of the Wenzhou people, who have faced harsh conditions such as natural geographic disadvantage and minimal state investment. Needless to say, Wenzhou's pioneering status in reform-era economic development benefits largely from transnational connections, which also enable the Wenzhou church to achieve a competitive edge in the domestic religious market.

Conclusion

Wenzhou boss Christians blend common business practices in Wenzhou's market economy with local church development. Dominating this so-called Wenzhou model of church development is an entrepreneurial class of church leaders who actively engage in massive production and consumption of sacred space across local, regional, and even national borders. The imposing Western-style church buildings enable these ascendant capitalists to display their newfound wealth and secure their social status. They also gain prestige, authority, and power in the local community by investing in church space. The specific pattern of the Wenzhou churches' real estate practice enables the entrepreneurs to translate their economic capital and channel their entrepreneurial logic and skills into daily church operations. The Wenzhou churches therefore mirror the local pattern of corporate ownership and are controlled by their investors. Aggressive practices of church property acquisition, moreover, facilitate church splits and multiplication that fuel Christian growth in a manner resembling the multiplication of local business.

The lack of an overarching church authority structure in managing religious practices and symbols has created space for this entrepreneurial class of church leaders to maneuver and shape the local Christian landscape, particularly through the strategies of outsourcing and copying. The outsourcing system has become a requisite for the Wenzhou churches' fast growth, given the shortage of qualified clergy. It also offers some boss Christians the opportunity to preach, further consolidating their cultural capital. Rapid imitation and duplication of the styles and concepts of overseas churches further enables the Wenzhou model of church development to be increasingly integrated into global Christianity.

Through self-conscious and deliberate endeavors to construct China's Jerusalem, Wenzhou boss Christians manage to refashion Chinese Christianity, a marginalized rural social institution in the popular imagination, into a modern urban institution with an entrepreneurial outlook. At the same time, they refashion their own class identity, from village entrepreneur with limited education to highly cultivated Christian leader. Thus they convert economic resources into cultural capital.

By examining Wenzhou Christian entrepreneurial logic on its own terms, I hope to shed light on the formation of a new local elite in reform-era urban China (cf. Chau 2006). Since money alone does not define elite status, a sense of social insecurity has developed among China's new rich. For many, the quest for respectability outweighs the simple desire to get ahead in the emerging market economy.[31] The Wenzhou model of church development is an important element of the local bosses' cultural strategies to distinguish themselves in a particular socio-symbolic world.[32] While the Wenzhou model of economic development serves as a microcosm of China's rural industrialization and modernization (Y. Liu 1992; A. Liu 1992), the Wenzhou model of Christian development reflects a widespread pattern of elite desire for cultural as well as economic capital. It may well be that some aspects of the Wenzhou model of Christian revival can and will be found in other localities, especially in overseas-oriented trading centers in coastal areas. These places would require certain regional autonomy, a mission-derived local faith tradition, and access to a multitude of mobile religious agents and transnational religious connections, all of which are key factors underlying the Wenzhou Christian revival.

Chapter 5

Gendered Agency, Gender Hierarchy, and Religious Identity Making

Alongside the locally developed entrepreneurial logic, gender is a fundamental organizing principle in the Wenzhou church community. The gender-separated seating arrangement during church services is a taken-for-granted practice. If asked, many would say it is just a "tradition," while neglecting to explain why; their tone seems to present the obvious reason. During evangelical meetings held in the church, there are always church workers (mostly female) who stand at the entrance and usher newcomers to sit separately, usually with males on the right and females on the left. This rule of gender separation is strictly enforced, though it often creates discomfort for those new to the Wenzhou church scene and coming with their spouse or a friend of the opposite sex. Less obvious gender separation takes place in a range of other church-related activities. Apparently, church rituals and programs serve not only to unite people of various social groups but also to give concrete expression to differences in gender and other social hierarchies within the same church group. This chapter adds a significant gender perspective on Wenzhou Christianity. I explore how gender differences and hierarchies are validated, modified, and reproduced through the experiences and practices of Wenzhou Christians in the changing context of regional capitalist economic development. I do so by examining meanings associated with gendered religious practices in the Wenzhou church community that have been conditioned by larger socioeconomic changes.

It has been noted that Christianity in the impoverished rural inland is an overwhelmingly female institution that mostly attracts the illiterate elderly. In economically advanced coastal Wenzhou city, the Christian revival is concomitant with the rise of a class of new rich entrepreneurs and professionals, the vast majority of whom are male. The rise of urban cosmopolitan Christianity in Wenzhou's capitalist development seems to reflect the rise of an elite, rational masculinity fostered by China's economic reforms. Enabled by a gendered reading of the sacred text, this group of affluent urban believers pursues a masculine approach to reconfiguring Chinese Christianity.

The Gendered Structure of Belief

I am sending you out like sheep among wolves. Therefore be as shrewd as snakes and as innocent as doves.

— JESUS SENDS OUT THE TWELVE DISCIPLES (MATTHEW 10:16)

As Jesus and his disciples were on their way, he came to a village where a woman named Martha opened her home to him. She had a sister called Mary, who sat at the Lord's feet listening to what he said. But Martha was distracted by all the preparations that had to be made.

— JESUS AT THE HOME OF MARTHA AND MARY (LUKE 10:38–40A)

Dominated by the male entrepreneurial class of believers, Wenzhou Christianity presents itself as rational, modern, and progressive. Shrewd male Christian bosses play a prominent role in negotiating space for church development in the state-steered economic transition (see Chapter Two). Not surprisingly, shrewdness is one of the most desired personal qualities for business-minded Wenzhou people, both men and women. For conservative evangelical Christians, this quality is more closely associated with masculinity, as the Matthew passage suggests.[1] Although devout and ambitious Wenzhou men, often self-positioned as Jesus' disciples, are struggling to transform society by being "as shrewd as snakes" and by being "salt and light" in the world, Wenzhou women are serving the church as loving and caring Marthas and Marys. The

Bible supplies a gendered structure of belief in which women are destined to contrast with men in their practice of the faith, but gender as practiced does not come from the text alone.

Despite the newly risen male middle class of believers, overall Wenzhou's female believers still outnumber their male counterparts. Overrepresentation of women in the Wenzhou churches might reflect the universal phenomenon of a male-female discrepancy in religiosity (see Stark 2002). Though the participant who attends daily church services is more often than not a woman, mainly middle-aged men lead the Wenzhou churches. Moreover, local preachers are predominately male. A young male preacher characteristically spoke of the Wenzhou church's gender ideal in a sermon: "Our church doesn't allow female pastors or female elders as the Bible says. Women can preach when brothers are incapable but they cannot become a pastor, because women tend to be emotional and first committed sin. Brothers are rational because men were the first created by God. Women are the hands and legs of men, while men are the head." In the Wenzhou church people generally agree with each other about what the Bible teaches regarding women in organizing and leadership positions. Nevertheless, women and men take roles and responsibilities in lay positions that may be in conflict with commonly held theological understandings in the church.

Although women are not allowed to lead the Wenzhou church, both materially and symbolically the male church leadership rests on women's productivity in the domestic sphere. Wenzhou Christian women often make the church space as intimate as a living room by taking care of the cleaning, cooking, reception, and other daily household duties in the church. Locally, such women are called "Mada" (the Chinese word for Martha in the Bible) for their spirit of service paralleling what the Bible recorded of the woman who received Jesus into her home. In fact, the role of Mada has been institutionalized in almost every Wenzhou church. As the female gender of Martha in the Bible implies, Madas do "women's work" in the church just as they do in the domestic space. It is unclear if the Mada phenomenon is unique in the Wenzhou church, though some Wenzhou Christians claim so.[2] Apparently, to use such a positive spiritual name to address those who furnish household services in the church is to glorify the apparently trivial and auxiliary work without which a church can hardly function properly. Nevertheless, the female Christian model of Mada further restrains the role of women in the local church.

Though Mada is usually conceptualized as a church sister (sometimes called Aunt Mada), in reality it can also be a man. I have seen male Madas actively present in the dining and kitchen area in the Wenzhou church. They do the same kind of work as the female Madas, but their number is extremely small. Since people generally view domestic work as women's duty, being a male Mada could damage an individual's masculine identity. Also, as the passage from Luke suggests, Wenzhou Madas always busy themselves during church services and therefore are often distracted from the sermon. To attend a service from start to end is truly a luxury. This limitation in part contributes to the marginalized status of women in the ritual life of the Wenzhou church.

Male control of public ritual life is not unusual in a patrilineal, patriarchal Chinese society (Sangren 2000). For local Christians, the idea that women are inferior to men certainly finds solid support in their literal interpretation of the Bible. There appears to be a striking parallel between traditional Chinese patriarchal ideology and the conservative evangelical ideal; both emphasize feminine submission, subordination, purity, piety, and domesticity. The notion of separate but complementary gender spheres can be found in evangelical Christianity elsewhere (Gallagher and Smith 1999) and traditional Chinese culture (Bray 1997). Not surprisingly, such constructed gender differences are seldom questioned in popular Wenzhou Christian discourse, but often naturalized and essentialized as biologically based sexual differences believed to be ultimately created by God. This is consistent with gender stereotypes immanent in the patriarchal Chinese family system. As Sangren put it, "Women are commonly said to focus more on their own interests and those of their children (especially sons) than are men, who are supposed to be more capable of identifying with broader concerns and more inclusive collectivities. In a word, women are said to be—and expected to be—more *xiaoqi* (self-interested), less *dafang* (generous), than men" (Sangren 2000: 179). The gendered extremes of the Wenzhou Christian experience—the elite male entrepreneurs and non-elite female Madas—reflect this ideology. Wenzhou Christian women invest their energy in household duties and in the domestic realm of the church, while Wenzhou Christian men, not unlike other Chinese men, are expected to be preoccupied with production of *guanxi* and *mianzi* (face) in a more public arena in order to develop and reposition the church in society, which is particularly the case for the newly risen entrepreneurial class of Wenzhou Christians. However, this stereotypical view of feminine Christianity must be understood in the context of a rising elite, rational masculinity in the urban Chinese church in the post-Mao era. The domains they occupy in the church reinforce the difference between Christian women and men.

The Rise of Textually Based Rational Masculinity and the Elite Male Circle

The post-Mao revival of religion accommodates mass participation for both the textually and nontextually inclined (Kipnis 2001b). A textual sector and a nontextual sector can be found co-existing in the recent Wenzhou Christian revival. My study demonstrates that these two modes of Christian participation powerfully communicate gender distinctions. Simply speaking, textually centered church activities such as theology lectures and courses appeal to male believers, while experientially based activities such as prayer meetings tend to attract females. As more urban, young, and well-to-do believers emerge and promotion of the "quality of belief" (*xinyang suzhi*) becomes a central agenda in the Wenzhou church, the charismatic tradition of the church is refashioned with the written literacy of Christian orthodoxy.[3] This trend is expressed in growing interest in theological study of Christianity, especially among many young and middle-aged Wenzhou Christian men. This growing emphasis on theology can be a result of Wenzhou Christians' intense desire for "culture" and cultural distinction.[4] In particular, for the younger generation of local believers being well equipped with theology often means possessing high cultural capital, which strongly appeals to the new rich class, most of whom received little schooling. Not surprisingly, such values or ideals also permeate the lower sectors of the church community.

Wenzhou Christians generally take theology as the highest knowledge. Some would expect anyone who holds a doctoral degree to know the Bible and be able to preach. Almost all Wenzhou Christians I met described themselves as theological fundamentalists who hold a belief in the inerrancy of the Bible. Although the Wenzhou church overwhelmingly emphasizes Bible reading (in part to represent themselves as authentic Christian believers), there are great gender variations as to how far one goes in pursuing serious study of textual orthodoxy and popular theological literature and how one understands the importance of the sacred text in daily practice.[5] The sacred text offers a structure in which both women and men engage in an interpretative understanding of faith, because its complexity and ambiguity can easily accommodate multiple interpretations (Kipnis 2002; Weller 1987).

The male entrepreneurial class takes a pragmatic approach to use of textual resources in daily business life. Many male Christian bosses are fond of the idea of using biblical knowledge in promoting business success. They like to buy books that focus on faith and business management, not only for themselves but also for their managers and workers to study (see Chapter Two). One male boss in his forties, named Zhong, emphasized that "one must study and apply the Bible flexibly" (*shengjing yao huoxue huoyong*). He told me repeatedly that the Bible is a "management book" comparable to Sun Tzu's *Art of War* and *The Chronicles of the Three Kingdoms* (two Chinese classics on strategic interaction he grew up reading under his businessman father's guidance); the Bible teaches people how to handle interpersonal relationships. He believes the Old Testament teaches lessons (particularly the story of King David) that could be applied in daily business life, though the four Gospels are less applicable because they focus on "cultivation of spirituality." "Marketing and the Word are the same," he argues. At church meetings he shares stories in the Old Testament and relates them to his leather business. He has even written several essays on figures in the Old Testament (King David and Jonah) and their lessons for contemporary business practices. By emphasizing the "material base of faith," he believes that seeking worldly happiness in family life and one's personal career is also important for a Christian. He thus rejects the type of evangelism that labels these as a kind of "emptiness." This applied approach to the sacred text is not uncommon among Wenzhou bosses, who often have to break rules in order to survive and succeed in the perilous socialist market economy and who then subsequently attribute their business success to God's blessings. Brother Zhong used Sun Tzu's words to reconcile the Christian notion of honesty derived from faith and cheating strategies prevalent in the marketplace. As he said, characteristically, "To your subordinates, your family, and your church brothers and sisters, you need to say the truth, but to business opponents and enemies, you need to use strategies. Soldiers don't dislike deception [*bing bu yanzha*]. By telling the truth you won't be able to do good business." Many Wenzhou Christian businessmen like Zhong eagerly seek to attend short theology training classes in Wenzhou and beyond, in part because for them the Bible is not only symboli-

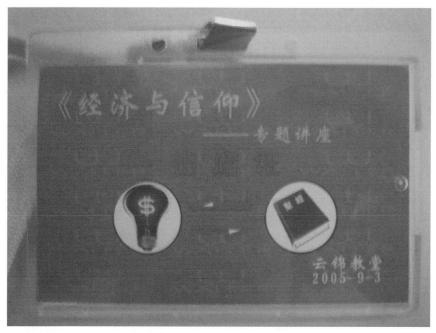

Figure 5.1 A specially designed badge for the participants in the monthly forum organized by the professionals' fellowship. (Photo by author.)

cally and spiritually important but pragmatically useful, and certainly more powerful than any Chinese strategy books.

The view of the Bible as a pragmatic management book does not preclude serious concern for salvation. Since the 1990s, Calvinist-based reformed theology introduced by Stephan Tong, an influential Chinese Indonesian preacher, has predominated in the Wenzhou church community. It champions the notion of "once saved always saved" (*yici dejiu, yongyuan dejiu*). This theology seriously challenges the older generation of church leaders, who were charismatically oriented (see Aikman 2003: 191). For many, it sends a clear message that no matter what bad things the believers do they can ensure salvation once they repent their actions. Because many claim that within the current corrupt business environment one can hardly preserve personal integrity, Tong's teaching offers the possibility of Christian salvation.

In the past decade or so, "theology fever" (*shenxuere*) has been associated with "diploma fever" (*wenpingre*) in the Wenzhou church.[6] The main stake-holders in this movement are overseas preachers, teachers, and young to middle-aged local men who strongly aspire to a rationalized understanding of the faith. The emphasis on textual knowledge of Christianity has quickly established a hierarchy of faith in the local church community, as many local believers realize that membership in this new elite circle is based on education, especially theological education.[7] Gifted youths are encouraged to attend seminaries in the West, and some have already taken this course of action. During my stay in Wenzhou, I attended three separate three-day-long theology lectures (*shenxue jiangzuo*) given by three well-known overseas Chinese preachers, all middle-aged men with doctoral degrees from U.S. institutions. The topics they addressed were "the Book of John," "general apologetics," and "spiritual theology and reflections on the charismatic movement." All three labeled their lectures as "rational theology." In one case, a young organizer emphasized at the beginning of his three-day course that this was not a spiritual cultivation meeting (a female-centered church event that will be discussed later) in order to set the tone for the event. These theology lectures were open for registration to only *selected* individuals rather than the whole church community. They were organized rather formally. To attend, participants needed someone's recommendation. Each participant was required to fill out an application form and pay 80 yuan in advance.[8] Applicants also needed to put one recommender's contact details on the form. The class size was strictly limited (to 150) and printed lecture materials were distributed. Assignments were given and a graduation certificate was issued at the end of the training course.[9] Participants in these theology lectures are predominantly male (more than 90 percent), with most between twenty and forty and coming from all over the greater Wenzhou region. These demographics show how theology studies have become an advantaged male-dominated Christian space. Interestingly, this situation is in line with the topic of one theology lecture, which openly engaged in rationalistic criticism of (an admittedly nonrational) charismatic movement that "particularly appeals to lower class or underclass marginalized groups." Some churchgoers, in particular the disadvantaged elderly members, deem it religiously unacceptable to be required to have an invitation and pay a fee to enter the church space. In contrast, the professional and entrepreneurial class has little difficulty accepting this arrangement, which is almost a norm in the business world.

The sharp gender discrepancy also occurs in a male Christian entrepreneur organized "economy and faith" monthly forum that is part of the activities of the Wenzhou Professionals' Fellowship. Like the theology training courses, this monthly forum too is held in a local church and attendance requires an invitation. Although there is no set fee, the boss participants are expected to make voluntary financial contributions to support this regular fellowship activity. All the guest speakers invited to lecture at the forum are male Christian celebrities holding a higher degree (professor, entrepreneur, writer, overseas pastor). They are literally expected to "teach" (*jiangke*), an act of passing on knowledge, rather than to "preach" (*jiangdao*), an act that is supposed to be moved by the Holy Spirit. Accordingly, people refer to their participation in such a lecture as "listening to a course" (*tingke*) rather than "listening to the Word" (*tingdao* or *ting daoli*), which is often used to characterize their regular church attendance.[10] Brother Liu, a main founder of the fellowship, once commented on this preference of scholar-type speakers: "People will listen to scholars more than peasants. It is all about who gives the talk" rather than what one says. Such lectures almost always involve nice PowerPoint presentations. The audience carefully takes notes, and some even tape-record the entire lecture. This highly controlled and tightly restricted setting of textual study in part reflects tactics to avoid state interference because large-scale religious activities involving foreign Christians are a sensitive issue.[11] Restricted admission also serves to encourage formation of an elite culture and the male elite circle of Christian entrepreneurs in the church. Noting that several women carrying their babies showed up at a monthly forum, one fellowship organizer (a young businessman) complained, "If too many nonprofessionals come, entrepreneurs won't like to get involved and will lose interest."

In addition to lectures and courses, elite male believers are also enthusiastic about promoting textual Christianity through publishing (*wenzi shigong*). Many have noticed the importance of church or fellowship newsletters in communicating with the international Christian community. Viewing it as a new direction in "cultural evangelism" (*wenhua xuanjiao*) and a way of representing an elitist form of Christian identity, many churches and fellowship groups started publishing their own magazines and newsletters, circulating them in the church circle and beyond in order to build the image (*xingxiang*) and enhance the cultural quality (*wenhua suzhi*) of Wenzhou Christianity. Another purpose of publishing is to network with overseas churches. A group of California-based Chinese American Christian entrepreneurs affiliated with the Full Gospel Businessmen's Fellowship International found their way to Wenzhou during the Chinese New Year holiday of 2006, soon after they read the newsletter of Wenzhou's newly established professionals' fellowship, their Chinese counterpart. They shared an agenda of combining business investment with evangelizing. The newsletter proved the key to their initial contact and later cooperation.

There is also competition among church publications. Most have a professional look with elegant covers. Many exaggerate a given church's achievements, often in the name of glorifying God. In the inaugural issue of a delicate-looking local church magazine titled "Wheat Seeds" published in 2006, the editor, a young man in his early thirties who later went on to pursue seminary education in the United States, proudly claimed that "the birth of this magazine reflects God's care about Wenzhou church's publication outreach and fills a blank area in the publications by Wenzhou churches." The growing publication efforts can be viewed as an important sign of the rise of rational masculinity in the post-Mao Wenzhou church.

New evangelical initiatives in the Wenzhou church community are also taking on an elite male perspective. This is in part a consequence of a self-conscious fashioning of the urban entrepreneurial and professional class of believers who are predominantly male. "Repositioning [*chongxin dingwei*] Christianity" has been a major evangelical concern and practice for these well-connected, economically and politically powerful believers. In so doing, male entrepreneurs repeatedly emphasize such notions as high end, professionalism, learnedness, and "linking up with the international track" as part of a "top-down, elitist approach" (*shangceng jingying luxian*) to spreading faith. While enthusiastically promoting a modern, cosmopolitan image of Wenzhou Christianity, they consciously refashion themselves as "high suzhi" believers and citizens. One young organizer of the professionals' fellowship states explicitly that besides evangelizing, one of their goals is to "use the church as a medium to promote the influence and role of these entrepreneurs and build an advantaged group." Both repositioning of Christian faith and refashioning of elite male Christians are pursued, often deliberately at the expense of the poor, elderly, female believers who have traditionally made up the majority of the Chinese Christian population. The male entrepreneurial class of believers not only distinguishes themselves from these "low suzhi" believers in daily rhetoric but also deny their equal access to certain church-related activities by requiring an invitation and charging an admission or membership fee.

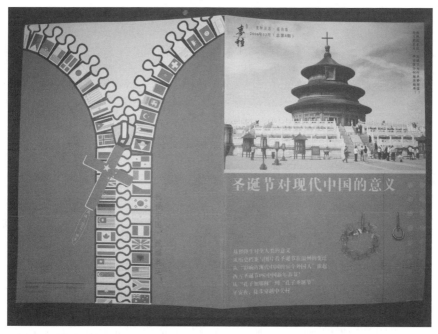

Figure 5.2 The front and back covers of a Wenzhou church publication. (Photo by author.)

Through a series of high-profile evangelical activities, affluent bosses seek to establish a new hierarchy in the church in which they occupy the highest position. Grand evangelical banquets are an example of these efforts. In these carefully positioned and produced grand occasions, the elite male Christian entrepreneurs focus on inviting the right guests, discussing the menu, decorating the tables, and making the seating plan. To clearly distinguish it from a migrant workers' evangelical meeting or a Christmas banquet, the organizers always strive to ensure that the banquet exhibits a high professional standard, good taste, a sense of learnedness, and an international outlook. For example, to cater for the taste of the "church's VIPs" at one banquet the organizers distributed more than a hundred copies of an *Esquire* magazine issue featuring an article titled "God Is My CEO," which told the success stories of several overseas Chinese Christian entrepreneurs.[12] At the banquet, several overseas Christian entrepreneurs gave testimonies on business management and family life. These personal business success stories and testimonies suit the local bosses' preferences and counter the stereotypical image of Christians as a disadvantaged group in mainstream society.

There is always more demand to attend such a banquet than can actually be accommodated. For many, being invited to such an event signals moving up the social ladder and into a new hierarchical world.[13] As an invitation-only event, it also serves to unite as well as divide people in the local church community. For the uninvited, disappointment could easily become anger. Feeling excluded, a well-known local church leader and retired high school teacher openly attacked the elite male entrepreneur circle as "forming a clique to pursue selfish interests" (*jiedang yingsi*). He was a major figure in the Wenzhou church in the Maoist era, but his influence has faded dramatically in the last two decades as the entrepreneurial class of believers grew in power. Reluctant to give up his position in the elite circle of the church, he literally sought almost every chance to be present and give his voice at various activities organized by this group of Christian businessmen.[14] However, he is also known for his sharp criticism of the new rich class in the church, which often upset the same businessmen. It did not take long for the professionals' fellowship organizers to block him from knowing about the details of upcoming events. Many believe that his bluntly spoken personal style puts him in a difficult dilemma.

This banqueting culture creates a hierarchical world among male Christians themselves; it also reinforces the gender hierarchy prevalent in the local church. In this elite male world, women's marginalized status is expressed in their role as receptionists. According to one middle-aged female believer at a planning meeting for a banqueting event, the church sisters who make invitation phone calls should have "sweet and beautiful voices" (*tianmei de shengyin*). This might be interpreted as an implicit gendered evangelical strategy to attract the male entrepreneurial class. An explicit criterion in the receptionists' selection is always "tall and pretty" young Christian girls. This gender hierarchy and gendered division of labor in the church are obvious when we look at the Mada phenomenon and the fact that females constitute the main body of evangelical performers on the stage. The ability to command the bodies of tall, pretty, sweet-sounding women, whether in the church or at work, is another status symbol for these men. For elite male believers, the feminine form of Christianity certainly needs to be appreciated, but it is being stigmatized (though often implicitly) in the context of a rising rational masculinity in the church.

Figure 5.3   Young Wenzhou Christian girls greet elite male participants as reception-ists at a high-profile evangelical banquet held in a local hotel. (Photo by author.)

Sometimes the negative theme of women's narrow-heartedness and lack of rationality emerges in the interactions among the elite male circle of be-lievers. Generally speaking, being like a Christian sister is a social stigma for male believers. For example, a young male preacher once criticized what he called "feminized preaching" (*nuxing hua jiangdao*) in the church. This pejorative term refers to the fact that some (male) preachers just focus on "is-sues of making money and their daughters' marriage" in their sermons and "have no big burden" (*meiyou da de fudan*). Similarly, one middle-aged male boss commented on his unhappy experience of working with a group of male house church leaders who still hold strong anti-TSPM emotions: "It is no use to argue with them. They are not like men. Being with them for too long, I feel I am also becoming more and more unlike a man." In contrast to men, women are more likely to be evaluated on the condition of their marriage and spouse relations (*jia de haobuhao*) than on their textual knowledge. For example, a young male boss once commented on the marriage problems of a sister who had received a graduate degree at a Singaporean seminary, saying that "she is not bad looking, but guys are most afraid of girls who have studied theology." For Wenzhou Christians, theological knowledge masculinizes women because it gives them a tool for making moral judgments—generally a male privilege in the church.

There is a widespread penchant to associate women with emotionality (*ganxing*) and men with rationality (*lixing*) in the local church community. Male believers' rational masculinity often clashes with experience-based feminine spirituality in the church. Once a male church leader was sharing his recent study of what he called "systematic theology" (*xitong shenxue*) in a somewhat self-conceited tone. Not knowing what the term was really about, a young woman insisted that she did not think reading theology had any significance in her personal relationship with God; the most important thing for her was simply to submit to God and pray to God. This "highly spiritual" comment quickly dampened the male church leader's enthusiasm about further sharing his systematic theology. The man responded: "Women just lack rationality." Repeatedly I heard church leaders complain that women are too emotional and narrow-minded and that overrepresentation of sisters in the church is not a positive thing. According to several male entrepreneur church leaders, a main challenge the Wenzhou church faces is that "yin rises while yang declines" (*yinsheng yangshuai*), referring to the fact that many church sisters perform men's roles on stage, and church brothers are less active in performing during various evangelical occasions. From an elite male Christian perspective, these negative feminine qualities make the church vulnerable to the charge of superstition that is often imposed on folk religion.[15] Despite this powerfully sexualized discourse, it is important to note not only how forms of male power over women are exerted and experienced in the church community but also how women fashion a peculiarly female version of religiosity. Wenzhou Christian women's emphasis on personal experience with the divine has opened up possibilities for them to claim spiritual authority and be highly involved in certain public church rituals.

Experientially Inclined Feminine Spirituality and the Women-Centered Context of Spiritual Cultivation

Men and women in the Wenzhou church have ties to different spheres of religious space, and correspondingly they have their own experiences of religious identity and interpersonal relationships. Unlike the highly controlled textual study or evangelical banqueting occasions that form the elite male modern church culture, the female Christian domain always encourages spontaneity and discourages any attempt at self-control or intentional refashioning. In contrast to the elite male circle's focus on developing particularistic, hierarchical relationships in front of God and managing outward appearance, the feminine form of Wenzhou Christianity can be characterized by women's pursuit of boundless and unconditional love from God and their deep concern about cultivating authentic emotional selves (cf. Kipnis 2002).

While elite male Christians brag about their worldly success and wisdom as evidence of God's work on them, local Christian women often see unusual bodily sensations as proof of God's spiritual presence in life. A recurrent theme in the narratives of the female believers is their direct experiential access to the divine. An elderly woman recounted her conversion in the midst of the Cultural Revolution and claimed to have been "caught by the Holy Spirit." She said she had never read the Bible at the time of conversion and was just like "a kindergarten kid," but God taught her about faith. She was able to see a vision from God seven days after starting to believe in Jesus in October 1973. She described vividly that on that day in a dream she saw a shining image of Jesus and a portrait of Mao both hanging in midair. According to her, the two images appeared quite close to each other but were actually far away. At the same time, she heard a voice: "Chairman Mao is the king in the world but Jesus is the king in heaven, the king of kings." The woman identifies the hallucinated external voice and image she experienced three decades ago as a strong sign of God's presence in her life. The term *Holy Spirit* (*shengling*) is widely used by local Christian women to denote the state of hallucination that is often evoked by prolonged prayer (see Luhrmann 2004).

Rong, in her mid-thirties, recalled how continuous prayer helped remove her doubt in faith two decades ago when she was a middle school student. She remembered attending a prayer meeting with hundreds of people during a summer break, which directly led her to receive baptism. On that August day in 1987, other worshippers were about to leave after hours of prayer, but she decided to continue praying while waiting for a pedicab to pick her up. Unexpectedly she was "caught by the Holy Spirit" (*dezhao*). As she put it, "I cannot use worldly language to describe the feeling, very joyful and unspeakable. Being accepted as God's child and filled with joy and being set free [*shifang*] . . . It is just like talking to your father, very joyful." Though the time of her additional prayer was more than thirty minutes, to her it seemed only a few moments, and she did not even want to stand up when others asked her to leave. "After standing up, everything seemed to have changed. The sky, the flying birds and the people all became extremely beautiful. I don't know if everyone needs this type of experience. But for me, it was very memorable [*kegu mingxin*]. Faith should be based on both the rational level such as Bible reading and the emotional level. There should be a combination of rationality and emotionality in daily [Christian] experiences."

Not a small number of Wenzhou Christian women are aware of the importance of achieving a balance between emotionality and rationality in faith, but many clearly take the spontaneous experience of being caught by the Holy Spirit as a privilege. Spirit-filled women are frequently able to experience closeness with God as friend, father, husband, and lover (see Griffith 1997). In a less dramatic but more intimate tone, Miao, who is in her early thirties, shared her emotional experience of God as if He is just one of her close friends. On our way back from a spiritual cultivation meeting (*peiling hui*) held on a nearby mountain, she said she had had problems (*nao bieniu*) with God for some time and admitted having been a naughty child, but she eventually discovered she had to listen to Him and decided to fully submit to Him so she could have peace and comfort. She said to me emotionally, "My most beloved person is God [with a pause], and the second one is still Jesus Christ; I love Him even more than my husband." The desired mind-body state pursued by these Wenzhou church sisters resembles what Tanya M. Luhrmann (2004) calls "metakinesis" in contemporary U.S. evangelical Christianity: the complex process in which individuals use language and bodily experiences to create a sense of the lived reality and build remarkably intimate relationships with God.[16]

In popular Wenzhou Christian discourse, the notion that "sisters emphasize life [*zimei zhong shengming*], while brothers emphasize truth [*dixiong zhong zhenli*]," speaks directly to the role of gendered agency in religious identity making. Women tend to stress prayer and the form of prayer meeting in their spiritual life. Compared with other religious practices such as church attendance, Bible study, testimony, and Christmas celebration, prayer is the single most important way for women to seek intimacy with God (cf. Griffith 1997). Ideally, they pray whenever an important issue rises (in relation to health, financial situation, marriage, career, and so on) and they need to make a decision. Sobbing women kneeling down on plastic or bamboo pads and making simultaneous prayers is a common scene in the church. Tissue boxes that people use to wipe tears are always prepared in advance at charismatically oriented prayer meetings. Wenzhou Christian men are much less likely to exhibit such dramatic emotionality in public, though a few certainly do.

Criticizing a well-known young male preacher who recently set up his own church, Miao said, "You must pray first and ask God to lead you rather than simply come up with your own plan." She deeply suspected that the young man had not prayed before starting the church, and she was also greatly concerned with whether his church had weekly prayer meetings. The purpose of such prayer is to "follow God's heart" (*heshen de xinyi*), a popular local Christian women's phrase. Therefore, one should not insist on things that go against God's heart. How to tell what follows God's heart and what does not mainly rests on unusual bodily and emotional experience of God's unconditional care rather than close textual reading of God's plan in daily circumstances.

When elite men pray, the emphasis is more often on propriety than emotional experience. The organizers may decide collectively who is to say or lead a public prayer. They usually choose the most respectable figure to perform this important ritual act, symbolizing and confirming his status among the elite circle. At banquet tables, Christian businessmen often politely decline a pre-meal prayer invitation from someone else; one gives this privilege to others as a gesture of modesty and respect.

Some male preachers dispute the heavy female emphasis on prayer, maintaining that without solid biblical knowledge one runs the risk of being led and filled by an "evil spirit" (*xieling*) rather than the Holy Spirit. A prayer is used to deliberately induce the state of being "caught by the Holy Spirit," and weeping is always its most evident expression. This is true for both men and women, though men are generally more refrained in their crying. Moreover, they mostly avoid charismatically oriented worship, which includes weeping, laughing, jumping, and dancing while praying. For many men, expressive self-disclosure of emotions in public ritual is a sign of immaturity and lack of self-control, and therefore damaging to masculine identity.

Almost all churches hold weekly prayer meetings that last about one hour, but usually only a small number of men participate. These "spiritual culti-vation meetings" (*peiling hui*) constitute a vital part of Wenzhou Christian women's narratives. In these female-dominated meetings, few participants carry a Bible. No blackboard writing or PowerPoint presentations are given; sermons are kept short and are filled with testimonies on miracles of heal-ing and a heavy emphasis on the role of prayer. Prolonged prayer sessions are mixed with lots of hymn singing. Participants usually pay little attention to the sermon and seem to be interested only in the prayer and worship ses-sion. Repeated acts of kneeling down, clapping, stretching hands, jumping, sobbing, singing, and shouting "amen" and "hallelujah" make the prayer ses-sion more like bodily exercise. This style of worship also manifests a strong therapeutic culture in Wenzhou Christianity. In one spiritual cultivation meeting attended by hundreds of middle-aged women and several elderly men, the worship leader, a middle-aged woman in old-fashioned dress, re-peatedly shouted via a microphone, "*baba, baba, baba, baba* [father] . . . *jiejing, jiejing, jiejing, jiejing* [purify] . . . *chongman, chongman, chongman, chongman* [fill] . . . *yizhi, yizhi, yizhi, yizhi* [heal]." The desire for spiritual and physical healing is obviously intense among the participants, but many also use such spiritual cultivation meetings to consciously pursue the experience of God's presence in bodily terms in order to demonstrate and strengthen the authen-ticity of their faith. Furthermore, they enjoy close contact with other women in these feminine spheres. These charismatically inclined women can achieve a degree of dignity, freedom, and security that would often be impossible in a mixed church service.

Sometimes, women's spiritual cultivation meetings are called "female mass meetings" (*nuzhong hui*) in the Wenzhou church. They promote a fe-male community of solidarity. According to the chairwoman of the Wen-zhou church women's ministry committee, since the Wenzhou church was allowed to reopen, there have been regionwide women's spiritual cultivation meetings every year, the goal of which is to "enhance church sisters' qual-ity [*suzhi*] in faith, revive their spiritual life, and further stimulate them to sacrifice themselves to love the Lord and the church" (Shen 2000: 19). In a spiritual cultivation meeting held in one of the largest churches in the city center, more than a thousand women from several districts and counties at-tended for three days. The theme was "to revive Deborah in current times" (Deborah is one of only five women called "prophet" in the Bible). As part of the meeting program, nine women's choruses took turns performing hymns. Three female preachers were invited from outside Wenzhou to preach, and several local church sisters helped interpret their sermons from Mandarin to Wenzhou dialect. In addition, nine prayer groups took turns praying for the meeting in an upstairs room whenever a sermon session was going on in the main church hall. Several dozen sisters helped out in the church kitchen to serve meals.

In emotion-filled prayer meetings, participants disclose publicly their private feelings, desires, pain, and suffering to seek divine assistance in a collective, religious way. This self-disclosure can cultivate an intense sense of intimacy with God and with other participants and sympathizers. Compared to the highly controlled and carefully positioned elite men-led church activities, which tend to produce and reinforce social hierarchies, female-dominated prayer meetings, with their focus on intimacy and healing, tend to break down social barriers among participants.

In their study of contemporary American evangelicals, Gallagher and Smith (1999: 230) argue that "those from charismatic and Pentecostal traditions were more apt to emphasize women's spiritual authority and women's rights to preach and teach in religious services." Compared with noncharismatics, these charismatic evangelical Christians placed more emphasis on personal experience than on biblical texts. The link between the church's charismatic style and its positive view of women's spiritual role also appears to be valid in Wenzhou. Wenzhou Christian women are empowered where charismatic worship is valued. This is particularly so for the middle-aged and elderly women who are often said to be "spiritually experienced" and "have the burden for prayers." Locally, such women are frequently referred to as "prayer-calling mothers" (*daogaopo*, colloquially called *apo*).

Daogaopo sometimes organize prayers in their houses twenty-four hours a day, seven days a week. They divide each day into twenty-four one-hour shifts. Such consecutive prayers are called "shepherding prayers" (*shouwang daogao*). When big typhoons hit Wenzhou during the summer, they pray for the city's security and safety, which has led to public acknowledgment. One woman describes how *daogaopo* serve a vital spiritual role:

> Because people don't know how to admit their sins and they just keep crying. Apo would ask, "Do you have such and such sins, you need to admit sins to God, God is trustworthy, and He will forgive your sins." Then those people would

follow apo's direction of thought and repent. After repentance they would feel released [shifang] and become very joyful. For some people who still cannot stop crying, apo would say something like, "God has already forgiven you. Now you need to study God's words, and let's pray together once more." This is to provide them with a method [of admitting sins] in that setting.

Clearly, the *daogaopo* is an expert in manipulating emotions. The "method" of admitting sins cannot be taught but has to be learned and practiced; it often involves unusual bodily practice such as speaking in tongues. The role of *daogaopo* is both recognized and denied in the church. Young male believers often ridicule them for their "ludicrous" bodily phenomena. Some attack the *daogaopo* phenomenon as a sad result of ignorance due to the lack of necessary "theological equipment," or they simply call it "earthy" (*tu*).

When asked how she acquired the ability to pray as a *daogaopo*, Sister Qin-xia, who is in her mid-forties, said:

> It is through exercise [caolian], the training [zaojiu] of your life by God. It is mainly like you stay with the Lord in the inner chamber and you must purify your mind and purpose to please God, then you will get rather close [to your goal] in your exercise and be on a fast track. If one has wrong motivations and polluted thoughts, then it won't work. Since God caught me and I found grace on the day when I was seventeen, I have been very strict with myself, never having any obscene ideas or thoughts. It is just purity [shengjie], and there are no other conditions [to achieve the ability to pray].

Many local believers (including some male bosses) went to her to request prayers in the hope of solving their personal problems, which keeps her busy all the time. Her miraculous power to communicate with God comes from her "exercise" and "training," in her own words. She was fasting on the day I interviewed her. Regular fasting apparently has had a negative impact on her health. Her doctor told her that her body looks like that of someone who is twenty years older than she is.

The direct link between bodily purity and efficacy (*ling*) associated with the Christian god was echoed and reiterated by other church sisters. For instance, one explained to me that few God-created miracles (*shenji*) occur today "because people are increasingly leading an impure life." She was mainly concerned about extramarital love and premarital sex.[17] According to such logic, spiritual efficacy depends not only on God's agency but also on the degree of the believer's bodily purity and sincerity. Indeed, Wenzhou Christian women tend to focus their religious practices on seeking bodily discipline and emotional submission. Conservative sexual morality appears to be the most salient feature of their religious identity. In contrast, elite men (particularly most entrepreneurs) do not emphasize the sexual behavior required by their Christian identity in their religious narratives. Business-minded Wenzhou men face strong pressure from the highly commercialized local society to embody a rational, "cool masculinity" (Zheng 2006). Such men are much more likely to be "tested" (to use an evangelical phrase) by the sex consumption that has become an integral part of urban Chinese business ritual (Liu 2002; Zheng 2006). Therefore, although women use bodily purity and discipline to construct their Christian identity and spiritual authority, men tend not to follow such practices.[18]

Spiritual cultivation meetings are a popular public community event open to all. In the mid-1980s, "running after spiritual cultivation meetings" (*gan peiling hui*) was a fashion among Wenzhou Christian women. They would attend those held by their home churches and go to other churches and places to attend spiritual cultivation meetings as well. Mengle, in her mid-thirties, recalls her past experience of running after such meetings: "Even on dark nights we would carry flashlights to attend spiritual cultivation meetings very happily. We ran after spiritual cultivation meetings every week, listened to sermons, said prayers, admitted sin, and repented. It was a great revival and felt very comfortable." She considered herself to be a rather rational person, who only felt emotional and excited after several rounds of admitting sin and crying. She thought she was unlike other people who would sing and dance immediately after admitting sin and be filled with the Holy Spirit. As a result, for not being willing to let God take over her body, she even called herself the "sinner of the sinners" (*zuiren zhong de zuikui*). However, she also noted that the feeling of being filled with the Holy Spirit did not last long. "So emotionality and rationally must be combined," she concluded.

Many church sisters claim that the work of the Holy Spirit was rather intense in the 1980s, when running after spiritual cultivation meetings was also at its peak. The importance of these meetings in the spiritual life of Wenzhou Christians has greatly declined since the late 1990s. As one woman said, "The method of God's work has changed. But we cannot deny it [the experience of being filled with the Holy Spirit] in the past. We really have cried and laughed. Now it is impossible, even with technological advancement" to induce participants' emotions. It seems that the declining significance of this particular form of spiritual cultivation today relates in part to the rise of a rationalized modernity in the larger society and to the impact of the rationalization process embraced by the elite male members of the church.

Nevertheless, this female world of emotion and ritual brings great joy, intimacy, comfort, and empowerment to participants and may even serve as a form of resistance against patriarchy by helping women oppose the pressure to fulfill masculine ideals. The collective nature of such ritual makes the desired emotions and feelings hard to replicate in the private sphere without the induction and stimulation of experienced worship leaders.[19] Some women describe their emotional outbursts at such spiritual cultivation meetings as a "transient feeling" (*chanajian de ganshou*) and a state of "being empty-minded" (*tounao yipian kongbai*). They also acknowledge that their passion would vanish soon after the meeting broke up, and they simply could not recall what really happened to them during that period. Therefore, these public ritual activities do not seem to empower women to embrace a renewed sense of self in daily life but only alleviate their anxieties momentarily while perpetuating patriarchal authority that might be the source of their anxieties. The logic of worship and prayer in this female context of spiritual cultivation reinforces and reproduces gender identity and stereotypes embedded in local culture and family ethos. There is a continuum between public ritual life and domestic life; women's emphasis on bodily practices seems to have roots in their productivity in the domestic sphere.

Embodying Feminine Spirituality, Reproducing Patriarchy

Today Wenzhou women and Wenzhou men have together created the Wenzhou Model of economic development (A. Wang 2003). Besides managing household and family business accounts, Wenzhou women play a visible role in the process of developing many specialized local markets, one of the main characteristics of the Wenzhou model. A local saying well captures women's role in Wenzhou's initial accumulation of capital: "Those engaged in supply and marketing are heavenly warriors, and those engaged in household production are the female warriors of the Yang Family" (*pao gongxiao de shi tianbing tianjiang, gao jiating shengchan de shi yangmen nujiang*; A. Wang 2003: 113).

Here heavenly warriors and the Yang female warriors denote Wenzhou businesspeople's powerful and invincible personal capacity. Although Wenzhou women are active participants in regional economic development, they are subject to gender inequality in patrilineally constructed families. This is partly due to the nature of the petty capitalist mode of production, in which gender inequality plays a key role in maintaining the economic security of the household and accumulation of petty capital, and in which women's traditional "narrow-heartedness" is often an asset in assisting and developing family business (Gates 1996). Furthermore, Wenzhou women's work is significantly devalued because their activities of economic production generally take place in the domestic space and are thus publicly invisible (Zhang 2001: chap. 5).

Although Wenzhou Christians (male and female) attack ancestor worship as "superstitious" idol worship, they readily embrace the traditional principle of male patriliny no less than local non-Christians do in their domestic life. Son preference is deeply rooted in local Wenzhou culture and is even more salient in the Wenzhou model of economic development.[20] Christians are no exception. Stories abound in local Christian communities about how individual believers avoid the one-child policy, with some preachers going overseas to have a second child. Moreover, the hope for a son and strategies to achieve this goal are generally viewed as morally positive in the local church. Contrary to the early Western missionary enterprise in Wenzhou that promoted gender equality by encouraging women's educational participation and the unbinding of women's feet (Soothill 1907), the Wenzhou Christianity that is led by male bosses plays a part in sustaining the patrilineal, patriarchal family structure. This patriarchy structures the desires of Christian women because the utmost concern of most married church sisters is to produce a son to continue the patrilineal mode of family.

Even though women far outnumber men in the Wenzhou church, Christian girls are always urged to marry Christian boys, while Christian boys may choose a nonbeliever since it is assumed that the new bride will follow her husband's faith after marriage. It would be unimaginable for a woman to reject the offer to participate in the ritual life (particularly funerals) of her husband's family. After hearing of her Christian friend's unhappy marriage into a Buddhist family, a twenty-three-year-old Christian woman expressed her worry about her future mother-in-law's Buddhist faith. She said she could accept a husband who was not a Christian; she would, however, strongly hope to live with her husband separately from his mother because otherwise her "superstitious" mother-in-law might take her child to a Buddhist temple one day and not allow prayer and hymn singing at home. There are numerous "tragic" examples of how devout sisters quit the church after marrying nonbelievers. More often, as a compromise, church sisters marry men from a Christian family background (with either one parent or both being Christian) who may seldom or never attend church. This gender difference in evangelical mate preferences corresponds to the gender hierarchy in the Chinese patriarchal family system. As the traditional Chinese saying goes, "If you marry a chicken, follow the chicken; if you marry a dog, follow the dog" (*jiaji suiji jiagou suigou*).

Young women constitute most of Wenzhou's "cultural and artistic" evangelization teams. For them, serving the church means leading hymn singing, playing the piano, and performing at all sorts of evangelical shows. However, they usually quit once they get married, because they are culturally expected to fulfill their life obligations as a good wife and mother. More than once, I heard female church workers describing the conflict between their family obligations and their church work.[21] For the church to serve its evangelical goal, the only practical solution is to recruit more young single women. One male evangelization team leader said to me that he was often caught in a dilemma; he worried both that these dedicated sisters would not have time to look for appropriate mates because of their busy evangelical schedule and that marriage would mean losing these well-trained and experienced performers.

Although Chinese women can seldom resist the traditionally defined obligation of childbearing, like women elsewhere they have physical control over this biological process. Through childbearing, women can also exercise limited power in their relations with men in the domestic realm. For local Christian women, biological reproduction offers the ultimate site of manipulating the body and producing feminine spirituality. However, in this process patriarchy is embodied and reproduced unintentionally.

Many women believers describe how the Holy Spirit has led them in selecting a mate and bearing children. Several women claimed they were able to know well in advance the sex of their infant, the time of birth, and the name of the local hospital because they had visions from God. Whenever these visions came true (*yingyan*), the women's faith deepened. A personal story published in the tenth anniversary special church brochure of a main local church to showcase "God's grace" reveals the church's religious and gender ideals. Titled "The True Light Entered My Home," it recounts how

Sister Mei converted to Christianity by marrying into a local Christian family and how she came to truly accept God in the unimaginably painful and troublesome process of bearing a son for her husband and his family. Though coming from a local Buddhist family background, Mei readily accepted her Christian mother-in-law's request to attend church weekly with her in order to please the husband's family as a new bride. At that time, she was not serious about the faith and admitted going to church simply for the excitement of sociality and to fulfill the new family's expectation.

Things changed after she gave birth to two daughters years later. The mother-in-law wanted badly for her to produce a male heir to the family, since Mei's husband was her only son. Mei became pregnant again, but a B-scan detected a female fetus. Under pressure from the family, she had an abortion. The abortion immediately drew criticism from the church she attended. Some church sisters came to comfort her and teach her about Christians' antiabortion stance. In addition, they prayed together for her to get a son. She was also asked to pray to God for a son herself. With consistent prayers, Mei became pregnant again. Once again, the B-scan showed a female fetus. Not unexpectedly, the desperate mother-in-law pushed her to undergo a second abortion. This time, with her better understanding of Christian teachings, Mei resisted.

The church sisters did not give up their prayers. Accompanied by a church sister who lived next door, Mei went to request a prayer from a spiritually experienced elderly woman (*daogaopo*) who was said to "have the burden for prayers." In a prayer the elderly sister claimed that God had promised her a child whose name was "true light." Days later, a test in the hospital showed she was actually carrying two fetuses, one female and the other male. The male fetus was not detected in the previous B-scan because of its tiny shape. Mei concluded her story:

> Because of this child's coming, I have seen the true light more clearly, recognized the true light, and accepted the true light. The true light is the Lord Jesus who shows sympathy for the people, loves them more than Himself, and sacrifices Himself for their salvation. Because He completely knows what I want and knows how to lead me to recognize and receive salvation, He is the true light in my life. When I was in the midst of darkness, sorrow, and despair, He guided me and brought me light. I deeply believe He will be my best companion in my life journey. I am willing to follow Him for life and lead my entire family to leave

the inherited faith [Buddhism], to please Him by walking on the path He has set. He is my savior and the true light over my family. I thank Him!

Mei, her mother-in-law, the *duogaopo*, and other sympathetic, warmhearted church sisters who continually prayed for her collectively all participated in producing a male heir, simultaneously perpetuating the patriarchal structure of the local community. The birth of the son testifies to the efficacy of the Christian god; notably, the son (rather than the three daughters and the previously aborted female fetus) becomes not only Mei's embodied way of accessing God but the metaphor of "true light" for the patrilineal, patriarchal family. In this way, traditional Chinese patriarchal insistence on producing male heirs and the Christian notion of salvation mutually reinforce each other. Through such bodily experiences as pregnancy, abortion, and delivery, women like Mei undergo a female-specific spiritual journey in which they come to intimately experience the presence of God and deepen their faith. Structured by a Chinese patriarchal family system, Wenzhou women's devotion to Christianity encompasses processes that "enlist women into complicity with a patrilineal mode of production of gender identities" (Sangren 2000: 184). Moreover, elite male believers largely endorse this authentic female Christian self.

A middle-aged Christian entrepreneur offers a male perspective on how feminine spirituality contributes to producing a son for his family. He has two children; the elder one is a daughter and the younger one is a son. During his wife's second pregnancy, the devout Christian woman wept a lot while praying to God for a son. This "sincerity" (*kenqie*) in the form of weeping, he emphasizes, is directly associated with the efficacy of her prayer. According to him, the birth of the boy was God's blessing. At that time the father was not a Christian and was not sure about whether his wife should get a B-scan to find out the sex of the fetus in advance, but eventually she persuaded him to fully trust God because resorting to a B-scan would be like testing God. "Fortunately we didn't have a B-scan. If we had, it might have been a girl again," he said retrospectively.

For evangelical women to convert their non-Christian spouses, hard bargaining is necessary in domestic issues, particularly childbearing. Sister Qinxia, a middle-aged *daogaopo*, married a non-Christian more than a decade ago. Though the man came from a Christian family background, he was not a believer and she was pressured by the church to convert him. She tried for three months to do so but failed. After the birth of their son, he did convert to Christianity. As she said:

> I was very clear about God's decree. God said my husband would repent. He repented gradually during my childbearing. He wanted a boy, just like other Wenzhounese. I prayed and told him that whether he wanted a girl or boy was up to God and he must repent. He repented for the child. It was not because I taught him much about the Bible. It was miraculous that he had a dream about the birth of a girl but he really wanted a boy. I said that you need to listen to the Lord. It is very convenient for God to give you either a boy or a girl. But the most important thing is that you need to repent. Later, very miraculously, God listened to his prayer. My husband repented and stopped playing poker [gambling] and started to listen to the Lord. I also prayed a lot. God gave me a vision that I would bear a boy, and the time of the birth was 6:30. I told him that God had listened to my prayer and promised me a boy. God even told me what the boy would look like. God has never lied to me.

Sometimes, opposition to premarital sex reflects a belief in divine causality and an intense desire for a son. A young Christian woman who is currently an elementary school teacher recalled how she successfully rejected the request for cohabitation from the man who was then her fiancé (he was from a Christian family but not a practicing believer):

> When there were many spiritual cultivation meetings, I had a good education about this [not having premarital sex]. They all said that living together before marriage was not good and would have an adverse impact on the younger generation. God does not approve of this. My husband did not know much about it. I told him that I had a relative who was like this [having premarital sex) and could not bear a healthy son. Only the third child survived. God's punishment is rather heavy. Then he was afraid that he would have a retarded son if he insisted [on cohabitation]. If so, it would all be his fault.

Wenzhou Christian women's ability to influence their spouses depends on their ability to link their Christianity to the production of a healthy son, which demonstrates the complex interplay among the female body, feminine spirituality, and female power in the domestic sphere.

Conclusion

The significant gender differentiation in Wenzhou Christians' religious expression and representation sheds new light on the nature of mass religious participation in the post-Mao era. Gendered agency and subjectivity cannot be ignored in analysis of the ongoing, massive revival of Chinese Christianity. In portraying gendered religious practices within Wenzhou Christianity, I do not intend to argue that there are two autonomous domains defined by separate gender roles or that Wenzhou Christian women and men are simply distinct creatures. Instead, my analysis focuses on the tensions that exist between these two types of expression and the representation of Christian faith that is conditioned by the larger socioeconomic context: the rationalized, hierarchical, elite masculine and the universally compassionate, boundless, non-elite feminine.[22] The former emphasizes the knowledge of written texts, while the latter often derives authority and authenticity from personal bodily practice and enactment of emotional expressiveness. In Wenzhou, female Christians focus on cultivating direct and immediate bodily experiences of God in their private chambers and female-dominated emotion-filled settings. Male Christians attend public textual study and banquets. The practice of gender in the Wenzhou church community epitomizes the gendering of public and private space in contemporary urban China as a consequence of macro processes of modernity (cf. Kohrman 1999). The gender stereotypes in the church generate different normative expectations for Christian women and men. The next chapter explores how such tensions are compounded by hierarchies of class, generation, and place in the rapid regional capitalist economic development that surrounds and enables the Christian revival.

As the phenomenon of *daogaopo* suggests, some Wenzhou Christian women's strategy to capitalize on this "God-given" vision of gender differences not only enables them to legitimate the feminine expression of faith but allows them to compete with elite men in their claim to spiritual authority. However, this strategy is also conducive to reproduction of gender stereotypes and patriarchal ideologies and prevents women from expanding the scope of female power in light of the rise of an increasingly rationalized powerful elite masculinity fostered by the rapid market transition. Clearly, Christian women are "destined" to be marginalized by a gender hierarchy that privileges men's religious experience and sentiment, although there is no fundamental contradiction between the elite male expression of faith and the feminine version of religiosity. In this context, the male ambivalence to feminine spirituality is expressed both in the form of an elite contempt for women's focus on emotions and bodily experiences at the expense of textual orthodoxy and in appreciation of women's day-to-day service as "Marthas." This "appreciation" is similar to that of women's productivity in domestic space, which is deeply rooted in the Chinese patriarchal system. In a sense, the gender hierarchy and gender boundaries in the Wenzhou church can be powerfully informed by construction of gendered spaces and gender politics in the larger (secular) Wenzhounese community. In her ethnography of a large Wenzhou migrant entrepreneurs' settlement in Beijing, Li Zhang (2001) discovers that some Wenzhou women become further disempowered and are subject to new forms of gender hierarchy in a highly commodified urban environment, because of Wenzhou men's increased control over the public (business) sphere and because of social limitation of women's spatial mobility.

In a regional political economy in which petty capitalist production continuously reinforces economic exploitation of women and perpetuates the stereotypical notion of women's narrow-heartedness, and in which daily business rituals espouse commodified female sexuality, gender hierarchy is ritualized, celebrated, and naturalized in the evangelical Christian domain. A notable example is the reconciliation of patriarchal values and individualized Christian spirituality in many church sisters' sincere, emotion-filled prayers for a male heir for the families of their husbands and friends.

Of course there are men and women who break gender stereotypes. Nevertheless, these structures are powerful. The experiential sector of the religion accommodates and fosters non-elite women's participation to the church in an overwhelmingly compassionate, intimate, and egalitarian way. The intense sense of divine intimacy cultivated through bodily sensations encourages Wenzhou Christian women to obey God's will in all circumstances, while male Christian entrepreneurs tend to emphasize flexible study and application of the Bible, because of their rational masculinity and need to tolerate sin to participate in the business world.

Chapter 6

Conversion to Urban Citizenship: Rural Migrant Workers' Participation in Wenzhou Christianity

As is the case in other economically developed coastal Chinese cities, since the 1980s rural migrants from inland provinces have flooded into Wenzhou seeking a new life. Without legal urban residency, they usually engage in nonagricultural activities in Wenzhou and work long hours for poor pay and few holidays. Large groups of new converts in the Wenzhou church are rural migrant workers who start to participate in church life regularly only after arriving in Wenzhou.

This chapter explores rural migrant workers' participation in Wenzhou Christianity in the context of their close interactions with the entrepreneurial class of believers, both in the church and at work. The Wenzhou church is a platform that gives full play to the range of desires and interests of its participants. For many migrant workers, what the church offers may not necessarily have to do with spiritual fellowship or moral compass. Some unmistakably take it as merely an entertainment program. As Andrew Kipnis (2001b: 43–44) indicates, "The joys of entering a particular symbolic universe involve arguing with other participants as much as agreeing with them, participating without believing, and manipulating towards private and variable ends." By focusing on "participation," I do not intend to give a full account of the diverse motivations for migrant workers' conversions to Christianity at the individual level but to show how they interact with and contribute to the making of a locally produced Christian identity. Robert Hefner (1993:

17) pointed out that conversion is "not a deeply systematic reorganization of personal meanings" but "the acceptance of a new locus of self-definition, a new, though not necessarily exclusive, reference point for one's identity." My interest is in sorting out how the urban middle class of Christians and the migrant worker class of believers negotiate and enact their religious and cultural identities in relation to each other.

In this chapter I first illustrate the immediate local social and cultural context in which migrant workers' mass participation in the Wenzhou church is made possible. Then I move on to depict how migrant workers imagine an urban-based modernity through the lens of local Christianity and how they (re)construct their identity and seek a meaningful life in the city by becoming and being a Christian. Finally, I examine how migrant workers' presence in local church space and local Christian discourse sustain and intensify a sense of place, class, and religious identity among the entrepreneurial class of local Christians.

The Condition of the Migrant Worker Class: Isolation and Discrimination

A survey titled "The Life and Work Conditions of the Floating Population in Wenzhou City" presents the general socioeconomic characteristics of the migrant worker class of Christians in my study (see Wenzhou Statistical Bureau 2004). It reports that by the end of 2003, the "floating population" (*liudong renkou*) in the city reached two million. These migrants are mostly young adults (age twenty to thirty-five), hailing from Jiangxi, Anhui, Hubei, Sichuan, and Henan, and have been absorbed into Wenzhou's labor-intensive, export-oriented backbone industries, manufacturing shoes, garments, eyeglasses, and lighters. Many experienced multiple migrations before coming to Wenzhou. Although less educated than the local population in Wenzhou city, this floating population is described as "having a higher cultural quality" than those left behind in their rural hometown.

Compared to the earlier wave or their parents' generation of migrant workers, whose primary concern was to seek a livelihood, today's young migrant workers have growing material aspirations, increasing demand for equality, and a strong desire for upward mobility and integration into urban life.[1] This is partly due to this younger generation of migrant workers having received more school education than those who migrated in the 1980s. Their greater access to education and popular media increasingly reorients them away from rural labor and life to an urban-based modernity. Seeking better self-development replaces economic interest as a primary motivator for their migration to Wenzhou.

In some sense, today's young migrant workers are rural only in their place of origin or *hukou* status, but not in their disposition because few had any extensive experience of farming back home. In their rural hometown, they might already have embraced a youth culture that is modeled on urban youth culture (Yan 1999). In Wenzhou, many young migrant workers, like their urban counterparts, are fans of the NBA, video games, and pop music from Hong Kong and Taiwan. In particular, consumption of cell phones is one of the most salient aspects of this youth culture among the factory workers I observed in Wenzhou.

Cell phones have become not only a necessary article for daily use but also an urban identity marker. Once I accompanied a worker to a shopping mall in the city center where he bought his cousin, a young teenage working sister (*dagongmei*) in the same factory, a stylish multifunctional NEC cell phone for ¥1,200, almost the amount of his monthly salary. She can use the cell phone not only to listen to MP3 music and take photos but also to watch downloaded movies (an important feature for her). Owning a fancy cell phone is likely the most sought-after fashion among these migrant workers who have few channels to keep connected with the outside world.[2] During artistic evangelization meetings held by the local churches, many migrant workers use a cell phone with built-in camera to take photos of the exciting performances. Use of modern media technology clearly distinguishes this tech-savvy new generation of migrant workers from the "earthy" elder generation.

These believers are often not the most disadvantaged among the migrant worker population. I find those actively involved in church work are ambitious and relatively better educated. They also tend to self-identify as capable, ambitious people, especially in comparison to others from their hometown. This is why they left their village for the city. Some of the young migrant Christians come to the city as a means to "broaden visions" (*kaikuo yanjie*) and "gain social knowledge" (*zengzhang jianshi*). This desire leads many to frequently change jobs and construct reality through conspicuous consumption (see Pun 2003). With intense upward aspirations, they are reluctant to return to the countryside. But their conditions of life and work in the city often put them in a very difficult dilemma. As nonresidents they are not accepted by the established urban social order. They lack "urban citizenship," the social entitlements associated with legal urban residency (Solinger 1999; Zhang 2002).

Though many of the legal requirements of urban citizenship have recently been relaxed, the concept is still a lens for understanding the (re)making of boundaries of urban identity and belonging in Chinese society. As previously mentioned, as a result of Wenzhou's rural past and dramatic urbanization today only a small portion of residents are nonagricultural *hukou* holders. In fact a great portion of the local population who are agricultural *hukou* holders have long been engaged in private business activities. In 2004 the state sector employed less than 6 percent of the total city workforce (Wenzhou Statistical Yearbook 2005). A Wenzhou city *hukou*, associated with few rights and entitlements, is therefore institutionally insignificant in the life of Wenzhou society. Symbolically, however, few migrants are imagined to be true members of the urban community (cf. Friedman 2004).

Easily identifiable by their inability to speak Wenzhou dialect, migrant workers are constantly treated as outsiders and encounter considerable discrimination from local dwellers. Local authorities seldom treat locals and migrants equally. Taxi drivers, who are predominantly rural migrants, are routinely given higher fines than local drivers for violating the same traffic rules at the same spot. Migrants who operate pedicabs often have them confiscated by the local police.[3] According to a migrant who has worked as a pedicab driver for five years in Wenzhou and who had eighteen pedicabs confiscated in the past year (each costs him 600–800 yuan), "No matter if you have a license or not, all outsiders face discrimination." Those migrants who rent a locally licensed pedicab for personal business operation can also be fined 50–100 yuan simply because they are outsiders. Behind this type of bureaucratic hassle is rampant discrimination against "noncitizen" migrant workers.

Along with discrimination, migrant workers in Wenzhou suffer much isolation, both physically and socially. They often live in cramped spaces, in a factory dormitory or a rented room shared with others at the urban-rural fringe zone where rent is lower. It is also not uncommon for migrant workers to live in temporary shacks built within factory workshops. Two people (of the same sex) sharing a single bed is a common scene in factory dormitories. Factory workers generally work twelve to fifteen hours a day, seven days a week, and have only a one-day break every month.[4] Many of them, with their IDs taken and the gate secured by private guards, live in an enclosed environment. There are also a great number of migrants working in Wen-zhou's service economy (in restaurants, hotels, bars, and night clubs, or as taxi drivers, pedicab drivers, salespersons, etc.). Few of them can afford to live downtown. Migrant workers also lack the time to pursue social advancement. Given the high intensity of work, just taking a rest is a luxury.

Since the 1990s, several migrant neighborhoods have gradually taken shape next to newly emerged industrial zones. These shabby districts are character-ized by a lack of basic hygiene, raw sewage, open garbage bins, and poor pub-lic security. The smell of burning leather and dark smoke coming from many small factories nearby constantly permeates the air, and the river that goes through the area has turned blue and black. These areas used to be rural farm-land a decade ago and were transformed recently by the local state-sponsored urban renewal project. Former villagers are now landlords who collect rental income from their migrant worker tenants. Living in a relatively enclosed com-munity for an extended period of time, these migrants often get to know each other. They shop for daily food at the same local market for agricultural prod-ucts and greet one another on the street in Mandarin or in their local dialect. Both the vendors and customers tend to be migrants. Migrants operate hair salons, video rental shops, poolrooms, miniclinics, food stalls, small groceries, payphones, pedicabs, motorcycle taxis, fruit stands, shoe and clothing stands, and so forth.[5] Many run their petty business without a license and encounter various bureaucratic inconveniences daily.

In the everyday life of such migrant enclaves, there is a mix of rural sen-sibilities and flashy urban lifestyle. Everywhere in these migrant enclaves, posters advertise rental properties, job openings, gambling techniques, and cures for sexually transmitted disease. This insecure environment nurtures a general sense of mistrust among the migrants themselves and between local residents and migrants. These districts share similar features with the urban villages Helen Siu (2007) researched in south China and termed "uncivil spaces." When I was looking for temporary housing in one such enclave, both my local church friends and the local housing agent (also a Christian) explicitly suggested I look for a local resident rather than a migrant to share an apartment with, for safety reasons. There is a sharp dichotomy between "locals" (*bendiren*) and "outsiders" (*waidiren*) or "migrant workers" (*dagong de*) in the daily language used among locals and migrants. A young migrant church worker once described a migrant worker district as a "mess [*luan*] because of the outsiders." The cramped condition of these migrant workers'

Figure 6.1 A Christian migrant worker's home in Wenzhou. Note the Wenzhou Christian calendar (as an identity marker) pasted on the door. (Photo by author.)

enclaves contrasts sharply with the splendid, modern local church buildings that give migrant worker participants a space for the fantasy of escaping the harshness of migrant work.

Imagining Urban Modernity

The local church has become a magnet for rural migrant workers, who often flock there by night with a sense of pilgrimage. Some large churches close to industrial zones turn on all their exterior lights and set off fireworks before evangelization meetings to attract the migrant workers who work and live nearby. Such evangelization sessions are usually a constellation of self-evident truths, fanatic passion, public spectacle, and artistic performance with the aid of multimedia technology. For many migrant workers, this "red and fiery" atmosphere in the church is reminiscent of temple festivals and other folk events in their rural hometown (see Chau 2006). When asked how they feel about a particular church service, some migrants simply use "atmosphere" (*qifen*) as a criterion. A "good atmosphere" includes loud music, glamour, glitzy stage lighting, and the presence of large crowds in a theaterlike church building with festival-like interior decorations.

With the adoption of modern technology, the Wenzhou church has fostered communal feeling and memory in some notably nontraditional ways. Many migrant workers wonder why the church does not charge them a membership fee, when its resources include large, luxurious, modern church buildings and the ability to host grand events. A Shaanxi migrant believer said he was initially afraid of going to a nearby church because he thought the locals who ran it would charge an admission fee. For isolated migrants, the church serves as a place to connect with a wider public. The spacious church building is a pleasant place where they can exchange job information and experiences of work and personal life, or simply kill time. During the hot and humid summer, when it is unbearable to stay in their rat-ridden rooms, attending a church service is a good pastime. Many arrive at the brightly lighted church hall well before the service starts to chat with people from the same hometown (*laoxiang*) and learn hymns as directed by local church sisters. In several migrant districts, the local church serves as an activity center for the migrant workers who work and live nearby.

For many, the church is also a modern schoolhouse for self-improvement and transformation through the teachings of local preachers. Local church preachers focus on scientific preaching (*kexue zhengdao*) to connect with migrant workers. This type of evangelical preaching uses rational methods and scientific terms to demonstrate the existence of God, and it usually draws on diverse sources (such as newspaper reports and research findings) to prove Christianity's rationality.[6] In one church evangelization session, I asked a young migrant worker from Jiangsu about his understanding of the faith. He said, "Like the Red Cross, there are a lot of things I didn't know before," while pointing at a Gospel tract titled "The Miraculous Cross," which claims that worldwide use of the Red Cross as a sign for a hospital is due to commemoration of Jesus. He continued, "This is an opportunity to learn." Migrant workers like to call Wenzhou church leaders and preachers "teacher" (*laoshi*), a term that refers to someone who is knowledgeable and respectable in Chinese society today. By referring to Wenzhou preachers as teachers and going to church as "going to class" (*shangke*), they affirm their desire for knowledge.

The fact that most Wenzhou church leaders and preachers are wealthy, male, and urban changes the social connotations many rural migrant workers previously associated with Christianity. Before coming to Wenzhou, they saw Christianity as a superstitious activity associated with illiterate old women and others who "have no way out" (*zoutouwulu de*). As shown in the previous chapter, throughout China the female gender and body are often associated with superstition, or backward and irrational belief. After coming to Wenzhou, migrants discover that "the richer and the more educated people are, the more they believe in God." Given that successful savvy male entrepreneurs dominate the pulpit and the public sphere of the Wenzhou church, Christianity has been not only made middle-class and masculine but transformed into a "reasonable" faith in the eyes of many migrant workers.

A young rural Anhui girl who works for a beauty salon said she used to think her late Christian grandmother was superstitious. When she was in middle school, she woke one night at the sound of her grandmother's prayer for her success in the next day's exams. At the time, she thought her grandmother was speaking to the air. After attending a weekly Bible study class in Wenzhou, she began to appreciate her grandmother's commitment to faith and became proud of her own newfound faith. She revealed her Christian identity whenever she could because, as she put it, "There is much reason and knowledge in it and God can care for me better than I do by myself."

Male migrants are often ashamed of the female-dominated church in their rural hometown but are willing to embrace the Wenzhou faith because of its links to elite rational masculinity. A newly converted male migrant from Henan attributed his previous lack of interest in Christianity to his misunderstanding of Christianity as a matter that pertains only to elderly women. He said that although he had worked in Wenzhou for more than a decade, he was just now learning the "theory of believing in Jesus." Before his experience at an evangelization session, he attended several Wenzhou Christmas parties, but only to watch the performances and seek the excitement of the sociality (*re'nao*). "Last year I didn't even know Jehovah is God," he said with a chuckle.

Some migrant believers express regret that their hometown lacks men who can preach with knowledge. They frame their experience of Wenzhou Christianity as part of a desirable new urban lifestyle. When asked what made him decide to be baptized in a Wenzhou church, one migrant worker from rural Anhui said he wanted to "experience it" (*tiyan yixia*), so he went for a "wash" (*xi yixia*).[7] To keep track of the extremely mobile migrant worker converts, many Wenzhou churches started issuing a baptism certificate with a photo (*shouxi zhengshu*) as proof of their Christian faith. A migrant believer who moves to a new church in Wenzhou is expected to show his or her baptism certificate. For migrant workers, this certificate, with its official church stamp and serial number, symbolizes an urban achievement to be cherished. Moreover, they are often told that their baptism certificate is accredited worldwide (*quan shijie tongyong*). In this context, baptism becomes an embodied experience of a cosmopolitan, urban modernity.

The urban-rural contrast in Chinese Christianity is also embodied in the material condition of the church community itself. Migrant workers like to speak of the Wenzhou church as "fully-equipped" (*shebei qiquan*), in contrast to the churches in their hometown, which often have only a few benches and perhaps an electronic piano. The Wenzhou churches' material environment is complemented by its integration into global networks of Christian modernity. More than once I heard migrant workers say, "The Wenzhou church is linked up with the international track." A Jiangxi migrant once spoke of the Wenzhou pastor in his church in an envious tone: "You see him one day, and then the next day you see him again. But in between he might have already made a trip to Italy to preach in the Wenzhou church there." Migrant worker Christians' fascination with "time-space compression" speaks to the cultural link between mobility and modernity in Chinese urban society (see Kohrman 1999). When asked to describe how he accepted faith in Wenzhou, Jianfu, a thirty-three-year-old Jiangxi migrant, recalled at length how a boss Christian took him to church on an imported motorcycle:

> At the age of twenty-four I accepted Jesus. There was a boss who believed in Jesus. One time he took me to a church using his motorcycle. He had a motorcycle because his father was the head of the local bureau of electricity. So that was the only motorcycle in the village at that time. It was a Honda 125. When the engine was working, it made a lot of noise. At that time it was very cool in the village, and he also had a mobile phone [dageda]. It was like a big brick, very thick . . .

Similar to Jianfu, some migrant workers are amazed by the fact that many Wenzhou Christians drive their own cars to attend church—an unthinkable scene in rural Christian communities. During my fieldwork, I accompanied two Wenzhou boss Christians to a large eyeglass factory where they lead a weekly Bible study group. The two brothers take turns driving a Mercedes-Benz or a Volkswagen to the factory, which is located in a suburb about forty minutes from the city center. They carry a laptop, an overhead projector, and an amplifier to facilitate their sermon. The well-dressed Wenzhou brothers, with their modern video-audio equipment and fancy cars, always draw much attention from the workers in the factory.

In sum, migrant workers' attraction to Wenzhou Christianity combines a desire for the red-hot sociality of large crowds and a quest for remaking their self-identity in terms of urban modernity. My migrant Christian informants use terms such as "proper" (*zhenggui*), "profound" (*shen'ao*), "pure" (*chunzheng*), and "solemn" (*yansu*) when talking about the services, sermons, and rituals of the Wenzhou church (often in comparison to the church in their rural hometown). Comments such as "the grand scene [*da changmian*] demonstrates a good faith" and "sermons preached in church buildings must be better than those in house gathering points" reveal the connection between the grandness of modernity and the legitimacy of Wenzhou Christianity in the imagination of many migrant workers.

Searching for Community Belonging

The worldly insecurity of migrants makes it difficult for them to imagine the future. Generally, the migrant worker class of Christians speaks positively of migrant work (*dagong*).[8] This is in part because they perceive no better alternatives and migrant work gives them access to a desired modern urban life. When asked about their future plans, they responded with a strong and pervasive sense of uncertainty. Some directly avoided talking about the future. They talked instead about their greatest fear (getting sick and being unable to work) and ultimately their dependence on "God's guidance." A young migrant woman said to me cheerfully in the presence of her husband, "We will continue to do migrant work until we are unable to . . . until our children come of age and can start to do migrant work." Clearly, their ambivalent status as rural migrants who have no legitimate claim to belong to the city leads to the ambiguity of their self-identity.

Christianity and church space are among the few resources to which migrants can turn in dealing with the problem of meaninglessness and reconstructing their self-identity. Many also find a channel for emotional expressivity in the church and a new community of belonging. Comments such as "I knew of the existence of God long ago but have only become close to Him after coming to Wenzhou," "It is God's grace that we can come out to do migrant work and see the outside world," "We came to Wenzhou from different parts of the country to make testimonies for Jesus," and "God has brought us to Wenzhou from 'five lakes and four oceans' (*wuhu sihai*)" reflect a shared narrative structure through which this group of migrant workers seek to make sense of their drastic life change from rural to urban and respond to an urban modernity in a collective, religious way.[9]

Through a range of activities such as Bible study, praying for one another's needs, hymn singing, the annual Christmas banquet, and group outings, the church offers a secure face-to-face community for isolated workers to derive pleasure from social interaction. Hymn singing with other migrants is a particularly memorable moment for many. One popular hymn repeatedly sung during migrant workers' services in a factory church is titled "Fellow Travelers" (*tongluren*). The lyrics go:

> Just because we are all fellow travelers, we have the same experience;
> Just because we are all fellow travelers, we have the same pursuit;
> Experiencing sweetness and bitterness together, only fellow travelers are the
>   most intimate;
> Shedding tears together, having happiness together, only fellow travelers are the
>   most sincere;
> Thank God for letting us meet on the road to truth and become fellow travelers.

This hymn, some migrant believers say, gives them a sense of "resonance" (*gongming*) because the lyrics reflect the reality of their lives in Wenzhou. They are fellow travelers, in a secular sense, who experience sweetness and bitterness together on the factory floor. The metaphor of fellow travelers, which appears in various church activities and rituals, creates a sense of belonging and warm bonding among migrant workers, facilitating their acceptance of Christianity.

However, the church is not just a place of sociality. It is also a moral community in which social belonging helps define how to live in the new urban environment. This is particularly important for those who feel they have been led astray by a criminal subculture. Pengjun, for example, sees

Christianity as a means to distance himself from past crimes. Along with some fellow migrants from Hubei province, he once engaged in blackmail and robbed long-distance bus drivers on the highway. He takes Christian faith as his salvation and the ultimate good. Now he asks himself, "Why not try to be a good person if all you have to do is to work hard?" He believes that without Christian faith he would have ended up in prison, like some of his earlier fellows. Currently working in a Christian-led eyeglass factory, he said he would feel uneasy if he missed a worship service now. He was led to God in another small factory where he previously worked. He described to me with a sense of joy the devoutness of his previous Christian boss and his wife; they would lead dozens of workers to kneel down in a big circle on the wooden floor during a weekly prayer session held in the factory on Friday nights, and on Mondays there would be a sermon that gave the workers a legitimate reason to stop their work and "go to listen to Jesus" (*ting yesu qu*). Such emotion-filled factory church gatherings serve as protection for those who are no longer bound by family ties after migration.

Many Christian migrants believe there are differences between Christian bosses and non-Christian bosses in their attitude to migrant workers. According to Yuexia, a female factory worker from Jiangxi, Wenzhou bosses generally are abusive, and she feels lucky to work in a Christian-led factory. She said she found peace and love in the religion, mainly thanks to a kind-hearted factory boss's wife (*laoban niang*). Yuexia shared the miraculous story of how the prayers of the boss's wife made her feel comfortable on the tough journey back home during the Chinese New Year. She usually feels carsick when riding long-distance buses or trains, but after the boss's wife held a one-hour prayer meeting to bless her before she set off she avoided motion sickness entirely. For migrant workers who take discriminatory treatment by factory bosses for granted, the prayers of Christian bosses seem like a gesture of unconditional kindness.[10]

Sympathy drives many migrant workers to church even though they find the Bible hard to understand. In a small Christian factory producing molds, the boss holds a weekly church service for about a hundred workers in the factory chapel. Those workers whose shifts collide with the service schedule and who decide to attend the service do not end up with their salary deducted once they sign in. This is an evangelical strategy to attract potential converts, and a "sacrifice" (*fengxian*) made by the ardent Christian boss. Sometimes the boss's wife greets the workers at the entrance of the chapel and distributes small snacks immediately after the service. Alienated workers enjoy this type of affective exchange with their Christian employers, which seems to be unimaginable for those working in a non-Christian factory.

The Christian mode of interaction enables many migrant workers to overcome their initial fear and anxiety in the new and strange place. Fuying, a female migrant from Jiangxi, recalled her first experience of going to a Christmas banquet in the local church a few years ago. Talking to me while inserting plastic sheets into the shoe tongues she had brought from the factory to her cramped room (shared with another Jiangxi couple), she said that back then she was afraid of going to the Christmas dinner since "they were all locals," but she eventually went with her Christian *laoban niang*, who offered great encouragement. Now she has much more confidence and has become familiar with the local congregants; she sometimes plays the piano in the church. "If I don't show up in the [weekly] Bible class, they later ask me what happened," she said with a smile. "Even though I have been here for quite a few years, my [spiritual] life [*shengming*] is still little like a child."

The Rhetoric of Change and the Embodied Knowledge of Faith

Therefore, if anyone is in Christ, he is a new creation; the old has gone, the new has come!

— 2 CORINTHIANS 5:17

Christianity has much to offer migrant workers who are struggling in a strange and difficult environment. When asked what it means to be Christian, Brother Liao, a factory worker from Shaanxi, said, "To take a million steps back, even if there is no afterlife, you can be a pleasant person to others [*meng ren xiyue*] in this world. It is worthy of your conscience [*duideqi liangxin*] to be an upright and righteous person. . . . If there is everlasting life, then that would be a heavenly gift that costs nothing [*tianda de pianyi*]. You only need to go to listen to a sermon once a week." For Liao, being a good person is more immediately important than having an everlasting life. According to him, he would have already lost his life on the street as a gangster if it were not for God's grace leading him to be a Christian. Although few migrants have experienced as dramatic a life change as Brother Liao, self-transformation is a recurring theme in migrant workers' narratives of Christian identity.[11]

In fact, as a marginalized social group migrant workers often come to the church with a quest for self-transformation (in secular terms) and social approval. The local church's evangelical teaching, which emphasizes that by believing in God one becomes a new creation in Christ, appeals to those who have little interest in Christian faith per se. Recounting his personal faith journey, one migrant believer told a "miraculous" story of how "a nonbeliever brought the Gospel to me." He said that he was desperate about his life in Wenzhou years ago, but it was a nonbelieving migrant friend who told him "You need to have a change" and "There is a Christian church nearby where you can change yourself."

For the workers, stressful work and long hours often lead to pain and suffering, significantly damaging their sense of self-agency. Their bodies become objects to be cured and saved. The learning of Bible knowledge works to convert their pain and suffering to God's agency and authority. Several Christian workers I interviewed had lost part of their fingers during factory work, and they took such injuries as "God's discipline" or a "reminder of sin." This attribution of divine causality is partly a consequence of the local church's evangelical practice, in which imposition of sin constitutes the core. As a young Wenzhou boss Christian preached in a factory church to a group of workers who work for an average of eleven to twelve hours a day with only one holiday a month:

> Why are you working such a job in the workshop and making so little money? Because you have sin and you have no knowledge. The sin is your weakness. Why are you not the president, why do you have quarrels with your wife? Because we are different from God who is all mighty. We are nothing. Since we have sin, there comes suffering. God looks at people from above and finds no one is righteous. Every one has committed sin. No one is a complete person. We still have sin in our life as Christians. University professors are not different from prisoners. Not much better. They all have sin. The only difference is the different conditions and environments in which they live.

This type of teaching supports the transformation of bodily experiences of pain into a strong moral sense. When workers find that their sin is responsible for their own fate, they then become docile bodies under capitalist domination. Wenzhou's labor-intensive industries come close to crude capitalist exploitation. In a sense, today's Wenzhou Christianity is strongly reminiscent of Methodism in early nineteenth-century England in terms of its role in forming the docile, industrious working class required by emerging capitalism (Thompson 1991).

As a deliberate evangelical strategy, the Christian rhetoric of change is reflected in various aspects of the Wenzhou church's evangelization among migrant workers. For example, large evangelization meetings targeting migrant workers have been titled "A Completely New You" (*quanxin de ni*) and "A New Creation" (*xinzao de ren*). Evangelical preaching is laden with promises of personal transformation in spiritual terms (e.g., from a life of emptiness to one filled with happiness), and it often forcefully links Christian conversion with upward mobility in socioeconomic life.

In one large evangelization meeting for migrant workers, a local preacher recited the many benefits of Christian belief and then finished his lengthy sermon by making an analogy. In his words, "If you believe in God, you will have countless blessings in life and eternal life after death," and "Believing in God is like accepting your uncle's invitation to be a boss in New York; not believing is like accepting a road-sweeping job your uncle offers you in Ethiopia." His tone was almost unquestionable, as if what he said was self-evidently true. Statements such as these reflect basic assumptions about the hierarchies of class, modernity, and capitalism among the Wenzhou Christian community on the one hand, and they offer a great promise for migrant workers to minimize these socioeconomic disparities through conversion on the other.

The rhetoric of change is also associated with the perceived behavioral changes that take place after a migrant worker's conversion. Male migrants often report quitting bad habits such as gambling and smoking, curbing a short temper (stop cursing), and improving their interpersonal relationships with others (coworkers or employers). Female migrants tend to report better relations with their mother-in-law, overcoming jealousy, and resisting premarital sex and abortion. Many of these positive behavioral changes lead to a disciplined migrant body. A migrant believer told me that faith can even transform one's posture and that his conversion made him feel more restrained while walking. Accordingly, he argues, he can tell whether someone is a Christian simply by how the person walks.

In contrast to the boss Christians' flexibility and manipulation of biblical messages, migrant workers tend to adopt a fixed understanding of moral prohibitions, particularly in relation to the Ten Commandments. Newly converted migrant workers are eager to exhibit signs of radical transformation in bodily terms. Many take bodily purity and discipline as the only route to personal well-being and success. Any violation could cause individual suffering. Wenfeng, a young Anhui migrant, recounted to me that he once ate a dead crab with blood still inside and got a severe headache later (the Old Testament forbids eating blood). However, because he got well five minutes after his prayer he felt that God answered him. He said Wenzhou brothers have good spirituality (*lingxing hao*), so they are rich. He regarded himself as not qualified to even talk about glorifying God, saying "I need to first enhance spirituality and then follow God's decrees, and in the end I can start a business and further develop it." He links good spirituality with such good habits as not smoking, gambling, having illicit sex, or getting drunk.

Wenfeng's story is worthy of close examination. First, it is doubtful one can find blood in a crab. I assume that Wenfeng, a recent convert in Wenzhou, just made up this story to demonstrate the dramatic change he had gone through, and to display his newly acquired Christian identity. Whether he is recounting things the way they really occurred becomes irrelevant at this point. Either way, his ability to reconstruct his body to fit with the Christian discourse of change is a telling example of how marginalized migrant workers tend to pursue an individualized bodily practice of faith. Indeed, in contrast to the bosses they have few cultural or economic resources, so the body is more likely to be manipulated and mobilized in achieving an authentic religious identity.

Workers' experience of poverty, humiliation, and discrimination contributes to a bodily knowledge that cannot be represented by anyone other than themselves. Having been beaten and verbally abused by local bosses and managers at work, Jiaoyou, a twenty-six-year-old who is currently a migrant preacher, recounted the unforgettable moment of rupture he experienced during an evangelization meeting that led to his conversion:

> At that time many people were determined to convert. When I made the determination, I just felt very painful [*ku*], the same as when I was working [in the factory]. I kept crying. When I was singing, I had tears on my face. I didn't know what the Holy Spirit was. That night I just felt I really longed for it. It is just like my life. I just wanted it. It was the most important thing for me. Many people were moved that night. Many were suffering. This is such a dark society.

You don't know how much pain the workers have had. I myself have experienced the pain.

Jiaoyou's conversion narrative illustrates the overwhelming emotional needs of migrant workers, and their resultant preference for individual closeness to God. To this God they can express their private emotions as well as feelings they cannot share with others. In doing so, they try to make sense of their hardships.

For long-term migrant Christians, adoption of the language of self-transformation is much less a public display of true Christian identity than a reactive response to the lived reality of social differentiation based on place and class, or an articulation of the desire for fast and smooth integration into the new urban world. During a local church-organized annual outing for migrant believers, Zhijun, a migrant preacher from rural Henan, preached a sermon on the ideal Christian transformation of migrants' outsider status in Wenzhou. Before he started, he expressed his willingness and happiness in coming to preach to an audience of outsiders—as an outsider himself. In the sermon, he said passionately:

> We know Jesus is the son of God. Jesus is the savior of mankind. Jesus is the only way through which we can enter Heaven. Since Jesus is the son of God, being in Christ we also become God's sons. This is very important. When you understand you are God's son, you will feel more honored than being a new Wenzhounese [xin wenzhouren]. Now, there is a slogan in Wenzhou that calls us migrant workers "new Wenzhounese."[12] I think this is not comparable to what Paul calls the "new creation." Neither is it comparable to being a U.S. citizen. Because we are citizens of the Kingdom of Heaven. The complete change of our identity and status in Christ is very unique. . . . You should not feel inferior because of your experience of migrant work here, for you know who Jesus is. Jesus is . . . God's son! [echoed by the audience] We are in Christ, so we are also God's sons. God is the Lord who has created everything. He is our father. As God's son, we should not bow our heads when we walk, but should hold our heads up and stride forward.

Oppressive work environments and the ideological category of outsider in the city generate a strong inferior sense of self for many migrants. The migrant preacher's repeated emphasis on their God's chosen status is to deliberately empower the disadvantaged migrant workers. Achieving a prestigious religious identity as a chosen one, however, does not necessarily lead to the desired change in one's identity and status in society. This is particularly frustrating for those migrant workers who have converted to Christianity mainly for the sake of pursuing a new life with respect and dignity in the city.

Struggling for Urban Citizenship

For rural migrant workers, there is a great gulf between urban employment and urban citizenship and also between conformity to local cultural norms and full participation in the institutional activities of the local society. In contemporary China, acquisition of urban citizenship by rural migrant workers resembles what classic assimilation theory calls "structural assimilation." Developed by Milton Gordon (1964), this term refers to the process by which minority groups enter the institutional life of the larger society at both primary (intermarriage and friendship networks) and secondary (employment and education) levels. Gordon notes that acculturation or cultural assimilation and structural assimilation are two separate stages, and that the former does not necessarily lead to the latter. This conceptual distinction between cultural and structural assimilation helps capture the ambivalent role of Christianity in shaping the adaptation of the migrant worker class in Wenzhou.

Given the sheer number of Christians, churches, and Christian-led factories in Wenzhou, Christianity constitutes a critical social institution of Wenzhou society. Christian conversion enables rural migrants to develop contact and social interaction with native-born members of Wenzhou society; it also reflects the assimilationist desires of Wenzhou migrants. As migrant workers make efforts to urbanize their dress, language, and customs, so do they urbanize their religious beliefs.[13] Newly converted migrant workers assume a locally produced Christian identity as a means to seek legitimate first-class citizenship (cf. Zheng 2007).

Church participation creates new possibilities for migrant workers to acquire urban citizenship. Their Christian identity—though frequently doubted by local believers—gives them (admittedly limited) access to jobs, housing, loans, social networks, and even potential mates in the Christian community. Nevertheless, it also creates new constraints. The experience of Chenbin, a thirty-year-old single male migrant and high school graduate from rural Anhui, highlights the complex and often contradictory role of Wenzhou Christianity in migrant workers' lives. Chenbin is one of the few ambitious migrants I came across in Wenzhou who sought to set up their own petty business. He was baptized in a Wenzhou church in August 2005, soon after attending a one-month church evangelization course.

When I first met Chenbin earlier in 2005, he was attending a Bible class in a local church at night while working as a chef during the day at a middle school canteen (a relatively easy job with a light workload, compared to most Wenzhou factory positions). In his first few years in Wenzhou, he had worked in factories producing shoes and glasses but did not make as much money as he expected, and he felt like a loser. In my conversations with him, he represented himself as a typical spiritual seeker disoriented by the life of migrant work. He said he was thinking about the meaning of his life in Wenzhou. After comparing Buddhism and Christianity, he decided that Christianity worked better for him because it emphasizes the "connection of people's heart" (*xinling de goutong*). He felt Buddhism was a money-making enterprise in which incense burning and monetary donations are done in exchange for material benefits. Moreover, he claimed to have seen foreign movies and TV programs in which there are often Christians and churches. He decided to be a full-time preacher just like the young man who preached to them (migrant workers) in the church evangelization session. If he were a preacher, "people would listen to me and that would feel great," he said. Moreover, he felt that his lack of money and power should not be a problem for this career choice. Dramatically, he referred to the Indian movie *Ashoka*, in which an emperor leaves the throne to pursue Buddhism, saying, "even the emperor went to preach." Chenbin's preacher dream seems to embody the migrant worker desire to counteract social stigma associated with rural outsider status.

A year later, I visited Chenbin in a suburban district (about a two-hour ride from the city center) where he had rented a small stall using borrowed money, to sell fake jewelry. He told me he had changed his mind about preaching. He realized that, unlike local church brothers who can afford to be a full-time preacher, first he has to do migrant work to make ends meet. Though he had kept reading the Bible every day, local church members criticized him for his lack of doctrinal knowledge. He felt Christians should treat each other as brothers, but even so he also encountered rejection on the part of local Christians. He had painful memories of a local church brother who ignored him outside the church.[14] As his frustration in the church grew, he abandoned his preacher dream and no longer attended church regularly.

Many single male workers try to avoid arranged marriages back home, resisting their parents' call for them to return to settle down. Some have not visited their rural home for years (even spending the Lunar New Year holiday in Wenzhou). Chenbin's mother also pressured him constantly to come home to marry, but he has his own standard and does not want to make a hasty decision. Migrant workers who are Christians often say they are waiting for "God's prepared marriage" in the city. Clearly, Chenbin's newly acquired urban ambition and strong sense of personal autonomy clash with his mother's rural sensibilities when it comes to mate selection. In rural China, parents often consider their children's marriage as their life obligation. Chenbin would end up arguing with his mother on the phone; he told me he would prefer to marry a local girl. This desire reflects both his drive for status enhancement and a personal economic calculation. According to Chenbin, getting a local wife would save him ¥10,000 a year in rent, which he could use as a gift to the mother-in law. He also fancied holding his wedding in the local Wenzhou church and then having a banquet in his home village during Lunar New Year.

Unfortunately he quickly found out that practically no local church sister would marry an outsider. He courted one local church sister but failed to win her love. When he asked a middle-aged local sister for help, she offered only her prayers. Later he tried to pursue another young local girl (also from a Christian family background). She said she liked him but her family would not accept an outsider. He answered by emphasizing that he would like to stay in Wenzhou forever, becoming a local. The girl then asked him if he could afford a new house. He said no, and the romance ended. There are similar cases in south China, where there are also many upwardly mobile families created by economic reform and where the demand for high marriage transfers among these families functions to exclude those at the lower end of the social hierarchy, particularly preventing the new underclass of migrant workers from marrying up (Siu 1993).

Such pain and disappointment is clearly felt more intensely by migrant workers who have high expectations of life and love. Realizing that people can distinguish outsiders from locals simply through appearance, Chenbin deliberately dresses like a local to avoid being considered earthy (*tu*, a derogatory term that city dwellers often use to characterize peasants). He is constantly reminded that he is an outsider in everyday affairs; for example, he had to pay a year's rent in advance for his stall rather than at the start of each quarter, which is the usual arrangement for locals.

Knowing I was doing research on Christianity, Chenbin once seriously asked me whether or not he needed to pay the local church a fee if he no longer believes, since he thought the church had spent money training (*peiyang*) him. I assured him this was not the case.

Chenbin's unsuccessful attempt to remake himself through Christian conversion is not unique. A subjectively experienced outsider status has much to do with discrimination and internalization of the entrenched institution of *hukou*, the hallmark of urban citizenship (Solinger 1999). When I asked Chenbin if a Wenzhou *hukou* is important and useful and could make a difference for him, instead of giving a direct answer he impatiently replied, "Of course, having a *hukou* means that you already have a home here. Without a home address here, they won't give you a *hukou*." *Hukou* has become a powerful metaphor here. In fact, it is almost impossible for an outsider to enter local social networks. The negative moral and ideological category of outsider has penetrated social interactions among local (Christian) communities, between local residents and migrant workers.[15] Chenbin told me he would never argue with the local people, including Christians, when they say outsiders are bad. Instead, he just wants to show them he is a good person.

Like Chenbin, none of my migrant worker informants ever expressed the simple intention to obtain an urban *hukou*, though they repeatedly emphasize incidents of perceived distrust and discrimination against rural outsiders on the part of ordinary urban residents. They generally view *hukou* status as ascribed and not amenable to change as they move from rural to urban areas and from one occupation to another. This subjective experience of *hukou* signifies an ideological and discursive exclusion that is critical for maintaining the entrenched urban-rural division and for perpetuating social inequality on the basis of the rural-urban spatial demarcation. It also confirms that Chinese urban citizenship is increasingly taking on new meaning and content in the reform era (Zhang 2002). Even though the rural-urban segregation justified by the *hukou* system has gradually diminished, as Lei Guang (2003: 638) aptly points out, "cultural distinctions of insiders (local) and outsiders (migrants) invoke and reproduce the rural-urban boundary on a constant basis."

Clearly, the insider-outsider dichotomy finds its expression in the local church. As Chenbin's case shows, the discrimination and prejudice migrants face within the church community causes some loosely committed believers to abandon the faith whenever it does not translate into upward mobility and first-class citizenship. Furthermore, the message migrant workers receive from the church, similar to that from the larger local society, tells them that because of their nonresident status they are inferior in spirituality.

A few migrants seek upward mobility in the church through advanced religious education. Though such educational opportunities are extremely rare for migrants in Wenzhou, a few "lucky" workers quit factory jobs and attend a yearlong theological training course using their personal funds.[16] Their parents back home cannot understand their choice, but they apparently have set their lives on a different track in the city. Their journey for migrant work has largely severed them from families in their rural hometown and from a set of traditional rural values. They tend to identify with elements of urban (religious) culture. For these migrants, who were initially driven to Wenzhou for urban employment, their willingness to afford great opportunity costs to attend this one-year study for no immediate financial gain attests to both their religious commitment and their strong desire for first-class citizenship.[17] This desire is quite reminiscent of some rural young Chinese who seek to secure urban jobs through embracing rigorous secular educational discipline (Kipnis 2001a). In both cases, young people of rural origin, with few opportunities for upward social mobility, aspire to remake themselves through educational attainment.

To a certain degree, such access to urban religious education has given elite migrant believers some privileges and further distanced them from the rural culture of their origin. Wenmeng, one migrant believer in the class, commented on the rural villagers' lack of appreciation for the important role of preachers: "Rural villagers [*nongcunren*] only know that [by being a preacher] one can make money without working; [if this were the case] then people would all try to be a preacher. They don't understand not everyone can preach." Systematic religious education distinguishes these migrant believers from the rest of the rural population while also significantly devaluing migrant work. The story of Jiaoyou, the single male migrant preacher from Guizhou, illustrates how Christian education managed by the local church simultaneously enables and constrains migrant believers' integration into Wenzhou society though shaping their attitude toward work.

On a hot August day, Jiaoyou received me in an air-conditioned church dormitory he shared with three other migrants in the class. Wearing a blue Ronaldinho soccer jersey, black jeans, and white sneakers, he shared with me the profound impact of the class on him. As the youngest of seven children, he had unhappy memories of how his parents and siblings derided his college dream as unrealistic (his mother told him not to forget who he was). He was forced to quit soon after entering middle school, for financial reasons. In 2000, one year after his arrival in Wenzhou, he converted to Christianity. He believes God has now led him to this spiritual training class, giving him the educational opportunity he longs for so much:

> To enter this [spiritual training] class has been a big wish of mine. When I was younger, I really hoped to go to college. I never regret entering this class. It is my most correct choice, even though I cannot gain financially. It makes me feel rich in my mind. It helps me change my values of life and guides me to know myself. . . . This is more satisfying than going to Beijing University and Tsinghua University. If God let me enter these universities, I may become proud of myself. God let me know myself. This is the biggest satisfaction God has given me.

Having suffered severe abuse at work, Jiaoyou finds that the spiritual training class is his cure and haven. Moreover, it fulfills his youthful dream of attending college and offers him more self-confidence and a sense of personal power.

Before Jiaoyou started the course, local churchgoers repeatedly questioned him about whether he was sure God had truly given him a clear vision to study theology. Though they did nothing to prevent him from applying to the local church-sponsored training course, these doubts "deeply hurt" him and perhaps even constituted a form of symbolic violence. He said he used to view the Wenzhou church as "spiritual" (*shuling*), but various experiences of local Christians' doubts and rejections have caused him to abandon this view.

Identifying with other migrant workers' experience of hardships and their attempt to seek a meaningful life in the new urban world, Jiaoyou admits his lack of communication with local Christians in the class and his preference for interacting with brothers and sisters from "five lakes and four oceans." Reluctant to return to his rural hometown to marry, as his mother constantly requests, he has made up his mind to proselytize full-time among the migrant workers in Wenzhou's industrial zones after completing the training class. He said with determination, "When I preach, I hope God can use me to help these worker friends and to let them receive God's love in their hearts." In his discussions with me, Jiaoyou often used cultural metaphors to sympathize with migrant needs. He drew parallels between today's migrant workers and the biblical "Israelis sojourning in Egypt" in Exodus. He also severely criticized Wenzhou factory bosses, for "showing no mercy to the poor and the sojourners, unlike what Jesus did to the 'children of Israel.'" He firmly believes that "Jesus loves migrant workers."

Although some elite migrant believers like Jiaoyou complain about the inequalities existing in local churches and factories, they unanimously speak of their own religious experiences with great pride and satisfaction. Expressions of growing personal autonomy and dignity pervade their narratives of personal religious identity. Commenting on their perception of personal transformation through faith, a number of newly converted migrant workers told me they used to "work for money" but now when they work they only "work for the Lord" (*wei zhu zuogong*) and try to "accumulate treasure in heaven" (*ji caibao zai tianshang*). By stressing the notion of working for the Lord, migrant workers attempt to transform themselves from subalterns to glorious agents of God. Nevertheless, most migrants' desire to completely remake themselves through participating in the local Christian domain may never be realized, given the local church's positioning of migrants as pedagogical objects and religious resources.

Migrant Workers as Pedagogical Objects and Religious Resources

For Wenzhou Christians, a key indicator of the church's revival is the scale of its evangelization, and evangelizing literally means proselytizing among rural people in inland provinces and migrant workers in Wenzhou's industrial zones. Since the rural migrant workers' encounter with Wenzhou Christians takes place in the context of a growing regional modernity embedded in the Wenzhou model of market economy, migrant workers are not only outsiders but also modernity's "others" in the imagination of many Wenzhou people. For Wenzhou Christian evangelicals, this view requires maintaining the boundaries between the urban civilizer and the migrant civilizee, between performative subjects and pedagogical objects, and restricting the range of possibilities that can be enjoyed by migrant converts.

In contrast to the emphasis by the local church on migrant workers' evangelical ministry (*mingong fuyin shigong*), local church leaders and preachers generally perceive evangelization among nonbelieving local residents as having an "insignificant effect" (*guoxiao bu mingxian*). Given the long-established tradition of Christianity and the large proportion of Christians in Wenzhou today, the local church holds the view that the rest of the local population remains non-Christian mainly because of their calloused hearts, rather than their lack of access to the Gospel. Nevertheless, Wenzhou Christians believe that God has led millions of migrant workers to Wenzhou the same way as He previously led Wenzhou (Christian) people to migrate and do business in other places (to spread the Gospel), all of which serve the "plan of expanding God's Kingdom" (*guodujihua*). As a result they do not now have to travel long distances to the rural inland for evangelization. The fact that migrant workers are the main target of evangelization today, however, has caused concerns for at least some local church workers, who doubt that the Wenzhou church is capable of conducting effective evangelization among the locals, particularly intellectuals. They attribute this limitation to the low quality (*suzhi*) of Wenzhou preachers, most of whom have only received elementary or middle school education. As one young preacher notes, "What we really lack is the rise of talented, high-quality evangelists" (*gao suzhi de budaojia rencai*). Both sides of the debate, however, agree that socioeconomic disparities between the evangelizer and the unevangelized play a determining role in shaping evangelization work.

In line with this cultural logic, local Christians tend to consider disadvantaged migrant workers "simple" (*danchun*) and "humble" (*qianbei*) because of their poverty and uprootedness, and they often speak of them positively as having a "teachable mind" (*shoujiao de xin*). A recurring theme in the Wenzhou church's evangelical narratives on migrants can be characterized as "double drifting" (*shuangchong liulang*), a metaphor local preachers like to use to refer to the condition of homelessness both in this urban world and in the spiritual world. Christian faith is said to be the only way for people to receive protection in this life and an eternal home for their souls.

THE GLORIOUS BURDEN FOR MIGRANT WORKERS
AND THE EXERCISE OF SYMBOLIC POWER

Do you not say, "Four months more and then the harvest"? I tell you, open your eyes and look at the fields! They are ripe for harvest. Even now the reaper draws his wages, even now he harvests the crop for eternal life, so that the sower and the reaper may be glad together.

—JOHN 4: 35–36

During the process of evangelization, Wenzhou Christians often position themselves as the sower and the reaper, and migrant workers as the crop waiting to be harvested. Bible verses carrying such terms as "crop" (*zhuangjia*), "harvest" (*shouge*), and "fields" (*hechang*) are frequently cited as local preachers address the importance of migrant workers' evangelical ministry. In this discursive context, migrant workers are transformed into agentless evangelical objects ready for remaking. Referring to John 4:35, a young local preacher said:

> Thinking of this Bible verse, my heart saddens [beitong]! The Wenzhou church now faces two million migrant workers, who are in a helpless situation. Are they not the fields that are ripe for harvest? Facing millions of suffering compatriots, how can we ignore them? Moreover, they are all evangelical objects [fuyin duixiang] who deliver themselves to our door. How can the church miss this opportunity?

Another local preacher describes the evangelization work of the Wenzhou church among migrant workers more in terms of a mission:

> Today a great vision is waiting for the Wenzhou church. The nationwide tide of migrant workers [mingong] has brought an unprecedented opportunity for the Wenzhou church. Among those who come to Wenzhou, many have never heard the Gospel. They may live in pathless [renji hanzhi] mountains, be ethnic minorities, or Muslims. They may not know who Jesus is at all. Many are atheists. Few of them have thought about the eternal spiritual life but hold a deep absurd [huangmiu] belief in the notion of "man can conquer Nature" [rending shengtian]. They work hard, hoping to use their hands to achieve a better life. Every young Wenzhou Christian should know that the heavy burden of this glorious ministry [rongyao shigong] is on our shoulders and the relay baton of the Gospel is already in our hands.

Terms such as "pathless," "minorities," and "absurd" vividly capture Wenzhou Christians' perception of migrant workers as a socially distant and uncivil category in need of enlightenment. Contrasting sharply with the "glorious" nature of the evangelical enterprise, this perception is framed with a linear Christian view of transformation via conversion. Lacking awareness of workers' real conditions and their internal differences, the Wenzhou church tends to work on an abstract stigmatized concept of *mingong*.

The Wenzhou Christian discourse on the "glorious burden for migrant workers" clearly represents an urban middle-class elitist approach to migrant workers, based on a sense of civility and progress (cf. Jacka 2006). For the elite circle of Christian entrepreneurs, evangelism can merge with an interest in controlling and policing migrant workers. For example, the organizers of the Wenzhou professionals' fellowship invited a Chinese American preacher and businessman to lecture on the necessity and urgency of evangelization work among migrant workers. In front of a group of Wenzhou entrepreneurs, the Chinese American brother used a PowerPoint presentation to give statistics, charts, and figures on the condition of the life of migrant workers and cited news reports, academic research, and his own anecdotal observations as the manager of an American company in China to construct an image of desperate and dangerous migrant workers needing Jesus Christ. The speaker further drew a comparison between today's Chinese migrant workers and black American slaves. According to him, the fact that the slaves were mostly docile workers under extreme racist oppression was due to their commonly held Christian faith, but in the case of Chinese migrant workers lack of faith has led to numerous cases of violent crimes against their employers, often reported by the popular media.

It is unclear whether or not this highly pragmatic preaching is a deliberate strategy to attract and strengthen Wenzhou bosses' commitment to Christian faith. Nevertheless, this invited presentation speaks to a reality of the Wenzhou church community in which migrant workers are completely objectified among the elite circle of Christian entrepreneurs. Realizing they have the capacity and convenience to both negotiate with the "top" (the Chinese state) and influence the "bottom" (migrant workers), this entrepreneurial class of Christians often represent themselves as the most strategically important group in the mission of Christianizing China. By stressing their strong sense of mission and by anticipating the ministry needs for millions of migrant workers, Wenzhou Christian entrepreneurs legitimize and reinforce their privileged social status, which is ultimately based on growing rural-urban disparities.

The discourse of the glorious burden for migrant workers enables the entrepreneurial class of Wenzhou Christians to romanticize their initial capital accumulation and exercise their symbolic power over migrant workers. This dual process of romanticizing and symbolic domination is particularly evident in the institutionalized practice of gift giving in migrant workers' ministry.

Since the early 1990s, in response to the mass influx of migrant workers in the city, many Wenzhou churches have set up weekly Mandarin evangelization sessions on Sunday nights. At such evangelization meetings, gift giving is a routine practice. Immediately after services targeting migrant workers, small gifts such as instant noodles, soap, toothpaste, oranges, towels, umbrellas, and other articles of daily use are distributed to the participants. One church even adopts a sign-in procedure to encourage the participation of migrants. Those individuals who continuously attend church over an extended period of time will be awarded a pressure cooker or a thermos. Sometimes cash (usually 5 yuan) is also used as a gift. The most grandiose form of giving, however, is the annual Christmas banqueting event, an occasion that draws migrant workers to the local church by offering great food and small gifts. Migrant worker believers get free admission to these Christmas dinner banquets and are encouraged to bring their non-Christian friends, while local church members have to purchase their own tickets (*canjuan*, usually 30–50 yuan per person).

This aggressive practice of giving, as a major method of attracting potential converts, affords the affluent urban middle class of believers symbolic capital and social prestige.[18] It allows Wenzhou Christians to draw a clear line between the morally superior and the morally inferior by giving, under a spiritualized framework of what many believe "God uses people's greed to lead them to Him." It is not uncommon for local believers to openly criticize some migrant workers for "only wanting food but resisting the Gospel" (*zhiyao shiwu buyao fuyin*). The local Christian assumption of greedy migrant workers has at times caused conflict between workers and local Christians in the church. In one case, an elderly local church leader expelled a migrant woman carrying a baby during an evangelization session because he presumed that she had only come for instant noodles. Migrant converts echo these beliefs in their conversion narratives. As one young male Jiangxi migrant believer said bluntly, "God uses instant noodle to attract greedy people like us."

For local Wenzhou evangelists, migrant workers are a practical tool to fulfill their evangelical ambition. Wenzhou church leaders and preachers see migrant workers as a key agent in the Wenzhou Christians' envisioned mission of leading the entire nation to return to the Lord (*zhonghua guizhu*). Jianfu, a Jiangxi migrant who leads a small Bible study group in a Christian-headed factory, once retold a local preacher's self-derisive statement: "We Wenzhounese are lazy and our evangelization depends on you the migrants." He explained:

> It is hard for Wenzhou people to evangelize in rural areas because of the language problem, the inconvenience of life, and high costs. This is why God has let Wenzhou develop first and then attract many outsiders to Wenzhou. They then accepted the Gospel here; I also believed in Jesus in Wenzhou. So I can use my own dialect to spread the Gospel among my fellow countrymen. It is convenient for me . . . I think he was telling a fact. It is perhaps God's work that Wenzhou is so developed [fada]. The Wenzhou church and its preachers have provided great support to our outsiders and invested a huge amount of money.

Jianfu notes that the Wenzhou church has extended financial support, audio equipment, and even furniture to the Jiangxi church back home. On various occasions, migrant worker believers set up a conceptual order: Wenzhou is God's blessed place, so Wenzhou has many private enterprises and entrepreneurs, Wenzhou is attractive to rural migrants as a destination for urban work, Christian entrepreneurs contribute great amounts of financial support to the church, many gifts are distributed at evangelical meetings, Christianity is attractive to migrant workers, migrant workers convert to Christianity, and finally migrant workers train for evangelization in China's vast rural inland. As migrant workers internalize their role as a vital religious resource of the Wenzhou church and as an indispensable part of this glorious mission of Chinese evangelism, they join a social order at the bottom of a new socioreligious hierarchy and become complicit in their symbolic subordination.

PRODUCTION OF CULTURAL DISTINCTIONS AND THE CHRISTIAN PROJECT OF "SENDING CULTURE DOWN TO THE COUNTRYSIDE"

As noted earlier, the role of migrants in the Wenzhou church community is largely confined by the interlocking hierarchies of class, place, and spirituality. Local Christian resistance to networking with migrant workers contributes to development of a distinct migrant worker's Christianity in Wenzhou. This migrant workers' Christianity is forced to exist in parallel to local Christianity, but not as part of it. Normally, migrant workers participate in separate and parallel church programs and activities (Bible study, hymn singing, performances, outings, communion, even baptism). Although they are not formally disallowed to sit through local residents' services (some may attend such services conducted in Mandarin), they can hardly assume teaching, leading, or performing positions there (even for long time believers) because of cultural boundaries existing in the local church.

The Wenzhou church certainly accommodates migrants in a much more equal style than the larger society does, but conversion or baptism itself does not guarantee full membership in the larger Christian community. Migrant believers must gain pragmatic awareness of the power relations operating behind the ritual and spiritual forms to be fully legitimate members of the faith community. Sister Hong, a Hubei migrant, learned this by participating in a main local church. She came from a Christian family background but says she truly got to know God only after coming to Wenzhou. Hong recounted her uneasy experience of joining a local hymn rehearsal group. During a church service held a month before Christmas, she heard an announcement asking those who wished to participate in the choir for the Christmas performance to stay after the service to learn hymns. She and several other migrant sisters decided to stay because they had always enjoyed singing hymns. But the local choir members did not welcome them. The local members looked down on them and said that she and other migrant sisters were "troublemakers" (*tianluan de*) to the choir because of their "poor Mandarin," "having no culture," and "being unable to catch up with the rhythm." Under great pressure, they quit attending the choir. Hong said desperately, "I want to be 'light and salt' (*zuoguang zuoyan*), but I am incapable without culture. I truly want to serve God, but there is no way I can do it." Performing is viewed as a privileged experience, signifying culturally superior status in the Wenzhou Christian community.

Those migrants who are chosen to serve the local church are always offered marginalized positions as ushers and cleaners rather than preachers, leaders, or performers. They can play a leadership role only at workers' services, and those who have received certain training from the Wenzhou church may preach or perform in front of an audience only of migrant workers. Few of them are aware of the processes of "othering" and objectification. Most local congregants view migrant workers as forever novices in spirituality and as pedagogical objects needing constant guidance from the local church. This implicit but deliberate rule regarding migrant workers in teaching, performing, and leadership positions must be understood both in the larger social context in which rural people are often associated with the notion of backwardness and in the local context of Wenzhou Christians' single-minded pursuit of cosmopolitan modernity (see Chapter Three).

Desiring to refashion Christianity as a modern cosmopolitan institution and to distance themselves from the rural church culture, Wenzhou Christian entrepreneurs produced a series of "high-end" activities involving guest speakers invited from outside. Once I attended a planning meeting among several Christian entrepreneurs who were organizers of the monthly forum for Wenzhou Christian professionals. The meeting started with a conversation about the importance of "packaging" (*baozhuang*) the nascent professionals' fellowship. The interlocutors generally agreed that where a guest speaker comes from matters to the audience. In their view, speakers coming from Western backgrounds are the most preferred, and the second-tier category consists of those from Beijing and Shanghai. As a middle-aged Christian boss put it, "people coming from the U.S. and those from Africa are absolutely two different classes (*butong dangci*). It absolutely matters." He then commented on a well-known professor from a Beijing university who had just given a popular speech at the forum, saying, "If he said he was from Jiangxi, we would not have received him in such a high-class manner." The professor currently works and lives in Beijing but was originally from Jiangxi, the inland province that has sent more rural migrant workers to Wenzhou than any other province in the last few decades.[19] Enthusiastic reception of Christian celebrities from Beijing, Shanghai, and the West constitutes, however, just one side of the story. On the other side, migrant workers, who are situated at the lowest ladder of the hierarchies of class, place, and modernity in Chinese society, basically have no right to lecture or be listened to in the local church.

Nor do migrants have the right to attend high-level Bible study classes. One main local church that was among the first to establish a migrant workers' ministry in Wenzhou and owns a grand church building located adjacent to a migrant district surrounded by factories runs an "outsiders' Bible class for potential or new converts" (*waidiren mudao ban*). Around thirty to forty migrant workers gather in a small classroom on the top floor of the church building every Sunday for the daylong Bible study class, which is taught by young local preachers. Established six years ago, this class emphasizes basic knowledge of Christianity. The church has advanced Bible classes at various levels for locals, but no advance study is offered to migrant worker believers. Many of the forty-some migrant believers have participated in the same outsiders' class and listened to similar, somewhat repetitive teachings for years, though there are always newcomers and old participants who leave from time to time. Confused and confined by the label of spiritual novices, several long-time migrant participants in this Bible class expressed their frustration about being unable to enter the higher levels of Bible classes dominated by locals. They also complained that the teachings received from local preachers are rather "unsystematic" (*bu xitong*).

Sometimes, "outsiders' services" (*waidiren juhui*) are interchangeable with "Mandarin services" (*putonghua juhui*) in the daily language of the church people. Because the so-called Mandarin services are created only for outsiders,[20] the term could be rather ambiguous even for many local church members. One local church leader takes Mandarin services in the Wenzhou church as a euphemism for separate migrant services: "Since we Wenzhounese also speak Mandarin, why are there still Mandarin services? Because we look down on them. So we leave them alone and don't care if they live or die" (*zisheng zimie*). He considers this division in the church to be a product of the larger Wenzhou culture, which stresses local pride. However, this element of local culture also reflects a general sense of urban supremacy. It is certainly unfair to view the Wenzhou church as xenophobic simply on the basis of a single statement, but the reality of institutionally segregated church services illustrates the othering process of the local church.

The labeling of migrant workers as outsiders seems incapable of changing even for those who have been involved in the local church for an extended period of time. At an annual Christmas party specially for migrant worker believers in a local church, a Wenzhou entrepreneur church leader introduced a long-time migrant believer who was going to perform in front of the crowd by saying, "Xiaohua is an outside brother [*waidi dixiong*] who has been in our church for ten years. He will sing the hymn 'God's love never changes.' Let's welcome him." The term "outside brother" points to the migrant workers' essential otherness to local congregants. Local Christians call migrant worker believers outsiders, and migrant workers themselves often also address one another as outside brothers and outside sisters in the church. This language reflects a bizarre combination of intimacy based on a commonly held faith and a distinction grounded in place of origin. For the Wenzhou church, rural migrant workers are needed religiously but kept away from locals culturally.

In sharp contrast with the Wenzhou church's general indifference to developing systematic church programs and activities suitable for outsiders, many large city churches enthusiastically send weekly evangelization groups to Christian-led Wenzhou factories and regularly stage large-scale public evangelizing meetings in the industrial zones (usually on national holidays).

Competition has developed among local churches to produce the largest and grandest possible cultural and artistic evangelization meetings (*wenyi budao hui*). I attended several big evangelical meetings targeting the migrant workers in Wenzhou's industrial zone. Each attracted thousands of workers from nearby factories. The biggest one I observed took place in a spacious factory workshop, with nearly three thousand migrant workers participating in the festival-like event. What are luxuries for migrant workers, such as laptops, overhead projectors, musical instruments, stereo systems, professional costumes, lighting equipment, and automobiles, are necessities for the production of these large evangelizing meetings. In this material context, urban privileges are conspicuously displayed and transformed into a modern Christian pedagogy.

This cultural and artistic form of evangelizing (dominated by singing and dancing, with the central theme of worshiping God) is, according to one evangelization group leader, "a free-of-charge evening party" that serves to fill the vacuum (*kongxu*) in the emotional and cultural life of migrant workers, most of whom cannot afford the cost of entertainment in wider Wenzhou society. In meeting migrant workers' need for cultural life, the Wenzhou church's factory evangelization work mirrors the "sending culture down to the countryside" movement (*song wenhua xiaxiang*), a central state civilizing project initiated in 1996 under which officials, artists, scientists, and college students go to the countryside to spread culture and scientific and literacy knowledge to rural areas.[21] Most visibly, this state-engineered urban-to-rural unidirectional movement has sent movies, troupes, and books to "poor, backward regions" (*pinkun luohou diqu*) in hopes of improving the image of the party-state. In a similar fashion, the Wenzhou evangelical enterprise, with its emphasis on the combination of preaching the knowledge of God and artistic performances, aims to metaphorically deliver the migrant worker audience a (free) gift from God.

Both the Wenzhou evangelical notion of presenting a spiritual gift and the official state notion of sending culture down assume a poverty of culture among rural people and imply their need to receive advanced (either Christian or socialist) culture in order to transform their own backwardness. Discursively, the arrival of new migrant workers contributes to continually supporting Wenzhou Christians' commitment to evangelism as well as to the affirmation of their class and place identities.

Figure 6.2 A large musical evangelization meeting in a Wenzhou factory. (Photo by author.)

Contesting and Remaking Boundaries of Urban Belonging

The Wenzhou church's strong urge to evangelize derives in part from a similarly strong desire to legitimatize a local faith tradition that has evolved at the margin of the state for a century. However, for migrant workers, their propensity to convert is driven by a recently developed upward aspiration to belong to the life of urban China.

Wenzhou bosses may not be unique in exercising symbolic power over the migrant worker class through the medium of Christian religion. This historical moment of Wenzhou seems to parallel that of the nascent English working class depicted by E. P. Thompson. In his analysis of the relationship between Methodism and social class in early-nineteenth-century England, Thompson views Methodism as "the religion of both the exploiters and the exploited" (1991: 412). He further spells out why many English workers, displaced by the Industrial Revolution, were willing to submit to Methodism's psychic exploitation:

> Indeed, for many people in these years the Methodist "ticket" of church-membership acquired a fetishistic importance; for the migrant worker it could be the ticket of entry into a new community when he moved from town to town. Within this religious community there was (as we have seen) its own drama, its own degrees of status and importance, its own gossip, and a good deal of mutual aid. There was even a slight degree of social mobility, although few of the clergy came from proletarian homes. Men and women felt themselves to have some place in an otherwise hostile world when within the Church [Thompson 1991: 417].

The English working people's longing for the Methodist sense of community may seem familiar given Wenzhou migrant workers' pursuit of urban belonging through Christianity, both being in the context of crude capitalist exploitation and aggressive displacement.

The rural migrants' encounter and interaction with local city dwellers in the Wenzhou church create new emotional contexts and cultural meanings for their respective identities. On the one hand, the Wenzhou Christian revival offers an unprecedented new opportunity for migrant workers with few economic resources or social networks to access urban space and keep pace with urban life (see Davis et al. 1995). On the other hand, the urban middle class of Christians has adopted definitions and terms such as *mingong* and outsiders to categorize and subordinate these migrants even within the supposedly "spiritual community of love." As self-perceptions of rural and urban identities are left open during processes of mass migration and rapid urbanization, Wenzhou Christianity furnishes a contested space of identity and a site for negotiating the boundaries of urban belonging.

Affirmation of a privileged urban-oriented Christian identity is dependent on a narrative construction of an uncivil migrant worker class awaiting the Gospel, and also on a spatial demarcation between local residents' church services and migrant workers' ministry. As the metaphor of the Christian project of sending culture down suggests, the Wenzhou church's evangelization work always involves one-way movement of people, knowledge, money, equipment, and performances from urban to rural. Some determined migrant believers, after being trained in Wenzhou and with the encouragement of the Wenzhou church, have returned to their hometowns to conduct evangelization, though it is not uncommon for them to come back to Wenzhou again for migrant work after encountering financial difficulties back home.[22] More often, they offer help and guidance to the rural church with their temporary return. Many take gospel tracts, Christian books, CDs or videos of sermons, hymns, and Wenzhou evangelical performances back to their rural village during the holidays.

Such short trips allow these elite migrant worker Christians to feel urban by "sending Christian culture down" to rural communities, as Wenzhou Christians have done before them. Jiahai, a Jiangxi migrant, is invited to preach at the church in his rural hometown whenever he goes back for a visit. Because he emphasized that he was not just an ordinary participant in the main church hall but a member of a Bible class in an upstairs classroom (higher status for him) in Wenzhou, he felt like a member of the elite in front of his fellow villagers back home. His fame in the local village church circle spread, and he has been invited to play a "ritual master" role by presiding at local villagers' funerals and wedding ceremonies. Even his father is given favorable treatment in the village church. According to Jiahai, whenever his father shows up in the church, he is asked to sit in the very front. On the street, local churchgoers greet him and say things like "He is Jiahai's father." Jiahai understands well that all the privileges he now enjoys in his home village come from his extended urban experiences, and he also consciously acts urban by preaching in the village church in Mandarin (he insists that his local Jiangxi dialect sounds too backward and non-Christian).[23] For migrant workers like Jiahai who converted to Christianity in Wenzhou, Christian faith is always a privileged, Mandarin-related, urban experience that they want to identify with but feel unworthy of at the same time.

For migrant worker Christians who desire to stay in the city permanently, a popular choice is to take up the task of spreading the Gospel among their fellow workers enclosed in the industrial zones and take a secular job at the same time, a combination they call "serving God with a job" (*daizhi shifeng*). Although struggling for a legitimate claim to belong to urban modernity, none of my migrant Christian informants want to spread faith among not-yet-converted local city dwellers. When asked why not, they would usually answer, "God did not give me such a vision." In a more concrete context, asked whether he had ever tried to spread the Gospel (*chuan fuyin*) to his neighboring stall owner, a Wenzhou local and Buddhist with whom he often plays cards, Chenbin admitted his reluctance and said with diffidence, "Both Christianity and Buddhism are Wenzhou traditions. . . . The Buddhists say Christianity is a superstition." This sense of inferiority, prevalent among migrant workers in confronting locals, testifies that distinctions of class and place are translated into differential claims to religious commitment and spiritual authenticity.

Much of the material in this chapter demonstrates that Christianity has become an important part of the ongoing process of translocalism in China, in which flows of people, capital, goods, images, and ideas circulate with increasing speed across the boundaries of the urban and the rural, continuing to result in new regional imbalance. Even if the household registration system were completely abandoned, the cultural distinction between the rural and the urban could hardly disappear soon. In this case, social differentiation is embodied in the practice of Christian space (cf. Liu 1997). Space produces distinctions and inequalities between disadvantaged migrant believers and privileged local churchgoers as it does between prosperous coastal Wenzhou and the poor inland. The migrant Christians' relationship with local Christianity resembles the coastal city's relationship with the rural inland in both social and spatial terms.

As a dominant urban institution that sustains norms of urban citizenship in this city, the Wenzhou church not only offers migrant workers a false promise of full membership in the urban Christian community but also fosters impossible dreams of first-class citizenship. The social hierarchies (local-outsider, urban-rural, boss-worker, Christian–non-Christian, saved-unsaved, spiritual-secular, civilized-backward, and male-female) structure migrant workers' interactions with local Christians, and how they construct their own identities and narratives. The Wenzhou evangelical enterprise embodies these dichotomies and contradictions in ways that are reminiscent of the Chinese state civilizing project in which ethnic minorities are treated as the Other (Harrell 1995). As the uneven processes of modernization and industrialization progress, urban-oriented Christian services and practices express the rural-urban divide and create new social hierarchies.

Chapter 7

Conclusion: Religious Revivalism as a Moral Discourse of Modernity

As in many parts of the contemporary world, Wenzhou refutes the once-popular prediction that capitalist modernity would lead to inevitable secularization. The city has gained fame as a regional center of global enterprises and, as "China's Jerusalem," a center for Chinese Christianity. Today's Wenzhou Christianity represents the urban elite phenomenon of religious revivalism in China's post-Mao modernization. At its core, and in contrast to local rural-based Chinese Christianities, this is a movement of an upwardly mobile class emerging alongside the rapid urbanization and industrialization of the region. The Wenzhou story shows that the presence of a business community organized at the grassroots level can not only negotiate changes in church-state relations but also move Christianity from the margin to the mainstream of Chinese society in everyday maneuvers.

I have argued against a dichotomous view of state domination and church resistance. Such a vantage fails to capture the social complexity of religious life. The reform-era Wenzhou church is not just a place where pro- or anti-state ideologies are played out. Multiple discourses are at work, and multiple subject positions are involved in local Christian revivalism. I have shown that Christianity is inextricably intertwined with class positions and dispositions, gender differentiation, place distinction, and everyday lived experiences in the local society. The church offers a site for formation of new social experiences and cultural identities among local groups of varying backgrounds.

Furthermore, preexisting folk ideologies fostered by the centuries-long petty capitalist mode of production have shaped an emerging Christian form of local social organization, even if it has not been entirely absorbed. Profoundly informed by a regional culture of commercialism, the resurgent and innovated Christian beliefs and practices in reform-era Wenzhou often contain a celebration of pragmatism and growing individualism, a supernatural justification of newfound wealth, and simultaneous commitment to religious faith and modern rationality. Wenzhou Christianity is not a monolithic religious or spiritual phenomenon.

Despite the specialties of the regional culture, the Wenzhou case can be viewed as a major instance of the rise of advantaged urban believers in the reform-era development of Chinese Christianity. These advantaged believers play an active role in shaping the public image of Christianity in local Chinese society. The political economic context of post-Mao reforms affords Christianity a greater place in local society, but too often Chinese Christianity is viewed as an autonomous entity, neglecting its engagement with other local sociocultural systems. This study shows that Wenzhou Christianity constitutes a popular domain in which the state and numerous local forces participate, rather than an autonomous symbolic universe that is inherently antistate and antihegemonic. By closely examining religious experience and meaning among Wenzhou boss Christians, it offers an opportunity to rethink post-Mao state-religion relations more dynamically and interactively.

Though the revival of Christian religion and the emergence of private enterprises appear to be signs of autonomous space for civil society being reclaimed from the totalizing state, Christian entrepreneurs and the post-Mao state actually share many important concepts, aspirations, and interests—particularly in the common pursuit of stability and development. Chinese Christians are not simply victims of the state modernizing project; nor is the post-Mao Christian revival a process of faithful believers resisting state ideology. Rather, the revival is better conceived as a dynamic process in which emerging socioeconomic groups embedded in local histories and memories try to claim their own space to practice long-established faith in the changing political and economic conditions of China. Wenzhou boss Christians not only seek to follow God's plan in the ongoing market transition but also produce, manage, and consume it. In doing so, they are helping to transform church-state relations and the overlapping domains of religious and secular practices in contemporary China.

While distinguishing urban-oriented Wenzhou Christianity from rural-based Chinese folk religiosity, which mainly revolves around seeking practical benefits (see Chau 2006; Weller 1987), the boss Christians' general interest in theologization and systematization embeds them in a global hierarchy of Christian modernity. Studying the Bible and other imported evangelical literature appears to symbolize authenticity and authority, and also a reorientation away from rural tastes and sensibilities toward Western modernity. Inspired by the Weberian argument relating religion, capitalism, and modernity, these Wenzhou bosses seek to legitimate their religious and entrepreneurial identities simultaneously by developing a regional religious model of modernity different from the secular one defined by the developmental state.[1] This project of alternative modernity in Wenzhou is captured by the popular local Christian slogan of "constructing China's Jerusalem." On the one hand, local bosses are often aware of the "original sins" committed during their accumulation of initial capital in the early years of economic reform. Now they are concerned with the moral authority and prestige that can be associated with "Jerusalem." As one boss said, "Wenzhou used to be known for counterfeits and fakes. Now we need to make Christianity a new brand of the city." On the other hand, the entrepreneurial class of church leaders self-consciously appropriates the market logic of property and ownership and a language of business for their projects of religious and cultural self-realization. Religious and capitalist economic practices are therefore mutually stimulated and interpenetrated in the "Wenzhou model" of church development. Huge amounts of economic resources have been channeled into various material forms of evangelism in the Wenzhou church across local, regional, and even national boundaries. Evidently, this is not a case of simple penetration of capitalist market relations but a contribution to the multicultural mode of global capitalism (Yang 2000).

What Max Weber (2001) calls "elective affinities" between Calvinist Christianity and capitalism unwittingly grant legitimating power for the new entrepreneurial class to unify their economic activity with symbolic participation in the post-Mao period. In describing elective affinities, Weber did not propose a causal relationship between Christianity and capitalism but argued that their association led to secular modernity in the West. Nor did Weber assert these affinities were universal. For Wenzhou Christians, however, these are not elective but absolutely intrinsic affinities. Wenzhou believers aspire to the form of modernity emerging in the West that has become the global prototype. They believe in the notion that Western capitalist modernity is a result of the spread of Christian faith. Consequently, to be modern is to be Christian and Western. As local preachers in their sermons cite Weber's thesis as a validation of their modern and progressive faith and as one reason for conversion, Weber becomes a "prophet" of universal Christian modernity.[2] For the Wenzhou church, Calvinism is *the* objective truth to be enacted as history. We may use the term "subjective affinities" to grasp the intentionality and human agency in the Wenzhou Christian conception of secular capitalist modernity as correlated to Christianity. The nature of the relationship between Wenzhou Christianity and Wenzhou's capitalist economy is thus not about whether the post-Mao city has followed a trajectory of Western modernization delineated by Weber or an "East Asian development model" informed by "vulgar Confucianism" (Berger 1988). Rather, it is about how local people creatively adopted and actively promulgated a powerful transnational cultural form to their self-transforming socioeconomic practices.

The Wenzhou Christian construction of subjective affinities between religion and capitalism and the fusing of religious and economic logic in practice should be understood as part of a larger moral discourse that champions the holistic distinction between the superior and the inferior. This holism, in many aspects, evokes the pervasive *suzhi* discourse in contemporary China. According to Kipnis (2006), this powerful term serves to justify all kinds of Chinese social and political hierarchies. Boss Christians are at the forefront of becoming high *suzhi* believers and citizens and of pursuing a holistic economic-spiritual-moral way of life. They seek to distinguish themselves in economic, symbolic, and moral spheres, or in their own words to contribute to both "material civilization" and "spiritual civilization" (a mimicry of a reformist state slogan). Embodiment of an overall superiority greatly appeals to the boss Christians who seek to throw off the stigmatized "village entrepreneur" label imposed on them since the rise of the Wenzhou model in China's rural industrialization and modernization. They seek to establish themselves as members of a new local elite through simultaneously embracing evangelical Christianity, rational masculinity, state connections, a freewheeling market, and Western lifestyle. In this process of self-remaking, these privileged men seek to cultivate all desired embodied qualities at once, while taking religious ideology as malleable and religious identity as fluid and open to improvising.

Wenzhou Christianity is certainly not unique in serving as a vehicle for creation of locality and moral leadership. To place the activism of Wenzhou boss Christians in the wider comparative context of Chinese religions helps link this case study to broader patterns in the relationship between religion and political economy throughout China. Various forms of temple-based religion have linked local communities to religiously sanctioned structures of moral authority in reform-era rural China. Wenzhou boss Christians are comparable to various local temple activists depicted by anthropologists working on popular religion in rural China (Chau 2006; Feuchtwang and Wang 2001; Wang 1996; Jing 1996). These local elites all sought to express their leadership aspirations and secure an alternative power base within geographic communities through wielding control over religious organizations and symbols.[3] A key difference between rural local temple elites and Wenzhou boss Christians is that the former's power is often legitimized by a traditional moral order shaped by Confucian statecraft ideology and reinforced by relatively closed local social networks, whereas the latter derives power, legitimacy, and resources from a global religious movement and from translocal and even transnational processes of religious evangelizing and economic expansion.[4] Furthermore, Wenzhou Christians' pronounced overarching loyalty to God and emphasis on congregational worship and moral discipline distinguish them from local community-based forms of popular religion (see Dean 2003) and the rest of local society.

In modernizing post-Mao cities, various forms of religious life generally face much greater ideological restrictions and state supervision than they do in rural areas.[5] This is particularly so for popular religion, which constituted an integral part of Chinese city life in the pre-Revolutionary era (Naquin 2000) but has since been attacked by modernist Chinese governments as "feudal superstition" incompatible with modernization (Anagnost 1994: Duara 1991). Today, urban Wenzhou residents apparently have great difficulty in channeling their newfound wealth from the private household economy into restoration of traditional ritual communities, mainly because of rigid state administrative boundaries existing in the city (cf. Yang 2004). Although popular religious practices triggered grand expansion of the communal ritual space in the countryside, the congregational life of Christian churches (many named after places and neighborhoods) plays a prominent role in forming collective identities and in defining the boundaries of local communities in the city district.[6]

In rapidly urbanizing Wenzhou, evangelical Christianity surpasses other major local religious traditions in its propensity to foster and embody significant grassroots religious activism among the upwardly mobile class. Besides its embrace of a cultural and moral language grounded in Calvinist theology that can be most effective at ideologically legitimating new categories of wealth and power, its lay leadership structure has the potential to institutionally integrate local economic elites into the power center of the church on a large scale.[7] By emphasizing the priesthood of all believers and deemphasizing good deeds and religious orders, the Christian church is more likely to serve as a local power base than any other religions will for members of the new rich, especially morally ambivalent businessmen. In the context of the religiously hierarchical Catholic Church and its celibate priesthood, apparently few busy entrepreneur believers would imagine themselves entering formalized liturgical structures to gain leadership status in the local community.[8] In the context of Wenzhou's intensely commercialized urban economy, it is equally unlikely that local businesspeople would literally renounce the world and join the clergy of Buddhist or Daoist temples in great number. In fact, a study done by local Wenzhou scholars indicates that clergy from poorer neighboring provinces who have hidden economic motives dominate Buddhist and Daoist temples in Wenzhou (Mo and Lin 1999). Some wealthy Wenzhou entrepreneurs compete for high social status in local communities through making lavish donations to popular temple organizations, yet they seldom participate in the daily operation of these organizations. Although temple-based popular religious institutions contribute to the revival of folk cultural practices and formation of a new power field in Chinese agrarian society (Chau 2006), Christianity has gradually emerged as a dominant form of Chinese urban religiosity and a major source of cultural legitimacy for the new rich class in the context of a modern commercialized economy. Given the differing socioreligious dynamics between the industrialized coastal zone and interior agrarian sphere, it is perhaps no accident that many Wenzhou entrepreneurs adopted Christianity as their outlet for negotiating identity, status, and morality, whereas local economic elites in rural China often turned to village temple groups, which are, for the most part, far more capable of generating a shared moral framework for the entire rural community than socially marginalized village churches (see Tsai 2007: chap. 5).

Furthermore, Christianity appeals to Wenzhou's private entrepreneurs partly because it helps to project a moral ideal and assert a unique regional identity differentiating Wenzhou from both China's vast inland, which is dominated by an agriculture-based economy, and Chinese metropolises such as Beijing and Shanghai, dominated by reformist state-led development.[9] As the nationwide debate on the Wenzhou model of development continues, Wenzhou's private entrepreneurs continue their painful search for national legitimacy.[10] As this study shows, some Wenzhou bosses are using global Christianity in an attempt to transcend a decadent state moral order captured by prevalent cadre corruption in both official and popular discourse. Even though there could be various reasons behind their conversion, Wenzhou boss Christians are not isolated spiritual seekers but members of a new type of post-Mao moral elite who have systematically pursued and promoted new categories of power and prestige in order to differentiate themselves from other groups.

Despite their lack of interest in serving the church full-time, boss Christians use their economic power to secure teaching and preaching positions in the church. They desire economic and cultural capital alike, and respect from society as both bosses and Christians. This local Christian reality contrasts sharply with places where people do not expect a successful businessman to be able to preach a sermon or see the capacity to engage in private business as vital to an evangelical preacher's mission. In Western contexts, altruism and economics are often considered separate spheres (Kipnis 1997: 24). In Christian Wenzhou morality, religion, and ritual are not separated from everyday life. As Weller (2000: 485) observes, the anthropological distinction between sacred and profane does not apply to parts of Chinese society. The economic instrumentality of Wenzhou bosses' Christianity often coexists with a fervent ambition for evangelism. The Wenzhou church community has not lost its moral high ground, even within the milieu of untrammeled entrepreneurialism, economic polarization, and the post-Mao consumerist local reality. Instead, Wenzhou Christian devotion sustains an old-fashioned communal narrative of divine causality that emphasizes the necessity of moral conservatism (especially in prevention of extramarital sex).[11]

Although it carries an explicit localist agenda for constructing China's Jerusalem, the Wenzhou church is fundamentally based on voluntary membership and claims a commitment to universal public morality. This seems to create the potential for its development into a base for a Western Enlightenment style of civil society, often manifested in the centrality of Christian moral discourse. However, it should be made clear here that Christianity as a world religion did not evolve within East Asian cultural traditions but was introduced from outside. Therefore, it is misleading to concentrate on the link between Protestantism and discourses of modernity as self-evident in the European sense.[12] In Wenzhou society, Christianity constitutes an alternative vehicle for social capital and a source of a uniquely Chinese modernity that is drawn on primarily by the new rich class. It seems unlikely that it will become any form of national civil association that contributes to China's successful political transformation.

Wenzhou Christianity articulates a crusade mentality when dealing with the competing interests of various local groups, and it uses a profound moral discourse to justify a variety of social hierarchies. This has to do with the Wenzhou model of development being an early capitalism phenomenon. Exploitation of rural migrant workers and the booming real estate industry enabled by massive private accumulation of land and property is reminiscent of Britain in its transition to industrial capitalism.[13] In this rapidly industrializing, post-Mao city, Christian moral discourse addresses the cultural ambiguity of the new rich identity and the need for free and open competition across diverse social spheres (rather than serving as an equalizing institution) among the ambitious new capitalists. It can be argued that Wenzhou Christianity plays a role similar to that of Methodism in nineteenth-century England in offering a moral context for formation of a new industrial capitalist social order (cf. Thompson 1991).

Parallel to Weber's Protestants, who view their devotion to work as a holy calling, Wenzhou boss Christians uphold the notion that "doing business is serving God." Although Wenzhou did not experience full colonization by the modern West, colonial and missionary modernity left a profound imprint on the collective psyche of Wenzhou society (Yang 2004). Wenzhou people's internalization of Western forms of modernity is certainly shaped by the historically transnational moment of the region. The project of constructing China's Jerusalem captures their worship of the Christian West and their determination to compete as an equal.

The Christian-inspired moral culture of modernity that has emerged is differentially related to individual churchgoers in Wenzhou society, where capitalist economic production led to growing class differentiation. In the local church community, class differentiation is reproduced and reinforced by differential access to this moral culture of modernity. On the one hand, underprivileged migrant workers seek urban citizenship by joining this modern urban form of religious, spiritual, and moral expression. Through emulating the privileged in language and bodily practices, they become complicit in producing subaltern identities and subjects. Although some migrant Christians contest the moral authority of the entrepreneurial church leaders by using their newly equipped canonical language, they lack the socioeconomic power to either adopt or challenge the holistic model of identity construction of the boss Christians.

At the same time, boss Christians strive to belong to a Christian modernity by exercising symbolic power over non-elite local women and migrant workers. They have invented a series of evangelical initiatives that exclusively serve their own cultural tastes and identity needs. Public textual study and banquets are ritual events that inscribe their hierarchical and patriarchal values. The evangelical practices of gift giving and of "sending Christian culture down" mark their socially advantaged and morally superior status in relation to unconverted or newly converted migrant workers from the impoverished rural inland. In this dual process of evangelization and conversion, local bosses often act as performative subjects while migrant workers serve as pedagogical objects subject to what E. P. Thompson (1991) calls psychic exploitation. Both parties participate in production and reproduction of a hierarchical moral order in distinct and meaningful ways.

By portraying and analyzing the heterogeneous and mutually contested practices of Christianity in Wenzhou, I have shown that Christianity is far from a coherent symbolic universe. Wenzhou Christianity as a historically complex regional construct has fully engaged local Chinese in a moral discourse of modernity in which emerging socioeconomic groups struggle to negotiate their social status and refashion and legitimate their identity. This moral discourse of modernity enables a bizarre combination of prosperity gospel, biblical fundamentalism, and moral conservatism whereby the upwardly mobile class can claim an overall economic, spiritual, and moral superiority. In short, Christian identity marks a larger hierarchical and moral distinction between the high and the low.[14]

The Wenzhou Christian creation of social hierarchies can be viewed as mainly a product of the earnest efforts of individuals to advance in the historical context of a modernizing China, concomitantly with their equally anxious search for a unifying meaning system and moral order whereby they can make sense of their experiences of growing inequality and dislocation in a rapidly changing society. In particular, the experiences of economically shrewd, politically connected, and moralizing Wenzhou boss Christians highlight the dynamism and contradictions of the postreform political economy. Their psychosocial self is reflective of the general Chinese mentality at this historical juncture. It is in these contexts of spectacular modernization and social polarization that the story of Wenzhou Christianity finds its wide resonance in contemporary China. Although Christian entrepreneurs still represent a minority within China's Christian population, active involvement of the upwardly mobile urban class in church life constitutes not only a trend but a likely future of Chinese Christianity in the context of China's embrace of a competitive globalizing economy. This is true insofar as enterprising Chinese citizens continue to feel a strong impetus toward ideological expressions that are congenial to their socioeconomic aspirations.

Finally, the Wenzhou story adds a new twist to the debate on human rights and religious freedom. It shows the growing religious freedom and declining persecution of Christians in the post-Mao context of decentralization and marketization. More important, the research sheds unique light on the persecution angle by emphasizing a subjective approach to religious freedom (as opposed to the dominant state-centered approach). It sees religious freedom through the eyes of local believers. Simplistic labels like resisting and suffering Christians do not do justice to the subjectivity of local Chinese Christians, who desire to fashion themselves as religious agents with social significance. The fact that many Wenzhou church leaders are eager to represent their religious practices and organizations as free of state control and intervention, often conspicuously shown in their grand church architecture and Christmas parties, points to the importance of this subjective approach (even though their churches or church organizations may not be completely independent of official supervision, or they have had to make compromises along the way). Whether or not the entrepreneurial church leaders are recounting their actual encounters and relationships with the state is less relevant. Their defiance of victimization and objectification in the religious domain attests to their quest for a sense of agentive and honorable self. By constructing the city of Wenzhou as China's Jerusalem, these socially and spatially mobile Chinese demonstrate both how anxious they are about constructing a sense of place in the rapidly urbanizing post-Mao era and how capable they are of contributing to world Christianity, not as God's martyrs but as resourceful negotiating agents.

Character List

bendiren 本地人

bing bu yanzha 兵不厌诈

Boteli 伯特力

bu lifa de falang 不理发的发廊

buneng buxin 不能不信

busan busi de 不三不四的

bu shuling 不属灵

butong dangci 不同档次

bu xitong 不系统

canjuan 餐卷

caolian 操练

cehua zhixing zu 策划执行组

chanajian de ganshou 刹那间的感受

chengzhongcun 城中村

chongman 充满

chongxin dingwei 重新定位

chuan fuyin 传福音

chunzheng 纯正

da changmian 大场面

dafang 大方

dageda 大哥大

dagong 打工

dagong de 打工的

dagongmei 打工妹

daizhi shifeng 带职事奉

dan 单

danchun 单纯

dao 道

daogao po 祷告婆

daoli 道理

da yihui 大议会

dazao pinpai jiaohui 打造品牌教会

Deng Xiaoping 邓小平

dezhao 得着

di cengci 低层次

dingshang balei 顶上芭蕾

di suzhi 低素质

dixiong 弟兄

dixiong zhong zhenli 弟兄重真理

dongshizhang 董事长

doudiao yishen tuqi 抖掉一身土气

duideqi liangxin 对得起良心

ernai 二奶

fada 发达

fangdang 放荡

fei wuzhi wenhua yichan 非物质文
    化遗产

fengxian 奉献

fu buguo sandai 富不过三代

fuyin duixiang 福音对象

fuzhai jingying 负债经营

gan peiling hui 赶培灵会

ganxing 感性

gaoduan 高端

gao suzhi de budaojia rencai 高素质
    的布道家人才

gongming 共鸣

guanxi 关系

guifan hua 规范化

guodujihua 国度计划

guojihua 国际化

guoxiao bu mingxian 果效不明显

hechang 禾场

hehe ben 和合本

heshen de xinyi 合神的心意

hongshui mengshou 洪水猛兽

houfang 后方

huangmiu 荒谬

Hu Guiye 胡归耶

hui 会

huikui 回馈

huise shouru 灰色收入

Hu Jintao 胡锦涛

hukou 户口

huore 火热

jia de haobuhao 嫁的好不好

jiaji suiji jiagou suigou 嫁鸡随鸡, 嫁狗随狗

Jianan 迦南

jiangdao 讲道

jiangke 讲课

jiangtan 讲坛

Jiangxiren 江西人

jianshe hexieshehui 建设和谐社会

jianshe Zhongguo de Yelusaleng 建设中国的耶路撒冷

jiantangre 建堂热

jiaoba 教霸

jiaohui zhuanzhi zhuyi 教会专制主义

jiating jiaohui 家庭教会

jiazhang zhi 家长制

ji caibao zai tianshang 积财宝在天上

jiedang yingsi 结党营私

jiejing 洁净

jingshen wenming 精神文明

kaikuo yanjie 开阔眼界

kegu mingxin 刻骨铭心

kenqie 恳切

kexue zhengdao 科学证道

kongxu 空虚

ku 苦

laoban jidutu 老板基督徒

laoban niang 老板娘

laoshi 老师

laoxiang 老乡

Lei Feng 雷锋

leji shengbei 乐极生悲

lianghui 两会

lihai 厉害

ling 灵

lingming de zaipei 灵命的栽培

lingming genji 灵命根基

lingqiao xiang she 灵巧像蛇

lingxing hao 灵性好

Li Peng 李鹏

Li Ruihuan 李瑞环

liudong renkou 流动人口

lixing 理性

long 龙

luan 乱

Mada 马大

maidian 卖点

maitang de enci 买堂的恩赐

meiyou da de fudan 没有大的负担

meng ren xiyue 蒙人喜悦

mianzi 面子

Mijia 弥迦

mingong 民工

mingong fuyin shigong 民工福音事工

mofang 模仿

muqu 牧区

muyang 牧养

nanxia ganbu 南下干部

nao bieniu 闹别扭

nongcunren 农村人

nuxing hua jiangdao 女性化讲道

nuzhong hui 女众会

paidan 派单

paigong 派工

pao gongxiao de shi tianbing tianjiang, gao jiating shengchan de shi yangmen nujiang 跑供销的是天兵天将, 搞家庭生产的是杨门女将

peida shifeng 配搭事奉

peiling hui 培灵会

peiyang 培养

pinkun luohou diqu 贫困落后地区

pubian endian 普遍恩典

putian tongqing 普天同庆

putonghua juhui 普通话聚会

qianbei 谦卑

qianfang 前方

qiangyang 抢羊

qi'e yangshan 弃恶扬善

qifen 气氛

qiye chengbao zeren zhi 企业承包责任制

quan shijie tongyong 全世界通用

quanyi zhiji 权宜之计

quanxin de ni 全新的你

re'nao 热闹

rending shengtian 人定胜天

renji hanzhi 人迹罕至

rili wanji 日理万机

rongyao shigong 荣耀事工

rushang 儒商

sanzi aiguo yundong weiyuanhui 三自爱国运动委员会

sanzi jiaohui 三自教会

shangceng jingying luxian 上层精英路线

shangke 上课

shanyu mofang 善于模仿

shebei qiquan 设备齐全

shehui zonghe suzhi 社会综合素质

shen'ao 深奥

shengdanjie 圣诞节

shenggong 圣工

shengjie 圣洁

shengjing yao huoxue huoyong 圣经要活学活用

shengling 圣灵

shengming 生命

shengshi 声势

shenji 神迹

Shenli 神力

shenxue jiangzuo 神学讲座

shenxuere 神学热

Shi Dakun 时大鲲

shifang 释放

shigong xueshuo 事功学说

shiyeren tuanqi 事业人团契

shouge 收割

shoujiao de xin 受教的心

shouwang daogao 守望祷告

shouxi zhengshu 受洗证书

shuangchong liulang 双重流浪

shuling 属灵

shuling ziyuan 属灵资源

shutian 属天

shutian de pinge 属天的品格

siling 司令

silu 思路

song wenhua xiaxiang 送文化下乡

suzhi 素质

tangwu weiyuanhui 堂务委员会

tangwu zhuren 堂务主任

tianda de pianyi 天大的便宜

Tianfeng 天风

tianluan de 添乱的

tianmei de shengyin 甜美的声音

tingdao 听道

ting daoli 听道理

tingke 听课

ting yesu qu 听耶稣去

tiyan yixia 体验一下

tongluren 同路人

tounao yipian kongbai 头脑一片空白

tu 土

tuanqi 团契

waibao 外包

waidi 外地

waidi dixiong 外地弟兄

waidiren 外地人

waidiren juhui 外地人聚会

waidiren mudao ban 外地人慕道班

waiguo de heshang hui nianjing 外国的和尚会念经

Wang Jie 王杰

wei jidu zhenghe ziyuan 为基督整合资源

wei zhu zuogong 为主作工

wenhua jidutu 文化基督徒

wenhua suzhi 文化素质

wenhua weiwen 文化慰问

wenhua Wenzhou 文化温州

wenhua xuanjiao 文化宣教

Wen Jiabao 温家宝

wenming Longgang 文明龙港

wenpingre 文凭热

wenyi budao hui 文艺布道会

Wenzhou minsu wenhua miaohui 温州民俗文化庙会

Wenzhou moshi de jiaohui 温州模式的教会

wenzhouren jingshen 温州人精神

wenzi shigong 文字事工

wo shu shangdi 我属上帝

wo shutian 我属天

wuhu sihai 五湖四海

Wu Yi 吴仪

wu zongjiao qu 无宗教区

xianjinxing 先进性

xiaojie 小姐

xiaoqi 小气

xiao yihui 小议会

xieling 邪灵

Xie Shengtao 谢圣弢

xin 信

xin daoli 信道理

xingxiang 形象

xinling de goutong 心灵的沟通

xinli xiangxin kouli chengren 心里相信，口里承认

xintu dahui 信徒大会

xin wenzhouren 新温州人

xinyang suzhi 信仰素质

xinyi ben 新译本

xinzao de ren 新造的人

xitong shenxue 系统神学

xi yixia 洗一下

xueqi 血气

xuexi 学习

xuezhe xing muzhe 学者型牧者

xunliang ru gezi 驯良如鸽子

yangjiao 洋教

yangqi 洋气

yansu 严肃

yesu de yangshi 耶酥的样式

yici dejiu, yongyuan dejiu 一次得救，永远得救

yidao zhichang 以道治厂

yigong 义工

yingyan 应验

yinjin 引进

yin jinlai, zou chuqu 引进来，走出去

yinsheng yangshuai 阴盛阳衰

yinxin chengyi 因信称义

Yisila 以斯拉

yixiang 异象

yi xue shenxue, jiu bian jiao'ao 一学神学，就变骄傲

yizhi 医治

yu guoji jiegui 与国际接轨

yuwan mian 鱼丸面

zaojiu 造就

zaoren 造人

zengzhang jianshi 增长见识

Zhang Rujing 张汝京

zhaoshang yinzi 招商引资

zhenggui 正规

zhengzong de　正宗的

zhiliposui de shenghuo 支离破碎的
生活

zhishi 知识

zhiyao shiwu buyao fuyin 只要食物，
不要福音

Zhongguo de Yelusaleng 中国的耶
路撒冷

Zhongguo jidujiao xiehui　中国基督
教协会

zhonghua guizhu 中华归主

zhuangjia 庄稼

zhuanye hua fengong 专业化分工

zhuquan 主权

zimei 姊妹

zimei zhong shengming 姊妹重生命

zisheng zimie 自生自灭

ziyuan youhua zuhe 资源优化组合

zong fuzeren 总负责人

zougou 走狗

zoutouwulu de 走投无路的

zuiren zhong de zuikui 罪人中的罪
魁

zuoguang zuoyan 作光作盐

Notes

1. "Guanyu zai shengdanjie qijian dui shiqu bufen luduan shishi jiaotongguanzhi de tonggao" *Wenzhou dushi bao* (Urban Wenzhou Daily), December 23, 2006, p. A2.

2. Aikman (2003: chap. 9) presents a journalist's account of Wenzhou Christians' pride in Wenzhou's reputation as "China's Jerusalem." An elderly Wenzhou church leader claims that he first used this term in the 1990s in an essay titled "Wenzhou: China's Jerusalem," which later circulated in the overseas Christian world.

3. According to Lambert (2006: 277), there were 750,000 Protestants, two thousand registered churches, and two thousand meeting points in the region in 2004. Some local church leaders put Wenzhou's current Christian population at one million. Shi (1997) estimates that a decade ago nearly 10 percent (six hundred thousand) of the local population was Protestant Christian, and there were more than eleven hundred churches and one thousand meeting points in Wenzhou.

4. In 1985, Catholics accounted for less than 1 percent (fifty thousand) of the total Wenzhou population (Kai 1989). Today the estimated number of Wenzhou Catholics is one hundred thousand. Many of them face state scrutiny from time to time for their loyalty to the Vatican and their reluctance to recognize the authority of the state-approved Catholic Church. There are no statistics on the number of Catholic churches in Wenzhou today. According to a source book on Wenzhou's religions (*Wenzhou zongjiao* 1994), Wenzhou had 130 Catholic churches in 1990, apparently all approved by the state. Although Catholic laypeople were active in reviving their faith communities after the lifting of the repression in the 1980s, government authorities have tightly controlled bishops and priests, reflecting troubled Sino-Vatican relations. Bishop James Lin Xili of Wenzhou, secretly ordained by the Vatican in 1992, was arrested in 1999 and was under state surveillance until his death in 2009. See "Underground Bishop of Wenzhou Dies on Episcopal Anniversary," *Union of Catholic Asian News* (www.ucanews.com), October 5, 2009. From the view of the Chinese government, the propensity to develop "underground" religious orga-

nizations and activities is greater for Catholics than for organizationally independent Protestant groups (Potter 2003). The relatively slow rate of Catholic growth in post-Mao Wenzhou might be attributed to both state restrictions and the legacy of the early missionary strategy of family-based conversion, which places more emphasis on intergenerational transmission of faith than on evangelism (cf. Lozada 2001; Madsen 1998). Buddhism, Daoism, and Popular religion have also revived in the region. The revival of local deity temples and Buddhist and Daoist temples appears to be visible in Wenzhou's rural areas but less significant in its city district (see Yang 2004).

5. On Wenzhou as a regional center of global capitalism, see a series of reports in *Economist*: "Winning in Wenzhou," December 10, 1988, pp. 32–33; "Boom Time in Capitalist Wenzhou," May 30, 1998, p. 43; "On the Capitalist Road," March 20, 2004, p. 14; "From Rags to Cigarette Lighters (and Dildos and Property Too): Wenzhou," June 4, 2005, p. 68.

6. On religious reenchantment as a feature of the changing global social landscape, particularly in postrevolutionary, postsocialist societies, see Comaroff and Comaroff 1999; Martin 2002; Taylor 2007b; and van der Veer 1996.

7. Chinese religion is certainly not unique in being treated as merely a dynamic of politicization and victimization. As Philip Taylor (2007b) points out, the dominant international discourse on religion elsewhere in socialist Asia (the relevant example here being Vietnam) has been overwhelmed by cases of human rights violations and of resistance to repressive states, and the diversity and vitality of religious activities has not received enough attention. Although many countries in the region are being integrated into the global capitalist political economy, we need to take seriously the role of religion as a key social and cultural agent in development processes.

8. This wildly popular view is exemplified in mainstream American journalists' accounts of Chinese Christianity, carrying such titles as "Jesus in Beijing: How Christianity Is Transforming China and Changing the Global Balance of Power" (Aikman 2003) and "The War for China's Soul: As Christianity Begins to Reshape the Nation, TIME Learns New Details About a Crackdown on One Church" (Elegant 2006). All these accounts fail to address the nature of Christian participation in today's China.

9. See also Yang 1961: 180–217. This state tradition needs to be understood within the larger historical context in which the world of popular culture was viewed as heterodox in relation to the state culture by late imperial times (Johnson, Nathan, and Rawski, 1985).

10. The sudden campaign of December 2000 to dismantle unregistered temples and churches in Wenzhou stirred immediate international concerns over the condition of religious freedom in China. The crackdown reportedly resulted in destruction of hundreds of church buildings in the city (see "China Blows up Churches and Temples in Religious Crackdown," Agence France-Presse, December 12, 2000). During my fieldwork in Wenzhou, I did not sense any local official opposition to Christianity. Unlike the antireligious campaigns of the Mao era seeking to eradicate

religion, the 2000 event appears to be a rare case in the reform era. It has had little lasting impact on local church development. Most important, it was not so much a matter of local opposition to Christianity as it was a crackdown led by provincial level leaders. Many local churchgoers I talked to suggest that the reported number of the demolished churches is a drastic exaggeration, and that the religious structures affected by the campaign were perhaps mostly unregistered popular religious temples.

11. For a number of case studies in the anthropology of Christianity that explore the situations in which meaning making has failed, see Engelke and Tomlinson 2006. These studies show that meaning is not an accomplished fact but a complex and contradictory process involving uncertainty and contestation.

12. The "Three-Self" principles include self-administration, self-support, and self-propagation. The churches registered with the TSPM are usually known as TSPM churches (*sanzi jiaohui*), and nonregistered churches are often called house churches (*jiating jiaohui*). For a discussion of the bitter divisions between TSPM and house churches and among the larger Chinese Christian community, see Dunch 2001b.

13. In his ethnography of a rural Chinese Catholic community, Lozada (2001) makes a similar statement on the diverse situations of China's Catholics in the reform era. On China's patriotic religious associations, Ashiwa and Wank (2006: 341) offered a more fruitful angle by seeing them as "key players in a fluid negotiating process between religious communities and the state control apparatus."

14. See also Brook and Frolic 1997 on the limits of the use of the Western notion of civil society (as opposed to the state) in understanding China's postsocialist transition. However, that the concept of civil society is tied to Western cultural assumptions does not render invalid everything built on that foundation. It is relevant to China's post-Mao modern transformations and to our understanding of the dramatic religious revival. See Yang 2008 for discussion of the separation of religion from state politics in the Chinese discourse of modernity and the need to see state formation and religious resurgence as twisted phases of modernization.

15. These anthropological studies of local Christianities demonstrate that Christianity is neither a homogeneous phenomenon that can be predicted in advance nor an arbitrary cultural category. For a historical and systematic account of Wenzhou Christianity, see Mo 1998.

16. See also Robbins 2007 on the actively produced neglect of the study of Christianity within anthropology.

17. The lack of fieldwork access certainly constitutes a great obstacle for anthropological research on Chinese Christianity, particularly for Western scholars, because the Chinese state views Christianity as a politically sensitive subject.

18. Joseph Kahn, "China's Christians Mix Business and God: Wenzhou Church Thrives on New Capitalists' Wealth," *Wall Street Journal*, June 16, 1995, p. All.

19. See Forster 1990a on violent factional struggles in Wenzhou during the Cultural Revolution that broke out between local rebel groups and Red Guard groups from Shanghai and Beijing.

20. See Rankin 1986 on accelerated commercialization and its social and political consequences in Wenzhou and other trading centers of Zhejiang during the late imperial era.

21. During the 1979 Sino-Vietnam war, the People's Liberation Army recruited Wenzhou code talkers just as the U.S. army employed Navajo Native Americans in World War II.

22. During the Maoist years, the cadres sent from the political center (*nanxia ganbu*) to Wenzhou experienced great difficulty in carrying out their political work, owing to their inability to communicate in Wenzhou dialect (see Forster 1990b: 55–56).

23. In contrast, the Catholic church in pre-1949 Wenzhou remained a Western missionary-dominated institution (see Wiest 2004). After 1949, it continued to maintain close institutional ties with the Vatican till the founding of the Wenzhou Catholic Patriotic Association in 1960 (Mo 1998: chap. 7). Wenzhou Catholics apparently faced harsher repression than their Protestant counterparts during Maoist anti-imperialism campaigns.

24. Don Lee, "China's Global Go-Getters," *Los Angeles Times*, March 12, 2007, p. A1.

25. In this context, "Jews of China" is a popular and respectable name for Wenzhou people. Although stereotypical, in the mind of the average Chinese Jews are known for their worldwide business achievements. Most Wenzhou people—both Christian and non-Christian—are proud of being called the "Jews of China."

26. Given that these rural migrant workers are not Wenzhou *hukou* holders, they are never included in the official calculation of the city's per-capita income. See Cheng and Selden (1994) on development of the *hukou* system of population registration and control.

27. Chinese sociologist Fei Xiaotong (1986) first systematically defined the term *Wenzhou model*. For an overview of the debate on the Wenzhou model, see Nolan and Dong 1990.

28. There are no direct statistics on the percentage of Christians among the broader population of private entrepreneurs in Wenzhou. One estimate claims that no less than 70 percent of Wenzhou's Christians base their livelihood on private business (see Chen and Wu 2005: 68).

29. On the general methodology for narrative analysis of life history, see Handel 2000.

30. This is a shortened expression of the Bible verse from Romans that reads, "That if you confess with your mouth, 'Jesus is Lord,' and believe in your heart that God raised him from the dead, you will be saved" (Romans 10: 9).

31. Bays (2003) has observed the popularity of this traditional theology among contemporary Chinese Protestants and attributed it to the legacy of the missionary past.

32. Many Christians I encountered in urban Wenzhou are not particularly against joining temple festivals. This is due to the fact that popular religious elements have been largely (if not completely) purged from major temple festivals held in the city. For example, the largest "temple festival" in Wenzhou is held annually in the Wenzhou Convention and Exhibition Center during national holidays and is officially called the Wenzhou Folk Cultural Temple Festival (*Wenzhou minsu wenhua miaohui*). It is sponsored by the municipal government and marketed by a media company as an event of fun seeking, shopping, and commodities exchange. Such folk events have been, to a large degree, appropriated and reconstructed by the local state as parts of an "intangible cultural heritage" (*fei wuzhi wenhua yichan*) to showcase the city's rich cultural tradition and promote the local tourist economy (see *Wenzhou shi fei wuzhi wenhua yichan minglu*, Wenzhou Bureau of Culture, Radio, Television, Press and Publication, 2007, updated in 2008 and 2009). Grand temple festivals characterized by pilgrimage and other popular religious practices are usually to be found in rural areas.

33. Webb Keane (2008) argues against the common assumption in the definition of religion that privileges inner belief over the materiality of religious practices and objects. See also Asad 1993 on his effective critique of the universality of the category of religion.

34. This is certainly also due to the ambiguity of the text and the paradoxical nature of Christian teaching.

CHAPTER TWO

1. By contrast, Christian entrepreneurs often use the words "low level" (*di cengci*) and "low quality" (*di suzhi*) to characterize the elders and rural migrant workers in the church. They seek to culturally engage the state through such a language of distinction.

CHAPTER THREE

1. There are no accurate statistics, given the fact that many Wenzhou people are illegal immigrants in Europe. According to a French government estimate, about one hundred thousand Wenzhou migrants live in "Wenzhou town" in Paris (Wang and Béja 1999). The figure resembles a small European city's population.

2. Ding Xiaoying, "Zhongrui shenxian manhadun" (Zhongrui's Involvement in Wenzhou's "Manhattan"), *Diyi caijing ribao* (First Chinese Business Daily), December 31, 2004, p. D3.

3. In 2004 only 19 percent of local residents were nonagricultural *hukou* holders (Wenzhou Statistical Yearbook 2005: 59).

4. Data cited in Hai Lan, "Wenzhou: Shiyong zhuyi de shehua" (Wenzhou: The Luxury of Pragmatism), *21 shiji jingji baodao* (21st Century Business Herald), May 16, 2007.

5. On Wenzhou's informal finance, see Tsai 2002: chap. 4.

6. In 2005, there were still 171 urban villages (*chengzhongcun*) in Wenzhou's three main city districts (Wang 2005: 21). But they are fading from the city landscape as new urban development projects proceed.

7. Zhang Yi, "Wenming Longgang" (Civilizing Longgang), *People's Daily*, December 18, 1999, p. 10.

8. In Wenzhou the current rate for private piano lesson ranges from ¥100–200 an hour.

9. In 2006 I searched piles of documents in the municipal archives of Wenzhou for the historical condition of the Wenzhou church. I list these documents as "Archives of Wenzhou Christianity."

10. Archives of Wenzhou Christianity.

11. Ibid.

12. "Flood and feral animals" is a popular Chinese idiom that refers to a great curse.

13. The China Christian Council (*Zhongguo jidujiao xiehui*) and the Committee of the Three-Self Patriotic Movement (*sanzi aiguo yundong weiyuanhui*) are colloquially called the two committees (*lianghui*). Established in 1954, the two committees are the officially recognized Protestant bodies in China. They functionally overlap and are often viewed as one organization.

14. Many Wenzhou Christians see Jews as God's chosen people and a type of Christian.

15. Young preachers formally affiliated with the TSPM church almost all hold a theology degree from a state-run seminary. However, some Wenzhou TSPM churches also regularly invite house church preachers to preach sermons.

16. It is often the case that only church members can access fancy facilities in the church. Though the church community is open to everyone, not all participants can be treated as equals. For example, a local young man in his mid-twenties wanted to register for a piano class in his parents' church, but his request was quickly rejected owing to his nonbeliever status, even though his parents are both long-time members of the church.

17. On the contemporary Chinese practices of localization and domestication of global cultural resources, see Yan's study (1997) of Beijing's McDonald's.

18. I have also seen overseas preachers who made English speeches and sermons in Wenzhou churches through the help of Chinese translators.

19. Use of foreign preachers in Wenzhou is facilitated by the lack of state inter-

ference. When I began my research, I soon noticed the frequency of certain terms used by my respondents. Several spoke of "internationalization" (*guojihua*) and "linking up with the international track" (*yu guoji jiegui*) when they were really referring to lax state religious governance and religious freedom. According to this logic, Wenzhou Christians believe they have enjoyed much greater religious freedom than rural inland churchgoers because Wenzhou is much more cosmopolitan and modern than the economically stagnant inland, as if Christian faith is an internal virtue of cosmopolitan modernity.

20. "Zhonggong zhongyang guanyu jinyibu zuohao zongjiao gongzuo de ruogan wenti de tongzhi" (Document 6: CCP Central Committee/State Council, circular on some problems concerning further improving work on religion), 1991, cited in Luo 2001: 434–37.

21. The aphorism underscores the value of patriotism, hard work and plain living, belief in science, consciousness of serving the people, solidarity, honesty and credibility, and observance of the law.

22. I was also told that given their authority, status, and power local church leaders can easily find beautiful wives from the church for their sons.

23. In 2005, a Wenzhou businessman's wedding involved five thousand guests, hundreds of banquet tables, and gift money of tens of millions of yuan. See "Wenzhou jinqian hunyin diaocha" (An Investigation of "Monied Marriages" in Wenzhou), *Qingnian shibao* (Youth Times), June 23, 2005.

24. In Yueqing Country, one of the most prosperous industrial areas in Wenzhou, the standard dowry is ¥300,000. The size is much lower, around ¥70,000, in Wenzhou city.

25. For local Christians, smoking is strongly discouraged but acceptable at a wedding banquet to produce the heated social atmosphere (*re'nao*) that is often seen as the most important and desired characteristic of a wedding. See Chau 2008 on the popular Chinese ways of producing sensorialized sociality.

CHAPTER FOUR

1. For an extended discussion of Wenzhou's village entrepreneurs, see Gong, Duan, and Chen, 1987.

2. This regional tradition of pragmatism can be traced back to the period of the Southern Song Dynasty about 850 years ago, when an influential school of thought known as Yongjia (the old name of Wenzhou) espoused the view that commerce was as important as agriculture, and that enriching the people should be the fundamental principle of government (see Cai 1999). The "theory of pragmatism" (*shigong xueshuo*), founded by the Yongjia school, challenged the dominant Confucian view of the day, which placed teachers and bureaucrats at the top of social rank and the merchant class at the bottom.

3. This situation is reminiscent of Paul Katz's portrait (1995) of the spread of the cult of Marshal Wen (a plague-fighting deity) in Wenzhou and other commercial centers in Zhejiang during the late imperial era. For Katz, traveling merchants rather than Daoist priests were usually behind the growth of Marshal Wen's temples.

4. The real estate craze is a reality across China today. Siu (2005) has portrayed and analyzed the transformation of a regional landscape in post-Mao Guangdong through the lens of the consumption craze for luxury private housing.

5. Kilde (2002) has discussed the connection between church architecture and religious experience and practice in nineteenth-century America.

6. Aikman (2003: chap. 9) also notes the rising number of Wenzhou Chinese churches in Europe.

7. Usually, the Wenzhou preachers and church leaders travel on business visas with invitation letters issued by immigrant Wenzhou Christian firms overseas. This convenient arrangement circumvents certain restrictions imposed by the Religious Affairs Bureau on cross-border religious exchange, and it greatly facilitates circulation of people, resources, and ideas between the Wenzhou churches overseas and those back home.

8. To dream big and be flamboyant is a modern urban virtue nowadays, not only in Wenzhou but across China. It helps boost one's confidence in business practices and presents the essential capacity and credibility in a transitional economy that is full of uncertainties.

9. For *honghuo* (social heat), a notion similar to *huore* that characterizes the most desirable mode of peasant sociality in rural China, see Chau 2006: chap. 8.

10. It is a common practice for Wenzhou people to pool their money together in a single investment project, and use of traditional self-organized credit associations (*hui*) is the most popular means of grassroots fundraising in Wenzhou society. See Shi, Jin, Zhao, and Luo 2002: chap. 10. On Wenzhou's ritual donation drives, see Yang 2000.

11. The annual general meeting is also called the big council (*da yihui*), which is composed of all the church members, in contrast to the small council, which is the power center of the church. Although Wenzhou churches have increasingly adopted the Western church council system as their authority structure, the small council is functionally equivalent to the traditional committee of church affairs and seems only a more democratic, international, and fashionable term used in the Wenzhou church community.

12. Bank loans are usually obtained by individual church members in the form of a personal housing mortgage.

13. This shows that nonproductive ritual economy of expenditure intimately co-exists with capitalist social processes in Wenzhou (see Yang 2000).

14. Quoted in Nicholas D. Kristof, "Christianity Is Booming in China Despite Rifts," *New York Times*, February 7, 1993, p. A16.

15. See Zhejiang Religious Affairs Bureau, "Zhejiang sheng zongjiao shiwu tiaoli" (Zhejiang Provincial Religious Affairs Regulations), *Zhejiang ribao*, April 4, 2006, p. 5.

16. Standardization is usually associated with another popular local term, "internationalization," or "to link up with the international track" in daily language use. So lacking "standardization" means lacking a conception of the most international, modern, and efficient ways of acting.

17. However, by adopting a voting procedure, Liu's church is one of the very few "democratic" churches in Wenzhou.

18. By outsourcing, local entrepreneur church leaders actually mean a process of flexible production based on specialized division of labor. They sometimes use the term in the church context with a slightly derisive tone.

19. The preacher-dispatch system may not work smoothly across the boundaries of the house church and the TSPM church. Although it is common for a TSPM preacher to be dispatched to a house church and vice versa, extremist house church groups strongly object to such arrangements.

20. These figures indicate the serious shortage of ministry and pastoral resources in the mid-1990s. After more than a decade of explosive Christian growth in Wenzhou, this shortage now seems even more striking.

21. Many Wenzhou Christians are striving to move upward in the hierarchies of economy and spirituality. A local Christian saying neatly captures this movement: "Bosses all want to preach while preachers all want to do business." Not surprisingly, there are few full-time preachers in Wenzhou; most have their personal business and serve the church part-time.

22. Among the many formal and informal lay training programs in Wenzhou, the Wenzhou Lay Training Center offers the most systematic training to help volunteers serve the church. Established in 1995 by the city-level two committees (*lianghui*), the center focuses on instruction in preaching, hymn and music studies, and church management (Shi 1997: 9).

23. In the case of cigarette-lighter production, some three thousand small Wenzhou firms have worked together, some specializing in components and some in final assembly. In 2002, Wenzhou made 750 million lighters, the equivalent of 70 percent of world demand. See "On the Capitalist Road," *Economist*, March 20, 2004, p. 14. A popular saying captures this flexible production within Wenzhou's family firms: "The eldest brother produces dresses, the second produces cloth, the third produces buttons, and their youngest sister is in charge of marketing and sales." Quoted in Li Jing, "Wenzhou Offers a Lesson in Economics," *China Daily*, April 26, 2004.

24. In Wenzhou's rural industrialization, many villages developed their own specialized industries and wholesale markets. There are ten major specialty market towns that integrate the activities of the household industries and the itinerant traders or sales agents.

25. This mirrors the diversified investment strategy of many Wenzhou boss Christians. All of these activities and efforts are for the evangelical purpose of Christianizing China.

26. Hamilton (2006: chap. 7) uses the term *reflexive manufacturing* to capture Taiwan's integration into the global economy. This also perfectly captures Wenzhou's current pattern of industrialization. I thank David Buck for pointing this out to me.

27. The entrepreneurial church leaders are copying the old-fashioned Western church style mainly because they want an "authentically" (*zhengzong de*) Western church building. When asked why, some simply say that "this is what a church should look like," and other styles may be considered "unspiritual" (*bu shuling*).

28. See Nyíri 2006 for a discussion of this global Chinese Christian civilizing project.

29. Some scholars have argued that Wenzhou's reform-era economic achievements were more a "renaissance" than a "takeoff" (e.g., A. Liu 1992: 698). This is not to argue that the tradition of entrepreneurship has remained unchanged for centuries, but that it influences the business practices of the Wenzhou bosses today.

30. In the 1980s, Wenzhou was notorious for making counterfeit products, particularly Western brand-name shoes, clothes, and lighters. Even today, in the minds of other Chinese, Wenzhou is still linked with fakes and counterfeits, although there has been great improvement in the quality of Wenzhou-made products.

31. Howard French, "Children of Rich Learn Class, Minus the Struggle," *New York Times*, September 22, 2006, p. A1.

32. See Kipnis 2001b on China's post-Mao religious revival as growing arenas of symbolic participation.

CHAPTER FIVE

1. When they talk about a flexible, strategic approach to engaging the state's regulation of religion, Christian businessmen often mention the phrase "as shrewd as snakes" (*lingqiao xiang she*) while rarely citing "innocent as doves" (*xunliang ru gezi*).

2. This gendered pattern of the Wenzhou church community, as reflected by the Mada phenomenon, is far from rare. At least in some parts of China, Mada refers to the entire group of female church workers who actively serve the church but lack doctrinal knowledge and basic secular education (Z. Wang 2003). Similarly, in her ethnography of a Hakka Christian community in the New Territories, Hong Kong, Nicole Constable (1994: 66) indicates that women there usually play a visible role in the "service" or "support" roles of the church, as Sunday school teachers, translators, secretaries, and itinerant evangelists.

3. For a detailed analysis of the contemporary Chinese Christian discourse of *suzhi*, see Cao 2009.

4. A popular saying in the Wenzhou church is critical of the desire for distinction

through studying theology: "Once you study theology you become proud immediately" (*yi xue shenxue, jiu bian jiao'ao*).

5. Almost every Wenzhou church decorates the walls with framed Bible verses written in Chinese calligraphy.

6. In the Wenzhou church many would agree that "theology fever" is mainly due to the great influence of Stephan Tong. Almost every young or middle-aged Wenzhou Christian man has listened to Tong's sermons (usually on tapes or discs) and read his books.

7. One male church leader emphasizes that attending church is not just about singing hymns and making prayers but about promoting church members' knowledge of many topics. Several churches have invited outside speakers to hold lectures on a variety of nonreligious topics (e.g., marriage and dating, civil manners, even Western literature). There are also reading clubs formed across local churches.

8. This admission fee was said to cover the costs of the host church and the honoraria of the overseas teachers.

9. Today, to secure a full-time position as preacher in the Wenzhou church one must have a seminary degree or a diploma obtained from training informally with overseas preachers. This shows the effort the local church has made to professionalize its clergy and modernize its institutional structure. Some also use this type of short-term theology training certificate to strength their application for graduate study in theology at an overseas institution. There are fewer charismatic leaders than ever in the local church community.

10. Under the influence of these overseas teachers, many local preachers seek to become "scholar-type preachers" (*xuezhe xing muzhe*) by combining preaching with teaching.

11. The presence of foreign teachers and preachers is also a unique "selling point" (*maidian*) of such activities, as one male organizer put it.

12. The Chinese edition of this magazine, published monthly in Beijing, is a product of a copyright cooperation with the well-known *Esquire* in the United States. It targets mature, successful male readers by introducing fashions, celebrities, and luxury lifestyles. Wenzhou boss Christians clearly identify with this social group.

13. Those invited to the banquet are expected to come with potential converts and be responsible for the cost.

14. Given his past influence in the church, local Christian bosses sometimes felt the urge to invite him to their high-end church activities, and as a token of respect he was sometimes invited to give a prayer at the end, partly because he was the oldest man present.

15. Women have often been associated with superstition in Chinese history. Overrepresentation of women in folk religion was responsible for its stigmatized label of superstition (Gates 1996). This is also true for the most part in present-day Wenzhou Christianity.

16. Luhrmann does not elaborate on any gender differences in the "metakinesis," though she notes that in contrast to women men tend to embrace Him as "more buddy than boyfriend" in the metakinetic state of "falling in love with Jesus" (Luhrmann 2004: 523).

17. In sharp contrast to female believers' somewhat emotional criticism of declining sexual morality in society, male believers seek to achieve a rationalized understanding using their theological knowledge while criticizing the phenomenon. One male preacher says that the fact of many Wenzhou bosses having a second wife is also God's "general grace" (*pubian endian*) because God's light shines on both good people and bad. This should be read not as an indication of Wenzhou Christian men's sexual liberalism but as their strong urge to theologize their day-to-day life in a decadent local social environment.

18. It is important to note that this gender difference in narratives is not necessarily a reflection of the difference in actual practice. In daily reality, Wenzhou Christian men certainly evince much more bodily discipline than non-Christian men. For example, some may offer cigarettes to their secular business partners but themselves refuse to smoke. See Kohrman 2007 for a discussion of the association between cigarette smoking and male sociality in the PRC.

19. For a discussion of the intimate relationship between charismatic experience and rhetorical performance of ritual, see Csordas 1997.

20. In 2004, the male-female ratio among newborn infants in Wenzhou was 124.7:100, far beyond the normal range; the birth of a second or third child in a family was mainly responsible for this serious gender imbalance (Wenzhou Statistical Yearbook 2005: 21). The one-child policy has not been consistently and strictly enforced in Wenzhou society, perhaps as a consequence of lax local governance. Yet slogans championing gender equality are common on the streets. The most often seen are "Having a son and having a daughter are the same," "Boys and girls are equally good," and "To be concerned with the well-being of girls is to be concerned with the future of the nation."

21. In contrast, men tend to struggle to combine their business life with church service and seldom complain about being hampered by domestic issues.

22. A similar gendered pattern of religious activities can be found in studies of Chinese folk religion (see Gates 1996; Sangren 1983).

CHAPTER SIX

1. According to the State Council's 2006 report on China's peasant workers, rural migrants today have shifted their focus from migration to the city to assimilation in the city, and from struggling for survival to seeking equality. According to a recent survey conducted in Hangzhou, Wenzhou, and Shenzhen, most young migrant workers today can be roughly categorized as the "new generation of rural migrant

workers," whose social identity is rather ambiguous, neither completely rural nor urban (Luo and Wang 2003).

2. I also found that many young workers are enthusiastic about Internet chatting and games. Of course, they are often unable to find this type of entertainment when working and living in a gated factory setting.

3. The pedicab is a major means of transportation in Wenzhou in addition to buses and taxis. Local people greatly rely on pedicabs in everyday life. A permanent pedicab license costs ¥300,000–400,000.

4. Those who work in factories headed by Christian bosses may have one weekend night to attend church each week. Workers' schedules also depend on the type and quantity of orders the factory receives. There are high and low seasons in every factory.

5. Almost all of these migrants had experiences of working in local factories, and they are ready to go back to factories anytime if they cannot do good business.

6. When it comes to evangelization among local people, the church shifts the emphasis of preaching to the relevance of a Christian god in one's life because, according to local preachers, many locals already accept the existence of gods.

7. The evangelical-minded Wenzhou church has no strict requirement for those who want to get baptized. Usually one has to answer several basic faith questions before baptism, but this procedure is largely a formality. Even those who fail this small test are seldom denied baptism. On the one hand, the local church encourages new converts to receive baptism as soon as possible. On the other hand, local believers hold deep doubt about the motivation for conversion among migrant workers, many of whom received baptism soon after they declared their determination to convert and thus might have little knowledge of basic Christian teachings.

8. In fact, I found many reported an older age to local authorities in their rural hometown to obtain an ID so they could move to the city for work as early as possible, before reaching the legal age of sixteen.

9. Asked about the condition of their faith, some migrant workers may feel too embarrassed to admit they are new to Christianity because they take Christian faith as part of a privileged urban lifestyle and advanced knowledge as preached in the Wenzhou church. In contrast, many local believers claim in testimony that they started to believe in Jesus when they were still in their mother's womb—a way of showing off their solid "spiritual foundation" (*lingming genji*).

10. This form of kindness should not be taken at face value. Writing on Wenzhou migrant entrepreneurs in Beijing, Li Zhang (2001: 122–23) interprets Wenzhou *laoban niang's* kindness to migrant workers as a strategy to shade class exploitation and secure worker loyalty to the boss's family.

11. Joel Robbins (2007) warns anthropologists to be aware of emphasizing continuity at the expense of rupture by exploring the contradiction between the Christian ideology of radical change and anthropology's central methodological concern about

continuity. This study shows that radical discontinuities can be an object of anthropological analysis among migrant worker Christians in Wenzhou.

12. The Wenzhou municipal government is certainly aware of the mounting stigma imposed on migrant workers in the city. Echoing the central state discourse on building a harmonious society, the so-called new Wenzhounese is a local state-advocated euphemism for the term *migrant workers*, which often conveys a very negative social meaning in local society.

13. Many migrant workers I came across in Wenzhou had learned to speak Wenzhou dialect.

14. This is not an isolated case. A female Christian migrant worker from Henan told me that "Wenzhou people are very ardent about spreading the Gospel, but when they step out of church, they don't recognize you anymore." She suggested that some migrant workers might be responsible for this, saying, "their caution is also due to those outsiders who fake their belief in Jesus in order to borrow money and seek other benefits."

15. However, foreigners or professionals from other places are never viewed as (or called) outsiders.

16. According to the migrant believers in the course, it offers forty places for advanced believers. To apply, one needs to complete an application form and submit two recommendation letters from local church coworkers who have known the applicant for at least two years. This sets a high standard. It must be economically practical for the migrants to pursue this type of full-time study for an extended period. I assume they have little burden for contributing to the family purse. Although they are offered free lodging and meals, it costs financially because of not being able to work. This demonstrates that they do not consider Christianity a savior of the poor but rather a means for status enhancement.

17. Their daily schedule involves six hours of theology classes and four hours of self-study. Their teachers come from different local churches.

18. The evangelical giving events can be seen as major hosting occasions in the local Christian community. See Chau (2006: chap. 7) for an inspiring discussion of the concept of "hosting."

19. Spatial categories and images are frequently invoked and mobilized in negotiating power and prestige in Chinese daily life today. The notion of Jiangxi people (*Jiangxiren*) itself carries negative meanings in Wenzhou society, mainly because the local media have stigmatized migrant workers from Jiangxi; they are viewed as responsible for the growing local crime rate. See also Liu 1997 on how sociospatial hierarchies have created new inequity among Chinese peasants and scholars in the reform era.

20. All Chinese, regardless of place of origin, are expected to be able to use Mandarin, the official Chinese language; therefore Mandarin loses its ability to define a particular locality or ethnicity.

21. The Wenzhou church has conducted large-scale evangelization in the rural inland in the name of Christian artistic performance groups sent to "convey cultural greetings and appreciation" (*wenhua weiwen*), both for safety concerns and for the purpose of drawing rural people's attention.

22. Migrant worker believers often speak of others' focus (and their own) on migrant work at the expense of church life being a result of "weakness" in spirituality.

23. Rural migrant workers also tend to speak to their fellow villagers in Mandarin in the church context. Several say that their rural dialects are unacceptable for preaching because the rural accent sounds uncivil, crude, and not humble.

CHAPTER SEVEN

1. For a discussion of world religions in the context of multiple modernities, see Hefner 1998b.

2. This is in sharp contrast with the usual reading of Weber. For Weber, modernity is closely associated with the process of secularization but does not necessarily take singular form (see Cannell 2006: 31–32).

3. See Brook (1993) and Duara (1988a, 118–57) on how local elites used temple patronage to seize power and legitimate their authority in local society in the Ming and Qing periods.

4. Although Wenzhou boss Christians are mobile and translocal religious agents, they demonstrate strong communitarian sentiment and have a localist moral agenda (cf. Fisher 2008). Fisher discusses the lack of local communal concerns among highly mobile urban Buddhist clergy and lay practitioners, who promoted construction of temples in faraway rural areas for the sake of earning merit and building morality for themselves.

5. Far more monographs have been written about religious life in rural China than about Chinese urban religious practices. Notable among the former are Chau 2006, Dean 1998, Dubois 2005, Jing 1996, Lozada 2001, and Mueggler 2001.

6. Popular religion exerts influence on the residents of urban Wenzhou not in the form of community-building or identity-shaping ritual activities but in the form of privatized religion, which involves such practices as burning incense to worship ancestors, consulting spiritual mediums for divine assistance on personal and family issues, and hiring fengshui specialists to site new houses and factory workshops. See also Fan 2003 for a case study of privatization of popular religion in the modern city of Shenzhen. Goossaert and Fang (2009) indicate a similar tendency toward privatization in the evolution of Daoism in contemporary urban China.

7. Having adopted the form of the Christian church, many Buddhist scripture recitation groups are actively present among Wenzhou's lay Buddhist practitioners, mostly middle-aged and elderly women as well as elderly men (Lin 2003). These Buddhist groups play a role in cultivating morality among lay practitioners, but by

emphasizing recitation (rather than interpretation) they have not developed a systematic language for their belief at the level of everyday life, as evangelical Christians have.

8. The clandestine tendency of Catholic practices, as a result of uneasy Sino-Vatican relations, may also discourage active involvement of high-profile businesspeople in church management.

9. The Wenzhou model exemplifies the role of private entrepreneurship in promoting China's rural industrialization. See Huang (2008) for an insightful analysis of China's postreform political economy, in which he highlights the important role of village- and township-based private enterprises in China's economic success and the continued significance of the state in the economic development of major cities.

10. Although the Wenzhou model is officially recognized as part of the "socialist market economy with Chinese characteristics," it is subject to continuous debate among Chinese scholars and officials today. For a popular lay discussion of recent problems with the Wenzhou model, see Zhang Jianjin, "Quanmian kandai Wenzhou moshi" (To Take a Comprehensive Look at the Wenzhou Model), *Zhongguo jingji shibao*, October 26, 2006. For a critical appraisal of the sustainability of the Wenzhou model by economic geographers, see Wei, Li, and Wang 2007.

11. Indeed, they are fascinating contradictory individuals, whose practices embody what Robert Weller (1999) calls "a split market culture" that encompasses both market and antimarket moralities.

12. In South Korea's postwar industrialization, Protestantism as an imported faith became "submerged" under the dominance of familial values and economic consciousness, thus contributing little to public affairs (Park 2000). In Taiwan's modern high-tech economy Buddhism, Daosim, and Confucianism rather than Christianity appear to be the bearers of a Taiwanese democratic modernity; these locally grown religious organizations act as "belt buckles" between social groups (Madsen 2007). It seems more meaningful to explore the role of historical contingency in the relationship among Christianity, modernity, and democracy in a comparative, inter-Asian context.

13. In official state discourse, the Wenzhou model is often positioned as being in the "primary stage of socialism," a catchphrase the Party uses to justify introduction of capitalist elements into the economy while acknowledging the country's current economic and cultural backwardness.

14. Through the vertical, hierarchical relationships fostered by the Wenzhou church, we may discern a lack of civility in this new space of grassroots organization, as is the case discussed in great detail in Madsen's study of Tianjin's Catholic churches (1998). For Madsen, some Tianjin churches are perfectly "civilian" because of their independent and self-governing organizational form, but in practice they manifest uncivil characteristics that are not conducive to the building of a civil society.

References

Aikman, David. 2003. *Jesus in Beijing: How Christianity Is Transforming China and Changing the Global Balance of Power*. Washington, DC: Regnery.

Anagnost, Ann S. 1994. "Politics of Ritual Displacement." In C. F Keyes, L. Kendall, and H. Hardacre, eds., *Asian Visions of Authority: Religion and the Modern States of East and Southeast Asia*, pp. 221–54. Honolulu: University of Hawaii Press.

Asad, Talal. 1993. *Genealogies of Religion: Discipline and Reasons of Power in Christianity and Islam*. Baltimore and London: Johns Hopkins University Press.

Ashiwa, Yoshiko, and David L. Wank. 2006. "The Politics of a Reviving Buddhist Temple: State, Association, and Religion in Southeast China." *Journal of Asian Studies* 65 (2): 337–60.

Bays, Daniel H. 1996. "The Growth of Independent Christianity in China, 1900–1937." In D. H. Bays, ed., *Christianity in China: From the Eighteenth Century to the Present*, pp. 307–37. Stanford, CA: Stanford University Press.

———. 2003. "Chinese Protestant Christianity Today." *China Quarterly* 174 (2): 488–504.

———. 2004. "A Tradition of State Dominance." In J. Kindopp and C. L. Hamrin, eds., *God and Caesar in China: Policy Implications of Church-State Tensions*, pp. 25–39. Washington, DC: Brookings Institution Press.

Berger, Peter L. 1988. "An East Asian Development Model?" In Peter L. Berger and Hsin-Huang Michael Hsiao, eds., *In Search of an East Asian Development Model*, pp. 1–11. New Brunswick, NJ: Transaction Books.

Bray, Francesca. 1997. *Technology and Gender: Fabrics of Power in Late Imperial China*. Berkeley: University of California Press.

Brook, Timothy. 1993. *Praying for Power: Buddhism and the Formation of Gentry Society in Late-Ming China*. Cambridge, MA: Harvard University Press.

Brook, Timothy, and B. Michael Frolic. 1997. "The Ambiguous Challenge of Civil Society." In Timothy Brook and B. Michael Frolic, eds., *Civil Society in China*, pp. 3–16. Armonk, NY: M. E. Sharpe.

Cai, Kejiao. 1999. "Wenzhou renwen jingshen pouxi" (An Analysis of the Wenzhou

Ethos). *Zhejiang shifan daxue xuebao shehui kexue ban* (Bulletin of Zhejiang Normal University, Social Science Edition) 2: 28–31.

Cannel, Fenella. 2006. "Introduction: The Anthropology of Christianity." In Fenella Cannel, ed., *The Anthropology of Christianity*, pp. 1–50. Durham, NC: Duke University Press.

Cao, Nanlai. 2005. "The Church as a Surrogate Family for Working Class Immigrant Chinese Youth: An Ethnography of Segmented Assimilation." *Sociology of Religion* 66 (2): 183–200.

———. 2007. "Christian Entrepreneurs and the Post-Mao State: An Ethnographic Account of Church-State Relations in China's Economic Transition." *Sociology of Religion* 68 (1): 45–66.

———. 2008. "Boss Christians: The Business of Religion in the 'Wenzhou Model' of Christian Revival." *The China Journal* 59: 63–87.

———. 2009. "Raising the Quality of Belief: Suzhi and the Production of an Elite Protestantism." *China Perspectives* 4: 54–65.

Chau, Adam Yuet. 2006. *Miraculous Response: Doing Popular Religion in Contemporary China*. Stanford, CA: Stanford University Press.

———. 2008. "The Sensorial Production of the Social." *Ethnos* 73(4): 485–504.

Chen, Cunfu, and Tianhai Huang. 2004. "Emergence of a New Type of Christians in China Today." *Review of Religious Research* 46: 183–200.

Chen, Cunfu, and Wu Yubo. 2005. "Chengshihua guocheng zhong de dangdai nongcun jidujiao" (Contemporary Rural Christianity Under Urbanization). *Shijie zongjiao yanjiu* (Studies in World Religions) 2: 65–70.

Cheng, Tiejun, and Mark Selden. 1994. "The Origins and Social Consequences of China's Hukou System." *China Quarterly* 139: 644–68.

Comaroff, Jean, and John L. Comaroff. 1991. *Of Revelation and Revolution. Vol I: Christianity, Colonialism, and Consciousness in South Africa*. Chicago: University of Chicago Press.

———. 1997. *Of Revelation and Revolution. Vol. II: The Dialectics of Modernity on a South African Frontier*. Chicago: University of Chicago Press.

———. 1999. "Occult Economies and the Violence of Abstraction: Notes from the South African Postcolony." *American Ethnologist* 26 (2): 279–303.

Constable, Nicole. 1994. *Christian Souls and Chinese Spirits: A Hakka Community in Hong Kong*. Berkeley: University of California Press.

Csordas, Thomas J. 1997. *Language, Charisma, and Creativity: The Ritual Life of a Religious Movement*. Berkeley: University of California Press.

Davis, Deborah S., Richard Kraus, Barry Naughton, and Elizabeth Perry, eds. 1995. *Urban Spaces in Contemporary China: The Potential for Autonomy and Community in Post-Mao China*. Cambridge and New York: Cambridge University Press.

Dean, Kenneth. 1998. *Lord of the Three in One: The Spread of a Cult in Southeast China*. Princeton: Princeton University Press.

————. 2003. "Local Communal Religion in Contemporary South-East China." *China Quarterly* 174: 338–58.

Diamond, Norma. 1996. "Christianity and the Hua Miao: Writing and Power." In D. H. Bays, ed., *Christianity in China: From the Eighteenth Century to the Present*, pp. 138–58. Stanford: Stanford University Press.

Dirks, Nick, Geoff Eley, and Sherry Ortner, eds. 1994. *Culture/Power/History: A Reader for Contemporary Social Theory*. Princeton: Princeton University Press.

Duara, Prasenjit. 1988a. *Culture, Power, and the State: Rural North China, 1900–1942*. Stanford, CA: Stanford University Press.

————. 1988b. "Superscribing Symbols: The Myth of Guandi, Chinese God of War." *Journal of Asian Studies* 47: 778–95.

————. 1991. "Knowledge and Power in the Discourse of Modernity: The Campaigns Against Popular Religion in Early Twentieth-Century China." *Journal of Asian Studies* 50 (1): 67–83.

Dubois, Thomas. 2005. *The Sacred Village: Social Change and Religious Life in Rural North China*. Honolulu: University of Hawai'i Press.

Dunch, Ryan. 2001a. *Fuzhou Protestants and the Making of a Modern China, 1857–1927*. New Haven and London: Yale University Press.

————. 2001b. "Protestant Christianity in China Today: Fragile, Fragmented, Flourishing." In S. Uhalley, Jr., and X. Wu, eds., *China and Christianity: Burdened Past, Hopeful Future*, pp. 195–216. Armonk, NY: M. E. Sharpe.

Elegant, Simon. 2006. "The War for China's Soul: As Christianity Begins to Reshape the Nation, TIME Learns New Details About a Crackdown on One Church." *Time* 168 (9): 40.

Engelke, Matthew, and Matt Tomlinson, eds. 2006. *The Limits of Meaning: Case Studies in the Anthropology of Christianity*. New York: Berghahn Books.

Fan, Lizhu. 2003. "Study of Modern Chinese Religious Beliefs: The Case of Shenzhen Economic Zone." CSRCS Occasional Paper No. 12. Chung Chi College, Chinese University of Hong Kong.

Fei, Xiaotong. 1986. "Xiaoshangpin da shichang" (Small Commodities Large Market). *Zhejiang xuekan* 3: 4–13.

Feuchtwang, Stephan. 2000. "Religion as Resistance." In Elizabeth J. Perry and Mark Selden, eds., *Chinese Society: Change, Conflict and Resistance*, pp. 161–77. London: Routledge.

————. 2001. *Popular Religion in China: The Imperial Metaphor*. Richmond, Surrey: Curzon.

Feuchtwang, Stephan, and Wang Mingming. 2001. *Grassroots Charisma: Four Local Leaders in China*. London: Routledge.

Fisher, Gareth. 2008. "The Spiritual Land Rush: Merit and Morality in New Chinese Buddhist Temple Construction." *Journal of Asian Studies* 67 (1) 143–70.

Forster, Keith. 1990a. *Rebellion and Factionalism in a Chinese Province: Zhejiang, 1966–1976*. Armonk, NY: M. E. Sharpe.

———. 1990b. "The Wenzhou Model for Economic Development: Impressions." *China Information* 5(3): 53–62.

Friedman, Sara L. 2004. "Embodying Civility: Civilizing Processes and Symbolic Citizenship in Southeastern China." *Journal of Asian Studies* 63: 687–718.

Gallagher, Sally K., and Christian Smith. 1999. "Symbolic Traditionalism and Pragmatic Egalitarianism: Contemporary Evangelicals, Family, and Gender." *Gender and Society* 13 (2): 211–33.

Gates, Hill. 1996. *China's Motor: A Thousand Years of Petty Capitalism*. Ithaca, NY: Cornell University Press.

Gernet, Jacques. 1985. *China and the Christian Impact: A Conflict of Cultures*. Cambridge: Cambridge University Press.

Gold, Thomas. 1990. "The Resurgence of Civil Society in China." *Journal of Democracy* 1 (1): 8–31.

Gong, Mu, Duan Jia, and Chen Shu. 1987. *Wenzhou de nongmin qiyejia* (Wenzhou's Village Entrepreneurs). Nanning: Guangxi renmin chubanshe.

Goossaert, Vincent, and Fang Ling. 2009. "Temples and Daoists in Urban China Since 1980." *China Perspectives* 4: 32–41.

Gordon, Milton. 1964. *Assimilation in American Life: The Role of Race, Religion, and National Origins*. New York: Oxford University Press.

Griffith, Marie R. 1997. *God's Daughters: Evangelical Women and the Power of Submission*. Berkeley: University of California Press.

Guang, Lei. 2003. "Rural Taste, Urban Fashion: The Cultural Politics of Rural/Urban Difference in Contemporary China." *Positions* 11 (3): 613–46.

Hamilton, Gary. 2006. *Commerce and Capitalism in Chinese Societies*. London and New York: Routledge.

Handel, Gerald. 2000. *Making a Life in Yorkville: Experience and Meaning in the Life-Course Narrative of an Urban Working-Class Man*. Westport, CT: Greenwood Press.

Harding, Susan. 1987. "Convicted by the Holy Spirit: The Rhetoric of Fundamentalist Conversion." *American Ethnologist* 14: 127–81.

Harrell, Stevan. 1995. "Introduction: Civilizing Projects and the Reaction to Them." In Stevan Harrell, ed., *Cultural Encounters on China's Ethnic Frontiers*, pp. 3–36. Seattle: University of Washington Press.

Hefner, Robert W., ed. 1993. *Conversion to Christianity: Historical and Anthropological Perspectives on a Great Transformation*. Berkeley: University of California Press.

———. 1998a. "Introduction: Society and Morality in the New Asian Capitalisms." In Robert W. Hefner, ed., *Market Cultures: Society and Morality in the New Asian Capitalisms*, pp. 1–38. Boulder, CO: Westview.

————. 1998b. "Multiple Modernities: Christianity, Islam, and Hinduism in a Globalizing Age." *Annual Review of Anthropology* 27: 83–105.

————. 1998c. "A Muslim Civil Society? Indonesian Reflections on the Conditions of Its Possibility." In Robert W. Hefner, ed., *Democratic Civility: The History and Cross-Cultural Possibility of a Modern Political Ideal*, pp. 285–321. New Brunswick, NJ: Transaction.

Hu, Hongwei. 2004. *Wenzhou chaofang tuan* (Wenzhou's Property Stir-Fryers). Hangzhou: Zhejiang renmin chubanshe.

Huang, Yasheng. 2008. *Capitalism with Chinese Characteristics: Entrepreneurship and the State*. New York: Cambridge University Press.

Hunter, Allan, and Kim-Kwong Chan. 1993. *Protestantism in Contemporary China*. Cambridge: Cambridge University Press.

Jacka, Jerry K. 2005. "Emplacement and Millennium Expectations in an Era of Development and Globalization: Heaven and the Appeal of Christianity for Ipili." *American Anthropologist* 107 (4): 643–53.

Jacka, Tamara. 2006. *Rural Women in Urban China: Gender, Migration, and Social Change*. New York and London: M. E. Sharpe.

Jing, Jun. 1996. *The Temple of Memories: History, Power, and Morality in a Chinese Village*. Stanford, CA: Stanford University Press.

Johnson, David, Andrew Nathan, and Evelyn S. Rawski, eds. 1985. *Popular Culture in Late Imperial China*. Berkeley: University of California Press.

Kai, Di. 1989. "Wenzhou zongjiao qingkuang de diaocha yu sikao" (An Investigation of the Condition of Religion in Wenzhou). *Shehuixue yanjiu* 2: 60–61.

Katz, Paul R. 1995. *Demon Hordes and Burning Boats: The Cult of Marshal Wen in Late Imperial Chekiang*. Albany: SUNY Press.

Keane, Webb. 1997. "Religious Language." *Annual Review of Anthropology* 26: 47–71.

————. 2007. *Christian Moderns: Freedom and Fetish in the Mission Encounter*. Berkeley: University of California Press.

————. 2008. "The Evidence of the Senses and the Materiality of Religion." *Journal of the Royal Anthropological Institute* 14 (1): 110–27.

Kendall, Laurel. 1996. *Getting Married in Korea: Of Gender, Morality, and Modernity*. Berkeley: University of California Press.

Keyes, Charles F. 2002. "Weber and Anthropology." *Annual Review of Anthropology* 31: 233–55.

Kilde, Jeanne H. 2002. *When Church Became Theatre: The Transformation of Evangelical Architecture and Worship in Nineteenth-Century America*. Oxford: Oxford University Press.

Kindopp, Jason. 2004. "Policy Dilemmas in China's Church-State Relations: An Introduction." In J. Kindopp and C. L. Hamrin, eds., *God and Caesar in China: Policy Implications of Church-State Tensions*, pp. 1–22. Washington, DC: Brookings Institution Press.

Kipnis, Andrew. 1997. *Producing Guanxi: Sentiment, Self, and Subculture in a North China Village*. Durham, NC: Duke University Press.

———. 2001a. "The Disturbing Educational Discipline of Peasants." *The China Journal* 46: 1–24.

———. 2001b. "The Flourishing of Religion in Post-Mao China and the Anthropological Category of Religion." *Australian Journal of Anthropology* 12 (1): 32–46.

———. 2002. "Zouping Christianity as Gendered Critique? An Ethnography of Political Potentials." *Anthropology and Humanism* 27: 80–96.

———. 2006. "Suzhi: A Keyword Approach." *China Quarterly* 186: 295–313.

Kohrman, Matthew. 1999. "Motorcycles for the Disabled: Mobility, Modernity and the Transformation of Experience in Urban China." *Culture, Medicine and Psychiatry* 23 (1): 133–55.

———. 2007. "Depoliticizing Tobacco's Exceptionality: Male Sociality, Death and Memory-Making Among Chinese Cigarette Smokers." *The China Journal* 58: 85–109.

Lambert, Tony. 2006. *China's Christian Millions*. Oxford: Monarch.

Lee, Joseph Tse-Hei. 2003. *The Bible and the Gun: Christianity in South China, 1860–1900*. New York and London: Routledge.

Lefebvre, Henri. 1991. *The Production of Space*. Trans. Donald Nicholson-Smith. Oxford: Blackwell.

Leung, Beatrice. 2007. "Christianity in Post-Mao China. Legalism and Accommodation." In Peter Chen-main Wang, ed., *Contextualization of Christianity in China: An Evaluation in Modern Perspective*, pp. 277–96. Sankt Augustin, Germany: Institut Monumenta Serica.

Leung, Ka-lun. 1999. *The Rural Churches of Mainland China Since 1978*. Hong Kong: Alliance Bible Seminary Press.

Li, Pingye, et al. (on behalf of United Front Department). 1999. "90 niandai Zhongguo zongjiao fazhan zhuangkuang baogao" (A Report on the Development of Religion in China in the 1990s). *Jidujiao wenhua xuekan* (Journal of Christian Culture) 2: 201–21.

Li, Qingpeng. 1999. *Zhongguo de Youtairen: Shenmi de Wenzhouren* (Jews of China: The Mysterious Wenzhounese). Beijing: Jingji ribao chubanshe.

Lin, Shundao. 2003. "Zhejiang Wenzhou minjian nianfo yongjing jieshe jihui diaocha yanjiu" (An Investigation of Grassroots Buddhist Scripture Recitation Associations in Wenzhou). *Shijie zongjiao yanjiu* 4: 59–67.

Liu, Alan P. L. 1992. "The 'Wenzhou Model' of Development and China's Modernization." *Asian Survey* 32: 696–711.

Liu, Xin. 1997. "Space, Mobility, and Flexibility: Chinese Villagers and Scholars Negotiate Power at Home and Abroad." In Aihwa Ong and Donald M. Nonini, eds., *Ungrounded Empires: The Cultural Politics of Modern Chinese Transnationalism*, pp. 91–114. New York: Routledge.

————. 2002. *The Otherness of Self: A Genealogy of the Self in Contemporary China*. Ann Arbor: University of Michigan Press.

Liu, Yia-Ling. 1992. "Reform from Below: The Private Economy and Local Politics in the Rural Industrialization of Wenzhou." *China Quarterly* 130: 293–316.

Lozada, Eriberto P., Jr. 2001. *God Above Ground: Catholic Church, Postsocialist State, and Transnational Processes in a Chinese Village*. Stanford, CA: Stanford University Press.

Luhrmann, Tanya M. 2004. "Metakinesis: How God Becomes Intimate in Contemporary U.S. Christianity." *American Anthropologist* 106 (3): 518–28.

Luo, Guangwu. 2001. *Xin Zhongguo zongjiao gongzuo da shi yaojian* (Outline of Major Events in Religious Work in the New China). Beijing: Huawen chubanshe.

Luo, Xia, and Wang Chunguang. 2003. "Xinshengdai nongcun liudong renkou de waichu dongyin yu xingwei xuanze" (Motivations for Migration and Behavioral Choices of the New Generation of Rural Floating Population). *Zhejiang shehui kexue* 1: 109–13.

MacInnis, Donald. 1996. "From Suppression to Repression: Religion in China Today." *Current History* 95: 284–89.

Madsen, Richard. 1993. "The Public Sphere, Civil Society and Moral Community: A Research Agenda for Contemporary China Studies." *Modern China* 19 (2): 183–98.

————. 1998. *China's Catholics: Tragedy and Hope in an Emerging Civil Society*. Berkeley: University of California Press.

————. 2007. *Democracy's Dharma: Religious Renaissance and Political Development in Taiwan*. Berkeley: University of California Press.

Martin, David. 2002. *Pentecostalism: The World Their Parish*. Oxford: Blackwell.

Mo, Fayou. 1998. *Wenzhou jidujiao shi* (A History of Wenzhou Christianity). Hong Kong: Alliance Bible Seminary Press.

Mo, Fayou, and Lin Hong. 1999. "Cong Wenzhou zongjiao xianzhuang kan zongjiao de shisuhua" (The Secularization of Religion Through the Lens of Wenzhou's Religions). *Zongjiao yanjiu* 1: 92–7.

Mueggler, Erik. 2001. *The Age of Wild Ghosts: Memory, Violence, and Place in Southwest China*. Berkeley: University of California Press.

Naquin, Susan. 2000. *Peking: Temples and City Life, 1400–1900*. Berkeley: University of California Press.

Nolan, Peter, and Dong Furen, eds. 1990. *Market Forces in China: Competition and Small Business: The Wenzhou Debate*. London and New Jersey: Zed Books.

Nyíri, Pál. 2006. "The Yellow Man's Burden: Chinese Migrants on a Civilizing Mission." *The China Journal* 56: 83–107.

Ong, Aihwa. 1996. "Anthropology, China and Modernities: The Geopolitics of Cultural Knowledge." In Henrietta Moore, ed., *The Future of Anthropological Knowledge*, pp. 60–92. London and New York: Routledge.

Ouyang, Houzeng. 1996. "Wenzhou jiaohui yipie" (An Overview of the Wenzhou Church). *Tianfeng* 1: 11–12.

Palmer, David A. 2007. *Qigong Fever: Body, Science, and Utopia in China.* New York: Columbia University Press.

Park, Yong-Shin. 2000. "Protestant Christianity and Its Place in a Changing Korea." *Social Compass* 47 (4): 507–24.

Parris, Kristen. 1993. "Local Initiative and National Reform: The Wenzhou Model of Development." *China Quarterly* 134: 242–63.

Potter, Pitman B. 2003. "Belief in Control: Regulation of Religion in China." *China Quarterly* 174: 317–37.

Pun, Ngai. 2003. "Subsumption or Consumption? The Phantom of Consumer Revolution in 'Globalizing' China." *Cultural Anthropology* 18 (4): 469–92.

Rankin, Mary. 1986. *Elite Activism and Political Transformation in China: Zhejiang Province 1865–1911.* Stanford, CA: Stanford University Press.

Robbins, Joel. 2004. *Becoming Sinners: Christianity and Moral Torment in a Papua New Guinea Society.* Berkeley: University of California Press.

———. 2007. "Continuity Thinking and the Problem of Christian Culture: Belief, Time, and the Anthropology of Christianity." *Current Anthropology* 48 (1): 5–38.

Sahlins, Marshall. 1996. "The Sadness of Sweetness: The Native Anthropology of Western Cosmology." *Current Anthropology* 37 (3): 395–415.

Sangren, P. Steven. 1983. "Female Gender in Chinese Religious Symbols: Kuan Yin, Ma Tsu, and the 'Eternal Mother.'" *Signs* 9 (1): 4–25.

———. 2000. *Chinese Sociologics: An Anthropological Account of the Role of Alienation in Social Reproduction.* London School of Economics Monographs on Social Anthropology, Volume 72. London: Athlone Press.

Seligman, Adam B. 1992. *The Idea of Civil Society.* New York: Free Press.

Shen, Enzhen. 2000. "Xingqi shidai de dibola: Wenzhou jiaohui funu peiling hui ceji" (To Revive Deborah in Current Times: A Report on the Wenzhou Church's Spiritual Cultivation Meetings). *Tianfeng* 2: 19–20.

Shi, Chenghui. 1997. "Wenzhou jiaohui shi ruhe kaizhan yigong peixun gongzuo de" (How the Wenzhou Church Volunteers' Training Work Is Conducted). *Tianfeng* 10: 8–9.

Shi, Jinchuan, Xiangrong Jin, Wei Zhao, and Weidong Luo. 2002. *Zhidu bianqian yu jingji fazhan: Wenzhou moshi yanjiu* (Institutional Change and Economic Development: The Study of the Wenzhou Model). Hangzhou: Zhejiang daxue chubanshe.

Siu, Helen F. 1990. "Recycling Tradition: Culture, History and Political Economy in the Chrysanthemum Festivals of South China." *Comparative Studies in Society and History* 32: 765–94.

———. 1993. "The Reconstitution of Brideprice and Dowry in South China." In Deborah Davis and Stevan Harrell, eds., *Chinese Families in the Post-Mao Era*, pp. 165–88. Berkeley: University of California Press.

————. 2005. "The Cultural Landscape of Luxury Housing in South China: A Regional History." In Jing Wang, ed., *Locating China: Space, Place and Popular Culture*, pp. 73–93. London and New York: Routledge.

————. 2007. "Grounding Displacement: Uncivil Urban Spaces in Postreform South China." *American Ethnologist* 34 (2): 329–50.

Solinger, Dorothy J. 1999. *Contesting Citizenship in Urban China: Peasant Migrants, the State, and the Logic of the Market*. Berkeley: University of California Press.

Soothhill, William. 1907. *A Mission in China*. Edinburgh: Oliphant, Anderson & Ferrier.

Stark, Rodney. 2002. "Physiology and Faith: Addressing the 'Universal' Gender Difference in Religiousness." *Journal for the Scientific Study of Religion*. 41: 495–507.

State Council. 2006. *Zhongguo nongmingong diaoyan baogao* (A Report on China's Peasant Workers). Beijing: Yanshi chubanshe.

Strand, David. 1990. "Protest in Beijing: Civil Society and Public Sphere in China." *Problems of Communism* 39: 1–19.

Swidler, Ann. 1986. "Culture in Action: Symbols and Strategies." *American Sociological Review* 51: 273–86.

Taylor, Philip. 2007a. *Cham Muslims of the Mekong Delta: Place and Mobility in the Cosmopolitan Periphery*. Singapore: National University of Singapore Press.

————. ed. 2007b. *Modernity and Re-Enchantment: Religion in Post-Revolutionary Vietnam*. Singapore: Institute of Southeast Asian Studies.

Thompson, E. P. 1991 [1963]. *The Making of the English Working Class*. London: Penguin.

Tonnies, Ferdinand. 1974 [1955]. *Community and Association (Gemeinschaft und Gesellschaft)*. Trans. C. P. Loomis. London: Routledge and Kegan Paul.

Tsai, Kellee S. 2002. *Back-Alley Banking: Private Entrepreneurs in China*. Ithaca and London: Cornell University Press.

Tsai, Lily L. 2007. *Accountability Without Democracy: Solidary Groups and Public Goods Provision in Rural China*. New York: Cambridge University Press.

Uhalley, Stephen, Jr., and Xiaoxin Wu, eds. 2001. *China and Christianity: Burdened Past, Hopeful Future*. Armonk, NY: M. E. Sharpe.

van der Veer, Peter, ed. 1996. *Conversion to Modernities: The Globalization of Christianity*. New York: Routledge.

Wang, Aimin. 2003. "Wenzhou nuxing de chuantong tezhi yu Wenzhou jingji" (Wenzhou Women's Traditional Characters and the Wenzhou Economy). *Wenzhou shifan xueyuan xuebao* (Bulletin of Wenzhou Teachers' College) 24 (4): 112–16.

Wang, Chunguang, and Jean Philippe Béja. 1999. "Wenzhou ren zai bali: yizhong dute de shehui rongru moshi" (The Wenzhounese in Paris: A Unique Model of Social Integration). *Zhongguo shehui kexue* 6: 106–19.

Wang, Mingming. 1996. *Shequ de licheng: Xicun hanren jiazu de ge'an yanjiu* (A Community's Path: A Case Study of a Han Lineage in Xicun). Tianjin: Tianjin renmin chubanshe.

Wang, Xin. 2005. "Jiedu Wenzhou chengzhongcun xianxiang" (An Interpretation of the "Urban Village" Phenomenon in Wenzhou). *Wenzhou daxue xuebao shehui kexue ban* (Journal of Wenzhou University, Social Science Edition) 18 (1): 21–27.

Wang, Zaixing. 2003. "Jidujiao shequn zhong de mada xianxiang jiqi shehuixue genyuan" (The Mada Phenomenon Among Chinese Christian Groups and Its Social Origin). *Zongjiao yanjiu* (Religious Studies) 1: 129–33.

Wank, David L. 1995. "The Alliance of Entrepreneurs and Officials: Private Enterprise in a Chinese City." In Andrew G. Walder, ed., *Departures from Central Planning: The Origins of Political Changes in Communist States*, pp. 153–83. Berkeley: University of California Press.

Watson, James L. 1985. "Standardizing the Gods: The Promotion of T'ien Hou ('Empress of Heaven') Along the South China Coast, 960–1960." In David Johnson, Andrew Nathan, and Evelyn S. Rawski, eds., *Popular Culture in Late Imperial China*, pp. 292–324. Berkeley: University of California Press.

Weber, Max. 2001 [1904]. *The Protestant Ethic and the Spirit of Capitalism*. Trans. Talcott Parsons. London: Routledge.

Wei, Yehua Dennis, Wangming Li, and Chunbin Wang. 2007. "Restructuring Industrial Districts, Scaling up Regional Development: A Study of the Wenzhou Model, China." *Economic Geography* 83 (4): 421–44.

Weller, Robert P. 1987. *Unities and Diversities in Chinese Religion*. Seattle: University of Washington Press.

———. 1995. "Matricidal Magistrates and Gambling Gods: Weak States and Strong Spirits in China." *Australian Journal of Chinese Affairs* 33: 107–24.

———. 1999. *Alternate Civilities: Democracy and Culture in China and Taiwan*. Boulder, CO: Westview Press.

———. 2000. "Living at the Edge: Religion, Capitalism, and the End of the Nation-State in Taiwan." *Public Culture* 12 (2): 477–98.

———. 2005. "Introduction: Civil Institutions and the State." In Robert Weller, ed., *Civil Life, Globalization, and Political Change in Asia: Organizing Between Family and State*, pp. 1–19. London and New York: Routledge.

Wenger, Jacqueline. 2004. "Official vs. Underground Protestant Churches in China: Challenges for Reconciliation and Social Influence." *Review of Religious Research* 46: 169–82.

Wenzhou Statistical Bureau. 2004. "Wenzhou chengshi liudong renkou shenghuo ji jiuye zhuangkuang diaocha baogao" (The Life and Work Conditions of the Floating Population in Wenzhou City). www.wzstats.gov.cn/infoshow.asp?id=2105. (Accessed May 10, 2008.)

Wenzhou Statistical Yearbook. 2005 and 2007. Beijing: Zhongguo tongji chubanshe.

Wenzhou zongjiao. 1994. In *Zhejiang zongjiao zhi* (The "Religions of Wenzhou" Volume of the Collection of Sources on Religions in Zhejiang Province). Wenzhou: Zhejiang zongjiao zhi bianweihui.

White, Jenny B. 1996. "Civic Culture and Islam in Urban Turkey." In Chris Hann and Elizabeth Dunn, eds., *Civil Society: Challenging Western Models*, pp. 143–54. London: Routledge.

Whyte, Bob. 1988. *Unfinished Encounter: China and Christianity*. London: Fount.

Wiest, Jean-Paul. 2004. "Setting Roots: The Catholic Church in China to 1949." In J. Kindopp and C. L. Hamrin, eds., *God and Caesar in China: Policy Implications of Church-State Tensions*, pp. 77–92. Washington, DC: Brookings Institution Press.

Wuthnow, Robert. 1991. *Vocabularies of Public Life*. New York: Routledge.

———. 2002. "Religious Involvement and Status-Bridging Social Capital." *Journal for the Scientific Study of Religion* 41 (4): 669–84.

Xiang, Biao. 2005. *Transcending Boundaries*. Trans. Jim Weldon. Leiden, Neth.: Brill.

Yamane, David. 2000. "Narrative and Religious Experience." *Sociology of Religion* 61: 171–89.

Yan, Yunxiang. 1997. "McDonald's in Beijing: The Localization of Americana." In James L. Watson ed., *Golden Arches East: McDonald's in East Asia*, pp. 39–76. Stanford, CA: Stanford University Press.

———. 1999. "Rural Youth and Youth Culture in North China." *Culture, Medicine, and Psychiatry* 23: 75–97.

Yang, C. K. 1961. *Religion in Chinese Society*. Berkeley: University of California Press.

Yang, Fenggang. 2005. "Lost in the Market, Saved at McDonald's: Conversion to Christianity in Urban China." *Journal for the Scientific Study of Religion* 44. 423 41.

Yang, Mayfair M. 2000. "Putting Global Capitalism in Its Place: Economic Hybridity, Bataille, and Ritual Expenditure." *Current Anthropology* 41 (4): 477–509.

———. 2004. "Spatial Struggles: Postcolonial Complex, State Disenchantment, and Popular Reappropriation of Space in Rural Southeast China." *Journal of Asian Studies* 63: 719–55.

———. 2008. "Introduction." In Mayfair Yang, ed., *Chinese Religiosities: Afflictions of Modernity and State Formation*, pp. 1–40. Berkeley: University of California Press.

Zhang, Li. 2001. *Strangers in the City: Reconfigurations of Space, Power, and Social Networks Within China's Floating Population*. Stanford, CA: Stanford University Press.

———. 2002. "Spatiality and Urban Citizenship in Late Socialist China." *Public Culture* 14 (2): 311–34.

Zheng, Tiantian. 2006. "Cool Masculinity: Male Clients' Sex Consumption and Business Alliance in Urban China's Sex Industry." *Journal of Contemporary China* 15 (46): 161–82.

———. 2007. "Performing Media-Constructed Images for First Class Citizenship: Political Struggles of Rural Migrant Hostesses in Dalian." *Critical Asian Studies* 39 (1): 89–120.

Zhou, Yongliang, and Dong Xiguang. 2003. *Wenzhou ziben* (Wenzhou Capital). Beijing: Zhongguo fazhan chubanshe.

Index

INDEX OF RESEARCH PARTICIPANTS

East-West Center Series on

CONTEMPORARY ISSUES IN ASIA AND THE PACIFIC

Protest and Possibilities: Civil Society and Coalitions for Political Change in Malaysia
By Meredith Leigh Weiss
2005

Opposing Suharto: Compromise, Resistance, and Regime Change in Indonesia
By Edward Aspinall
2005

Blowback: Linguistic Nationalism, Institutional Decay, and Ethnic Conflict in Sri Lanka
By Neil DeVotta
2004

Beyond Bilateralism: U.S.-Japan Relations in the New Asia-Pacific
Edited by Ellis S. Krauss and T. J. Pempel
2004

Population Change and Economic Development in East Asia: Challenges Met, Opportunities Seized
Edited by Andrew Mason
2001

Capital, Coercion, and Crime: Bossism in the Philippines
By John T. Sidel
1999

Making Majorities: Constituting the Nation in Japan, Korea, China, Malaysia, Fiji, Turkey, and the United States
Edited by Dru C. Gladney
1998

Chiefs Today: Traditional Pacific Leadership and the Postcolonial State
Edited by Geoffrey M. White and Lamont Lindstrom
1997

Political Legitimacy in Southeast Asia: The Quest for Moral Authority
Edited by Muthiah Alagappa
1995